BEAUVOIR AND *THE SECOND SEX*

Feminism, Race, and the Origins of Existentialism

MARGARET A. SIMONS

ROWMAN & LITTLEFIELD PUBLISHERS, INC.
Lanham • Boulder • New York • Oxford

ROWMAN & LITTLEFIELD PUBLISHERS, INC.

Published in the United States of America
by Rowman & Littlefield Publishers, Inc.
4720 Boston Way, Lanham, Maryland 20706
www.rowmanlittlefield.com

12 Hid's Copse Road
Cumnor Hill, Oxford OX2 9JJ, England

British Library Cataloguing in Publication Information Available

The hardback edition of this book was previously cataloged by the Library of Congress as follows

Simons, Margaret A.
     Beauvoir and the second sex : feminism, race, and the origins of
existentialism / Margaret A. Simons.
          p. cm.
     Includes bibliographical references and index.
     ISBN 0-8476-9256-6 (cloth : alk. paper)
     1. Beauvoir, Simone de, 1908–1986—Deuxieme sexe. 2. Beauvoir,
Simone de, 1908–1986—Criticism and interpretation. 3. Feminism.
4. Existentialism. 5. Race relations—Philosophy. I.Title.
HQ1208.S532   1999
305.42—dc21   98-37998
                                                                          CIP

ISBN 0-8476-9256-6 (cloth : alk. paper)
ISBN 0-7425-1246-0 (pbk. : alk. paper)

Printed in the United States of America

♾™ The paper used in this publication meets the minimum requirements of American National
Standard for Information Sciences—Permanence of Paper for Printed Library Materials,
ANSI/NISO Z39.48–1992.

To my French family
In loving memory of Papa, Tonton Léon, and Philippe

CONTENTS

IN MEMORIAM (1986)

I was twenty-six years old and a graduate student in philosophy when I first met Simone de Beauvoir. It was 1972, and I had won a French government grant to work with her on my doctoral dissertation on *The Second Sex*. I sold everything I could find to make the trip to France, my secretarial clothes, my car, my books. I was down to the essentials, my Red Wing boots, t-shirts, and Levi's. It sounds like a pilgrimage. But when my philosophy professor Calvin Schrag had first suggested in 1971 that I try for a Fulbright to study in Europe, I had asked, "With Habermas?" When he replied, "No, with Simone de Beauvoir," I was stunned. How could I write a philosophy dissertation on *The Second Sex*?

As a feminist activist, I was committed to developing feminist theory, but had found it difficult to do in philosophy seminars. I had first written a paper on Simone de Beauvoir's ethics after a professor had referred to her disparagingly as Sartre's girlfriend. I had once tried to present a seminar paper developing a critique of Habermas based on Shulamith Firestone's *The Dialectic of Sex* but had been discouraged by the misogynism of the all-male classroom. By 1970 I had already begun presenting papers for the newly founded Society for Women in Philosophy on Simone de Beauvoir's feminist philosophy. But a dissertation? Without the support of the secondary literature that a graduate student habitually leans on, without even a context within philosophy for defining the issues, how could I proceed? Philosophy professors in the all-male departments where I had learned how to do philosophy had never addressed a topic about women in any discussions or assignments. The few female philosophers we had read never discussed being women; Simone de Beauvoir herself denied being a philosopher and saw herself as a literary writer.

But I took up the challenge and arrived in Paris with fantasies, soon to be dispelled, of sitting down to dinner with Simone and Jean-Paul. When I called her at the assigned time to arrange a meeting, she sounded brusque and impatient with my poor French. When I eventually found myself at the door to her apartment, I was very nervous. I walked around the block several times in an effort to arrive exactly on time. I was shocked when she opened the door. In spite of looking old and wrinkled, she had the audacity to wear lipstick and bright red nail polish! I was offended to the puritanical core of my radical feminism. During our interview we were both on edge. Chain-smoking, in another affront to my "natural" values, she blew smoke in my face as I struggled to ask my questions in French. I wanted to ask her about the development of her philosophical perspective. I hesitantly posed my first question about the influence of the interpretations of Hegel by Kojève and Hyppolite on *The Second Sex*. Of course she had read them, she replied, but I must remember, she said leaning toward me in emphasis, that the only important influence on *The Second Sex* was *Being and Nothingness* by Jean-Paul Sartre.

I was taken aback. Here was the forbidden name, the name that I had in angry reaction consigned to footnotes in all my papers, moved back to center stage. Although I knew from her autobiographies that she saw Sartre as the real philosopher, I had hoped that as a feminist she would no longer see her philosophical work as merely derivative from Sartre's. I was unprepared for the forcefulness of her reply. It was impossible to see her in a passive role, as merely a follower of Sartre. Yet it was this very image of her work that she seemed to be defending so forcefully. Later I perceived her attitude as a defense of Sartre, who was still under attack for his late support of the May 1968 uprising. The fate of her own work concerned her much less. But how was I to proceed if she wouldn't go along with my efforts to trace the autonomous development of her philosophical position that was the focus of my dissertation research? I wanted her to be as docile as the texts that I studied in school. I could tell that dealing with a real person was going to be a challenge.

She enjoyed discussing feminist politics much more than my digging into the philosophical origins of *The Second Sex*. In our second interview she answered all of my questions in one word, either yes or no, and then asked eagerly, "tell me what's going on in the States." I threw up my hands and protested that I had spent three months working on those questions. I came to realize that it was a trade-off, she'd put up with my probing questions about *The Second Sex* in exchange for discussion of the women's liberation movement. But it was the last time I asked her questions that allowed for one-word answers.

She wanted to know what I was reading, and when I left I gave her all the feminist books I had brought to France with me. I wanted to repay her generosity. I had never been included in those dinners with Jean-Paul. But she gave me all the help she could. Someone had sent her a manuscript with a detailed bibliography, and she got down on her hands and knees to search through piles of manuscripts to find it for me. "I've lost my eyes," she complained in frustration as she tried to keep her glasses in place while she crawled across the floor. Once she lent me a book that she found particularly important; when I got back to the Cité I discovered that it had been autographed to her.

In our first discussions of feminist politics I took refuge from my intimidation in the supremacy of political correctness, especially when she told me that she was most in agreement politically with Juliet Mitchell's *Women's Estate*. As the weary veteran of painful years—well, months—of political struggle with leftist men at my school, I had abandoned compromise with socialism for the purity of radical feminism. I remember asking her with smiling condescension later that year if she still found the notion of feminine culture meaningless. Yes, she said, although she knew there were many feminists who disagreed with her. Only the fact that it was our last scheduled interview gave me the courage to state simply that I was one who saw nonservile feminine characteristics such as nurturance as part of a positive feminine culture.

In the years that followed, our relationship continued to grow. We met several more times for interviews and discussions of my various research projects. Once I had the pleasure of meeting Sylvie Le Bon and another time of sharing an interview with Jessica Benjamin, who helped me learn how to argue with Beauvoir about her work and its relation to Sartre. The publication of her book on Sartre's death came not long after my father's suicide and helped me deal with my grief. It also gave me the courage to talk with her in a more personal way about my feelings. In our last interview in 1985, after getting the tape recorder ready, I blurted out that I was still nervous after all these years of meeting with her. Her response was to offer me a Scotch. When I agreed she slowly got up from the sofa and walked, shuffling, bent over now, into the kitchen for two glasses and back to the refrigerator where she kept an enormous bottle of Scotch. It makes me cry to think of her again; I wish she could have lived forever. I'm glad her death has brought together those of us who loved her so much.

Reprinted from *Yale French Studies* 72, 1986, by permission of Yale University.

PREFACE

When I first began working on Beauvoir's philosophy and *The Second Sex* in 1969, I never dreamed that thirty years later major discoveries about her philosophy would still be made. But that is exactly what has happened. The general resurgence of interest in Beauvoir following her death in 1986, the growing influence of feminism in philosophy, and the posthumous publication of Beauvoir's and Sartre's letters and diaries have launched a renaissance in Beauvoir scholarship among philosophers. Research by Bergoffen (1997), Fullbrook and Fullbrook (1994 and 1998), Le Doeuff (1991), Lundgren-Gothlin (1996a), Simons (1995), and Vintges (1996) have brought significant breakthroughs. Traditionally considered Sartre's follower, Beauvoir, who was a trained philosopher, is being increasingly read for her own original contributions to both existentialist ethics and feminist philosophy. The most radical challenge to the traditional interpretation comes from Kate and Edward Fullbrook (1994) who use Sartre's *War Diaries* (1984) and Beauvoir's *Letters to Sartre* (1992) to argue that Beauvoir's metaphysical novel *She Came to Stay* (1943), long assumed to be an application of Sartre's philosophy, was instead largely completed before Sartre began writing *Being and Nothingness* (1943) and might thus be more accurately described as the model for Sartre's philosophy, rather than its application.

But these efforts to define Beauvoir's philosophical difference from and influence on Sartre have been plagued by our inability to establish a beginning point for an analysis of Beauvoir's philosophical development. Until recently, no manuscripts predating Beauvoir's relationship with Sartre were known to exist. But that situation changed in 1990, when Sylvie Le Bon de Beauvoir, Beauvoir's adopted daughter and literary executor, deposited Beauvoir's diaries dating from 1926 to 1930 in the

French Bibliothèque Nationale, where they would be available to scholars. Inspired by the Fullbrooks' discovery, I traveled to Paris in 1994 in the hopes of finding some evidence of Beauvoir's early philosophy in the diaries that dated from her years as a philosophy student at the Sorbonne. In her handwritten diary from 1927, I made an important discovery.

The findings, which I detail in chapter twelve, "Beauvoir's Early Philosophy: The 1927 Diary" (1998), include a moving account of Beauvoir's struggle against despair and the temptations of self-deception, which anticipates her later concept of "bad faith." Beauvoir turns to a philosophy based on a description of her own experience to define a theme prominent in both *Being and Nothingness* and *The Second Sex*: "the opposition of self and other." Working from a transcription of the 1927 diary prepared by Barbara Klaw and myself, and verified by Sylvie Le Bon de Beauvoir, I have uncovered previously unrecognized philosophical influences on Beauvoir, including that of Bergson and of Beauvoir's mentor Jean Baruzi, author of a controversial 1924 description of mystical experience, who may have provided Beauvoir with an early introduction to phenomenology. Merleau-Ponty, whose friendship with Beauvoir is recounted in her 1927 diary, is also often assumed to have influenced her. But the diary suggests the reverse: Merleau-Ponty's concept of embodiment was influenced by Beauvoir.

Of particular interest to feminist ethicists may be my discovery in the diary of a woman's moral voice affirming connection rather than separation. The problem of the Other does not arise for Beauvoir as it is does for Sartre, within a solipsistic context with the necessity of proving the existence of the Other. For Beauvoir, the problem of the Other arises within an intersubjective context with the necessity of realizing the self while desiring fusion with the Other. The lure of Being, in the flight from despair, can be the temptation to faith in an absolute God or a temptation to abdicate oneself for the sake of a human Other, made absolute. Beauvoir's initial formulation of the problem of the Other and the desire for domination and the theme of "the opposition of self and other," could thus provide an important historical context for interpreting not only her novels and essays, including *The Second Sex*, but also contemporary feminist ethics.

The renaissance in Beauvoir scholarship has also brought an interest in lesser-known texts that have transformed our understanding of her philosophy, as in Murphy's (1995) reading of Beauvoir's Algerian War writings, Bergoffen's (1995) reading of Beauvoir's essay on Sade, and Holveck's (1995) innovative reading of "Literature and Metaphysics." In chapter eleven, "Richard Wright, Simone de Beauvoir, and *The Second Sex*" (1997), I argue that Beauvoir's *America Day by Day* (1948), along with diaries, interviews, and correspondence from the era, can transform our understanding of the development of her feminist philosophy. I have discovered evidence that Beauvoir relied upon Richard Wright, the African American author of *Native Son* (1940) and *Black Boy* (1944), in defining the radical feminist politics of *The Second Sex* (1949). In addition to providing a broader interpretive context for reading *The Second Sex* and understanding Beauvoir's philosophical development, the research described in this chapter should help correct the provincial view that all trans–Atlantic intellectual influence extends westward and that Wright, as an expatriate writer, was only a passive recipient of French influence. The broadest significance of this research may be in furthering the recognition within the canons of history and philosophy of the significance of theorizing about race and racial oppression.

My research in this volume has often been inspired by recent work in feminist movement history. In "*The Second Sex* and the Roots of Radical Feminism" (1995), for example, I draw on Alice Echols's (1989) study of the history of radical feminism to respond to dismissive readings of *The Second Sex* as historically insignificant. I argue that Beauvoir's text laid the philosophical foundation for radical feminism and defined many of the points differentiating contemporary socialist feminism from traditional Marxist analysis. Beauvoir, I argue, was a model for later radical feminists, a social constructionist with a critique of Freudian psychoanalysis and a methodology privileging women's experiences and rejecting essentialist definitions of woman's identity. The connection between theory and action/movement building in my research may also interest students of movement history. Chapter two, "Racism and Feminism: A Schism in the Sisterhood" (1979), for example, reflects an important era when feminists undertook feminist self-criticism of the movement and sought to make it less exclusive. But the criticism that feminist theory ignores racial/cultural differences is still relevant today.

Issues of difference and the attractions and dangers of identity politics are also central to two other chapters in this volume, chapter six, "Motherhood, Feminism, and Identity" (1984), and chapter nine, "Lesbian Connections: Simone de Beauvoir and Feminism" (1991). In the chapter on motherhood, I analyze the conflict between the feminist individualist ethic in Beauvoir's *The Second Sex* and the effort by philosophers such as Sara Ruddick to valorize maternal practices within feminist theory as individual women struggle to integrate it into their public lives. My challenge is to respond to this feminist reclaiming of motherhood while arguing that choosing not to become a mother should be recognized as an authentic alternative for women, especially given the problems of breaking the cycle of abuse in families. This chapter on motherhood, like the other chapters that have previously been published, has been shortened to highlight the arguments, eliminate redundancy, and remedy inconsistency, thus making it more useful in the classroom.

Chapter nine, "Lesbian Connections: Simone de Beauvoir and Feminism" (1991), challenges the popular conception of Beauvoir as heterosexual through the analysis of her posthumously published diaries and letters from the 1940s and unpublished diaries from the late 1920s. I argue, against Bair (1990b), that Beauvoir's relationships with women are irreducible to her heterosexual relationships and that her love and concern for women of the next generation, for whom she wrote *The Second Sex*, illustrates the "lesbian continuum" described by Adrienne Rich. Drawing on Judith Butler's analysis of *The Second Sex* as making sexual difference primarily cultural rather than biological, I argue that *The Second Sex* provides an historic link between lesbian and feminist that conservative feminists would deny and that it goes further than critics such as Claudia Card have seen in challenging the institution of heterosexuality.

In 1979, Jessica Benjamin joined me in interviewing Simone de Beauvoir. It is a fascinating interview, which is published here in its original, unedited form for the first time. The highlight of the interview, for me, is our discussion of Beauvoir's influence on Sartre. Beauvoir agrees with me that her interest in childhood may have influenced Sartre. But she rejects, as usual, my suggestion that she had any philosophical influence on Sartre; Sartre was the philosopher, she was not. I remember leaning back on the couch, discouraged, only to see Jessica leaning forward to ask a question of her own: "So when you wrote in *She Came to Stay* that Françoise says that what really upsets her about Xavière is the fact that she has to confront in her another consciousness;

that is not an idea that particularly came because Sartre was thinking about that, or it was something that you were also thinking about?" Beauvoir's answer, and the exchange that followed, astonished me. Beauvoir replied, "It was I who thought about that! It was absolutely not Sartre!" Jessica responded, "So that is an idea which it seems to me appears later in *his* work." Beauvoir (laughing): "Ah! Maybe! . . . In any case, this problem was my problem. This problem of the consciousness of the Other, this was my problem." I was too stunned to speak, afraid that Beauvoir might recant her statement. Now, with the discovery of Beauvoir's 1927 diary, we finally have clear textual evidence to support this claim that she formulated the philosophical problem of the Other.

In the 1982 and 1985 interviews included here, I ask Beauvoir about her philosophical differences with Sartre on the issues of voluntarism vs. social conditioning and embodiment, individualism vs. reciprocity, and ontology vs. ethics. We also discuss her influence on Sartre's work, the problems with the current English translation of *The Second Sex,* her analyses of motherhood and feminist concepts of woman-identity, her experiences of sexism in school, feminist critiques of her novel *The Woman Destroyed,* the problem of women sacrificing themselves for men, and the feminist movement in France.

Several of the chapters in this book address the problem of interpreting Beauvoir's relationship with Sartre and challenge the sexist practices that have excluded her from the philosophical canon. Chapter three, "Beauvoir and Sartre: The Question of Influence" (1981), challenges the conventional view of Beauvoir as merely Sartre's philosophical disciple. I present evidence that Beauvoir's analysis in *The Second Sex* of the influence of history and society on individual socialization and development, that is, the importance of childhood on delimiting and shaping one's choices as an adult, appears later in Sartre's *Saint Genet* and *Search for a Method.* Chapter eight, "Sexism and the Philosophical Canon: On Reading Beauvoir's *The Second Sex*" (1990), was inspired by the work of feminist literary critics, including Annette Kolodny (1985) and Patrocinio Schweickart (1986), who expose the sexism at work in the shaping of the literary canon and provide an alternative feminist approach to reading women-authored texts. I provide a critical examination of the interpretations of *The Second Sex* and Beauvoir's philosophy in major texts on existentialism, as well as in the *Encyclopedia of*

Philosophy, to demonstrate how sexism has shaped the philosophical canon much as it has the literary canon.

My critique of the treatment of Beauvoir's texts continues in chapter five, "The Silencing of Simone de Beauvoir: Guess What's Missing from *The Second Sex*" (1983). As I explain in the synopsis that originally accompanied the article:

> In that 1952 translation by a professor of zoology, Howard M. Parshley, over 10 percent of the material in the original French edition has been deleted, including fully one-half of a chapter and the names of seventy-eight women in history. These unindicated deletions seriously undermine the integrity of Beauvoir's analysis of such important topics as the American and European nineteenth-century suffrage movements, and the development of socialist feminism in France.[1]

Mistranslations of key philosophical terms compound the confusion. The Hegelean term, "for-itself," which identifies a distinctive concept from Sartrean existentialism, has been rendered into English as its technical opposite, "in-itself." These mistranslations, and others, obscure the philosophical context of Beauvoir's work and give the mistaken impression to the English reader that Beauvoir is a sloppy writer, and thinker. But for Parshley, such considerations are irrelevant since, as he wrote in his preface, "Mlle de Beauvoir's book is, after all, on woman, not on philosophy."

The research in this book was made possible by grants from the National Endowment for the Humanities and the National Science Foundation, and the support of the Graduate School, the former School of Humanities, the College of Arts and Sciences, and the Department of Philosophical Studies at Southern Illinois University at Edwardsville. My research has benefited over the years from the comments of members of the Society for Phenomenology and Existential Philosophy, the Society for Women in Philosophy, the American Philosophical Association, the National Women's Studies Association, the Simone de Beauvoir Society, and the Beauvoir Circle, where much of this research was presented. I am also grateful to the students and faculty of the philosophy departments and women's studies programs at Washington University, Loyola University, Indiana University, Webster University, and Southern Illinois Universities at Carbondale and Edwardsville, as well as the congregation of the Alton Illinois First Unitarian Church, the members of Metro-East NOW, and the participants in the SIUE Conference on African Americans in Illinois History, and the 1997 Research Symposium on The Existential Phenomenology of Simone de Beauvoir sponsored by Florida Atlantic University and the Center for Research in Phenomenology for their stimulating discussions of various aspects of this research.

I would like to thank Helene Vivienne Wenzel for the boost she gave to Beauvoir scholarship as editor of the Beauvoir issue of *Yale French Studies* and for the opportunity to write my reflections on Beauvoir's death. I am indebted to Nancy Fraser and Sandra Bartky for their encouragement and helpful suggestions during the long process of preparing the 1982 and 1985 interviews for publication in *Hypatia*; to Martha Nelson at *Ms.*, who encouraged my research on the Parshley translation of *The Second Sex* and first expressed an interest in publishing my "Silencing" article, and to Dale Spender at *Women's Studies International Forum*, where it was finally published; and to editors who have published this research: Clare Moses, Alan Schrift, Lenore Langsdorf, Yolanda Patterson, Gene Redmond, Lester Embree, and Dorothy Leland. I owe special thanks to Cal Schrag and Bill McBride for launching me on the path where I have found such intense enjoyment, to Maureen MacGrogan for believing in the value of this project, and to Luann Reed-Siegel for treating my manuscript with such care.

It was a great pleasure to have Jessica Benjamin join me in our March 13, 1979, interview with Simone de Beauvoir. I treasure the memory of that day. For the arduous task of transcribing and translating the interviews with Beauvoir, I would like to thank Jane Marie Todd and Veronique Zaytzeff, who also provided invaluable assistance in subsequent communications with Beauvoir. For their encouragement and helpful comments on my research, I would like to thank my students and colleagues at Southern Illinois University at Edwardsville, with special thanks to Theresa Love, Wilbur McAfee, Rozanne Alvarado, Mary Ellen Blackston, Joyce Aschenbrenner, Sundiata Cha-Jua, Shirley Portwood, Chuck Corr, Cathy Surack, Tom Paxson, Carol Keene, Bob Wolf, Ezio Vailati, and Anne Valk. I'm very grateful as well for the critical comments of Alison Jaggar, Elizabeth Eames, Sue-Ellen Jacobs, Kathryn Pyne Parsons, Sandra Bartky, Rhoda Kotzin, Sheila Bruening, Azizah al-Hibri, Ann Ferguson, Maryellen MacGuigan, Julie Ward,

Debra Bergoffen, Ronald Aronson, Kristana Arp, Sonia Kruks, Eleanore Holveck, Peg Brand, and Eva Lundgren-Gothlin.

I gratefully acknowledge the kind assistance of Mauricette Berne and her staff at the Bibliothèque Nationale; Elva Griffith at the Rare Book Room, Ohio State University Library; and Timothy Young at the Beinecke Rare Book and Manuscript Library, Yale University. Finally, I owe special thanks to the following persons: Steven Hansen, at the SIUE Graduate School; Michel Fabre, who generously lent me the tape of his 1970 interview with Beauvoir; Ellen Wright, for sharing with me her insights into the life and work of her late husband Richard Wright and her dear friend Simone de Beauvoir; and Barbara Klaw, for sharing with me her transcription of the 1927 diary. To Sylvie Le Bon de Beauvoir, whose efforts have made possible the current renaissance in Beauvoir scholarship, and her adoptive mother, Simone de Beauvoir, who so generously agreed to meet with me and respond to my questions, providing me with invaluable support and encouragement, my gratitude goes beyond words.

Finally I would like to thank my friends Jane Zientek, Marc White, and Jamie Pelle for their early encouragement; Juliette Vaux, Marianne Anache, and Catherine Mouillon for their warm hospitality and patience with my American ways; my friend Pam Decoteau, for reminding me not to take myself too seriously; and my sisters Dot White and Jacqui Hill, my mother Nina Simons, and my husband Mikels Skele, whose love and support have made it all possible.

NOTES

1. Excerpts from this synopsis are used without acknowledgment in the following section from Bair's introduction to the 1989 Vintage edition of *The Second Sex*: "One of the most extensive cuts was in the 'History' section, where he deleted fully half the chapter and the names and histories of seventy-eight women. Since there is no note to indicate these deletions, much of Beauvoir's subsequent analysis of nineteenth-century European and American suffrage movements is seriously impaired, as is her treatment of the development of socialist-feminism in France" (Bair 1989, xvi).

1

BEAUVOIR INTERVIEW (1979)

Margaret A. Simons and Jessica Benjamin

Nineteen seventy-nine, the thirtieth anniversary of the publication of *The Second Sex*, was a year in celebration of Simone de Beauvoir and her contribution to feminism. In New York, a Conference on Feminist Theory in September, sponsored by the New York Institute for the Humanities, would commemorate Beauvoir's initiation of a new era of feminist theory. *Feminist Studies* planned to publish a symposium on Beauvoir. National Public Radio produced a special program on her. Gallimard, the French publishing house, published a collection of her articles, prefaces, and interviews. The week Jessica and I arrived in Paris for our interview, a film composed of discussions between Beauvoir and her intimate friends was playing in Montparnasse. This anniversary year seemed like an appropriate time to invite Beauvoir to review with us her involvement in feminism, from the genesis of *The Second Sex* to her current activities in the international feminist movement.

We had hoped, as well, to come away from our interview with a clearer picture not just of the French women's movement, but of Beauvoir as a person. Specifically, we wanted to ask her about her relationship with the philosopher Jean-Paul Sartre, which has been much distorted by the American academic and popular press. Although the relationship certainly played a central role in her life, it has too often been described as defining her, such as when *Time* refers to Beauvoir as Sartre's "Long-time Companion." Actually, of course, the reality is quite different. As she pointed out in our interview, this failure to recognize women as autonomous persons is the result of a "phallocratic prejudice." From the standpoint of feminist theory, a most serious aspect of this sexist view of Beauvoir's relationship to Sartre is the discounting of Beauvoir as an original thinker and the refusal to acknowledge, analyze, and critically study her work as social theory and social philosophy. This view fails to recognize the originality of Beauvoir's insights and is thus unable to appreciate her considerable influence on Sartre's development of a social philosophy of existentialism, and on contemporary feminist theorists as well.

We were thus surprised to hear Beauvoir say that she had not influenced Sartre at all philosophically, because she felt that she was not a philosopher, but rather a literary writer. Why should she accept this view of her work as merely reflective of Sartre's perspective rather than philosophically innovative? Perhaps the most obvious explanation is that Beauvoir was simply describing their relationship as she had experienced it. And, in fact, an examination of her autobiographies and essays reveals that she often claimed to lack philosophical originality and to be merely a follower of Sartre's philosophy, applying it or defending it from critics. In *The Prime of Life*, Beauvoir describes with characteristic candor the difficulties—her timidity and lack of audacity—that prevented her and other women from embarking on the grand system building that she identifies with philosophy. We can also see from her accounts in *The Prime of Life* that although Sartre urged her to write, he was nonetheless apt to see her essentially as a critic, or even as a passive spectator of philosophical discourse, rather than as a true participant. For example, Beauvoir remarks that in a series of conversations between Sartre and Raymond Aron, she was excluded because her "mind moved too slowly for them" (Beauvoir [1960] 1962, 67).

These same factors, as well as the later failure of the philosophical community to recognize the significance of her contribution in *The Second Sex* to the articulation of a social, political philosophy bridging the gap between Marxism and existentialism, can account for her attitude. Once this total situation is understood, it is not surprising that Beauvoir came to regard herself as lacking in philosophical originality and as subordinate to Sartre philosophically, a follower and defender of his ideas, while in fact, she both redefined and transcended those ideas in her work. Beauvoir's attitude should remind us of the great difficulty women confront in accurately evaluating their own work, especially within an antifeminist context or discipline.

But it should also warn us of the tendency to idealize women such as Simone de Beauvoir. In seeking to find in her a model for their own lives, women only create further misconceptions about her life. Not that we must accept her evaluation of her own work! What is called for is an accurate understanding of both her life, including her relationship with Sartre, and of her work, which has thus far certainly not received the critical analysis it warrants—even from feminist philosophers.

Beauvoir has clearly rejected the role of model for feminists, in both her life and theory. In the film *Simone de Beauvoir*, by Josée Dayan and Malka Ribowska, she admits to Alice Schwarzer, the German feminist, that there have been episodes in her life, in her relationships with other people, for example, in which she can feel no pride. And she complains about those persons who would idealize her and try to force her life to conform to a rigid mold.

> People often ask me: "Why have you not created women who are positive heroines?" Because I have a horror of that; I have a horror of positive heroes; and books with positive heros don't interest me. A novel is a "problematique." The story of my life is itself a problematique. I don't have any solutions to give to people and people don't have to await solutions from me. It is in this regard that, sometimes what you call my fame, people's expectations of me, bothers me. There is a certain unreasonable demand that I find a little stupid because it would enclose me, immobilize me completely in a sort of feminist concrete block. (Dayan and Ribowska 1979, 75)

Although Beauvoir did not want to be encased in feminism as though in cement, she obviously considered herself a feminist and valued her participation in the feminist movement. And she rejected wholeheartedly the celebrity role of *the* theoretician of the feminist movement, a role that Americans seem especially prone to thrust upon her. She refused the request of *L'Arc*, a French literary magazine, to devote an issue to her in 1974, asserting that the issue must not focus on her as a personality, as a celebrity, but on the work of a group of French feminist theorists. The sense of her appreciation of other women in her development as a feminist is clear from another discussion in the film. In this instance, Sartre comments to Beauvoir that she had become a feminist in the best way, by writing *The Second Sex*. Beauvoir replies that she "became a feminist, above all, after the book had existed for other women" (Dayan and Ribowska, 67).

Our interest in Beauvoir's current involvement in the feminist movement was stimulated by the evidence we found that Beauvoir, at the age of 71, was as engaged in feminist activity as ever before. Her adherence to a leftist political perspective linked her ideologically with the editorial board of *Questions féministes*, a French journal to which she lent her political support and her name as *directrice de publication*. In another interview, Beauvoir defines this leftist feminist vision:

> It is the hope that history will bring within society more profound changes than have yet appeared, changes that will truly transform relations between men and women, among men and among women—everything that has remained unchanged in spite of collectivization and the nationalization of the means of production in the socialist countries. That is the leftist hope. (David 1979, 83)

Feminism, in Beauvoir's perspective, is the leftist movement that would most radically transform society.

Yet an event occurred in Paris during our visit that made very clear Beauvoir's commitment to preventing the feminist movement from becoming subsumed, or in any way negated, by a male-directed movement. This event was the founding of the International Committee on Women's Rights, whose first official action was to respond to a call for support of Iranian women in the midst of demonstrations against the imposition of highly restrictive dress codes. The committee's response was to send an international task force to gather information about the status of women under the new regime. One of the most electric moments of the news conference called to announce the committee's formation and project in Iran came when Beauvoir angrily denounced a male speaker who had been arguing that the demonstrations by Iranian women were endangering the success of the revolution and that the women should, in the interests of the revolution, suppress their own complaints. Beauvoir loudly proclaimed that she had seen many revolutions in her lifetime and that in every instance the women had been told that they must not press their demands, that they must wait for the sake of the revolution. But their time never came, and now women are no longer content to wait, they demand liberation now!

In the preface to a book about two women's experiences in the French Women's Liberation Movement, Beauvoir addresses the danger in a leftist movement that defines women's liberation as "secondary."

> Certain militants would have liked to subordinate the women's struggle to the class struggle; the Feminine-Masculine-Future group declared itself to be radically *feminist*. The women's struggle appeared to them primordial and not at all secondary. That is also my position. In the most diverse countries I have heard it said—by men but also by women—that it was necessary *first* of all to concern oneself with the revolution, with the triumph of socialism; . . . *later* one could interest oneself with the problems of women. But in my experience, this *later* means *never*. Certainly it is necessary to link the two struggles. But the example of the countries called socialist proves that an economic change in no way entails the decolonization of women. (Beauvoir 1977, 9)

When Beauvoir first became involved in the feminist movement in the early seventies, her primary focus of concern and action was the movement to legalize abortion. We learned during our visit that much of her energy was then directed toward the issue of violence against women. She supported, and on occasion provided, shelter for victims of wife abuse. In this activity she aligned herself with the League for Women's Rights, which led a campaign to combat sexism in numerous areas of French society. Beauvoir admitted that much of its activity was essentially reformist, but that it was nevertheless valuable.

> In my estimation, tearing reforms from the government may be a stage on the road to the revolution—on the condition, of course, that one is not satisfied with these reforms but makes them instead the starting point for new demands. While preparing the projects on anti-sexist laws, the League has dedicated itself to important actions that are very much to the point. The League initiated a campaign for the denunciation of rape and created *S.O.S. Alternatives* to come to the aid of battered women. It had recourse to legal means—seeking the intervention of Françoise Giroud—and illegal means—by the occupation of Plessis-Robinson—in order to assure a shelter for battered women. . . . Why must women throw down their hands and accept everything? A revolutionary attitude today has to be a compromise

with existing conditions. To deny us the means of revolting is to deny our revolt. (Beauvoir 1977, 11)

Toward the latter part of our visit to Paris, an article written by Beauvoir appeared on the front page of *Le Monde*, a leading French newspaper. The article argued for the necessity of a law to combat sexism. Beauvoir criticized a recent French court decision acquitting a man who had beaten his wife nearly to death and then left her in agony throughout the night until she died.

> What we challenge are the sexist motivations that led to this acquittal. For having broken several windows, some young men were sentenced to years on a prison farm. For having murdered his wife, Monsieur Leber will serve no sentence, under the pretext that this offense arises from the domain of "love" or from the conjugal relation. . . . Does loving, then, implicitly authorize one to kill?
>
> The verdict . . . seems to us in the highest degree to reveal a sexist mentality. Contrary to what people claim, we feminists do not wish to avenge ourselves on men. But the fact is that we have no choice. In order to protect women, it is necessary to incarcerate certain men. That does not satisfy us, we would like to suppress violence and in order to do that it is necessary to attack it at its very roots.
>
> We would like to act on the entire cultural environment which supports these masculine, aggressive attitudes against women: advertising, pornography, literature. An antisexism law would permit us to denounce each case of sexist discrimination before public opinion. In the long run, an antisexism reflex would be created which would have avoided the death of Mme Leber. She would not have accepted the beatings, he would not have dared to beat her systematically, the neighbors would have intervened, the social services would have reacted. (Beauvoir 1979, 1)

When asked about her plans, Beauvoir often said that she was no longer engaged in major literary projects. "I'm a little tired of writing," she told Catherine David in their 1979 interview. "Maybe because I have the impression of having essential work behind me. Nothing I could write now could add substantially to it" (David 1979, 82). But in her discussion with Claude Lanzmann in the film, she admits that in spite of her newfound enjoyment of idleness, there are many projects, such as the film itself, which continue to occupy her attention.

Besides it could be possible that tomorrow I will take up again . . . that the desire for something will come to me. If by chance I had suddenly the desire to write a long and difficult book, perhaps I would throw myself into it once again. These things can happen. (Dayan and Ribowska 1979, 87)

Recent years have seen an evolution of feminist theory, bringing into question many aspects of Beauvoir's perspective in *The Second Sex*. But this development has, in a sense, only confirmed its importance for feminism. For Beauvoir, in spite of her relative isolation in 1948, writing without the political context of a feminist movement, succeeded in defining the central issues that are still the focus of theoretical discussion within international feminism today. She subjected every fashionable intellectual (and male-dominated) current to rigorous critique from the standpoint of feminism: biological determinism, psychoanalysis, Marxism. Anticipating by a quarter of a century, and indeed sowing the seeds of, recent Marxist feminist writings, she suggested that Marx's and Engel's reduction of all antagonistic social relations to relations of production, their inattention to the relations of *reproduction*, made them unable to explain the bases of women's oppression in society.

Woman cannot in good faith be regarded simply as a worker; for her reproductive function is as important as her productive capacity no less in the social economy than in the individual life . . . it is impossible to regard women simply as a productive force; she is for man a sexual partner, a reproducer, an erotic object. (Beauvoir [1949] 1961, 52–53)

But *The Second Sex* also helped lay the theoretical foundation for radical feminist theory, with Beauvoir's insistence that the most personal relationships and activities of a woman's life are inherently political. She saw all aspects of women's lives as distorted by a patriarchal ideology common to all cultures throughout history and permeating our laws, religions, and literature. But she was also aware of the situations that divide women. Her comparative analysis of racism and sexism is more cognizant of their dissimilarities than are many of the theories of contemporary, white feminist theorists. Beauvoir also continued in the tradition of Mary Wollstonecraft, and she anticipated the focus of much of contemporary feminism, by focusing on the contradictions inherent in the lives of women confined to a limited domestic sphere. But she also recognized the reality of privilege that such a role can represent to the working woman, freedom from alienating labor in dead-end jobs and from the necessity, and anxiety, of having to support herself and her children.

Although *The Second Sex* reflects the Freudianism then predominant in psychoanalytic theory, Beauvoir attacked its sexist concept of normalcy that effectively condemned women to dependent, passive lives. She essentially turned psychoanalytic theory on its head, considering it as evidence of the psychological depths of woman's social and political oppression. She used these insights to demand woman's social, economic, and political autonomy and to argue for an end to sexist educational practices. Her critique of sexism and psychoanalysis encompassed, as well, a critique of heterosexism: the ways that patriarchal ideology is lived out in sexuality. She saw lesbianism as an authentic alternative for women in a sexist society that offers and legitimates only inauthentic alternatives.

Beauvoir's analysis of woman's oppression in *The Second Sex* is open to many criticisms: for its idealism, i.e., her focus on myths and images and her lack of practical strategies for liberation; for its ethnocentrism and androcentric view, i.e., her tendency to generalize from the experience of European bourgeois women, with a resulting emphasis on women's historic ineffectiveness. Still, we have no theoretical source of comparable scope that stimulates us to analyze and question relentlessly our situation as women in so many domains: literature, religion, politics, work, education, motherhood, and sexuality. As contemporary theorists explore the issues raised in *The Second Sex*, we can see that in a sense all feminist dialogue entails a dialogue with Simone de Beauvoir. And a discussion with her can be a way of locating ourselves within our feminist past, present, and future. [M.A.S.]

INTERVIEW: PARIS, 13 MARCH 1979

Margaret Simons: I have always been interested in the development of your work. But critics, feminist and antifeminist, always talk about Sartre's influence on your work, but they never talk about your influence on Sartre's work. What has been your primary influence on Sartre, on his work?

Simone de Beauvoir: I believe that we have had a reciprocal influence: that is to say that each has criticized the works of the other. I believe that, as you suggest in the question, it has been said that it was Sartre who had influenced me. That is because in France it is always supposed that it is the man who influences the woman and never the other way around. Anyhow, Sartre was a philosopher, and me, I am not; and I never really wanted to be a philosopher. I like philosophy very much, but I have not constructed a philosophical work. I constructed a literary work. I was interested in novels, in memoirs, in essays such as *The Second Sex*. But this is not philosophy. On the philosophical plane, I was influenced by Sartre. Obviously, I was not able to influence him, since I did not do philosophy. I criticized him, I discussed many of his ideas with him, but I did not have any philosophical influence on Sartre, whereas he had such an influence on me, that is certain . . . But he did not have any literary influence on me, because I wrote what I, myself, felt like writing; and the influence that he was able to have, it was solely to criticize me to the extent that I also criticized him. Each one criticizing the other on the basis of that which he knew the other wanted to do.

Jessica Benjamin: Do you ever remember telling him that you thought something that he did ought to be changed, or be different?

SdB: Of course! Many times!

MS: How did he respond?

SdB: Well! He did what I told him to do! When I told him that the first version of *The Respectful Prostitute* was very bad, he completely rewrote it. When I told him that the end of *The Sequestered of Altona* was very bad, he completely rewrote the end. And many of his essays, as well. I criticized the major part of his works, sometimes very, very severely . . . He would argue, but then he would admit that I was right. He would change things because he knew that I criticized him according to his own intentions . . . The same was true for his criticism of my work: it was according to my own intentions. Thus, we always followed each other's work with the eyes of a reader who would be at the same time the author—with more distance than the author could have—but at the same time, with the complicity that the author has with himself.

MS: I see certain parallels in the development in Sartre's work and the development of your work after the war. For example, your interest in *The Second Sex* in the social, historical development of woman's situation and in childhood. Do you think that you communicated this interest in the child and in child development to Sartre and that he gained some interest because of your own interest? He never wrote about women, but he wrote more and more about childhood.

SdB: Maybe, that's right! Because I, myself, was much more interested in my childhood than Sartre was interested in his. And I think that, little by little, I made him become conscious of how his childhood had also been very important for him. And when he wrote *The Words*, it was because he realized that it was necessary that he talk about his childhood. And that, perhaps, was partially due to my influence. It is very possible.

MS: It is hard for you to say, isn't it?

SdB: One never knows, because it must come from the interior of a person . . . You know, one receives influences if one is ready to welcome them.

MS: It is so hard! He never talks about your influence on him! You have written many times . . .

SdB: What I'm telling you is that this is a question of philosophy. I was influenced by him in the philosophical domain, but not at all in the literary domain. When I wrote my memoirs, I was not influenced by Sartre. He never wrote any memoirs. When I wrote my novels, I was never influenced by Sartre, because it was my lived and felt experience that I rendered. I was never influenced by him there. I speak of his influence solely on the philosophical level; because he was a philosopher and I was not. There . . .

JB: So when you wrote in *She Came to Stay* that Françoise says that what really upsets her about Xavière is the fact that she has to confront in her another consciousness. That is not an idea that particularly came because Sartre was thinking about that, or it was something that you were also thinking about?

SdB: It was I who thought about that! It was absolutely not Sartre!

JB: So that is an idea which it seems to me appears later in *his* work.

SdB: Ah! Maybe! . . . (Laughter) In any case, this problem was my problem. This problem of the consciousness of the Other, this was my problem.

MS: It bothers me that you say you are not a philosopher. I don't know why. I suppose it is because I spend so much time treating your work philosophically. I don't know, maybe it is the definition in America that is looser.

SdB: Maybe . . . Yes . . . Because for me, a philosopher is someone like Spinoza, Hegel, or like Sartre: someone who builds a great system, and not simply someone who loves philosophy, who can teach it, who can understand it, and who can use it in essays, etc., but it is someone who *truly* constructs a philosophy. And that, I did not do . . . I never cared so much about doing it. I decided in my youth that it was not what I wanted.

JB: But your work is philosophical in the English sense, which means metaphysical. You see, I think that's the problem, that for us, it is very metaphysical, in a way. The categories that you think in are more metaphysical than an English person thinks in.

MS: It is because there is so much more concern with philosophical systems than in many American writers. Maybe that's true. *The Second Sex* is very difficult for many American readers, because it is so complicated. And *Ethics of Ambiguity*, that's philosophy.

SdB: For me, it is not philosophy, it is an essay. No, but, truly, if I take the word *philosophy* in a slightly elevated sense, I'm saying that the great philosophers are Descartes, Hegel, etc. Sartre, in my opinion, will be among them. But not I. There are very few philosophers in a century; there are perhaps two of them.

MS: Okay. Another question I wanted to ask you was about the influences on your work. When I first met you, I asked you about . . . Maybe it has to do with philosophy again. Maybe there is something I don't understand when we talk about philosophy. It could be. I asked about the influences on your work, Hegel's influence on your work, in *The Second Sex*, especially on the idea of the Other.

JB: I remember when you were saying to me yesterday, the question was how in your unconscious, in a way, this idea got to be so powerful about writing about women. In other words, not how you had the idea one day, but who, you think, might really have been important in the use for that, to make you think about that.

MS: Let me ask you in a little different way. *The Second Sex* is important for us, because it gives us a theoretical foundation. But when we look at *The Second Sex* it seems to be isolated from other feminism. What do you consider the feminist theoretical foundation for *The Second Sex*? You mentioned Virginia Woolf and Colette; you mentioned the woman's situation.

SdB: Virginia Woolf. But in any case, I wrote *The Second Sex* from my own experience, from my own reflections, not so much from some influences. Of course, I encountered Virginia Woolf in my readings. I liked *A Room of One's Own* very much. But I cannot say that I was influenced by it. I believe that I truly wrote the book in a very spontaneous manner, as one response to the questions that I asked myself, that I began to ask myself about the fact of being a woman. Then, at the time, I read books by men, by women, as well as books by antagonists such as Montherlant, Lawrence, who influenced me insofar as I understood how they understood women and how this was detestable. But I cannot say that there was someone in whose path I followed. The closest to me on this plane was, certainly, Virginia Woolf.

JB: When you read *To the Lighthouse* . . .

SdB: Ah! *To the Lighthouse*! . . . I don't recall that novel very well . . .

JB: I was curious because that is her most clearly feminist . . .

SdB: *Three Guineas* is also very feminist. But I had not even read it when I wrote *The Second Sex*. No, I cannot say that I was influenced by anyone in particular in *The Second Sex* . . . Or perhaps I was influenced by everyone. It was my stance with respect to the world and to literature, as I saw them.

MS: In the epilogue to *Force of Circumstances* you said that Sartre has been creative ideologically, and not you. And yet, *The Second Sex* is ideologically creative. It is spontaneous, it's crazy. It came out of your situation, as you say, it is very creative.

SdB: Yes!

MS: Sometimes, it is difficult for me to understand correctly your relationship with Sartre, and your autonomy. Your ideas of woman's situation, and of the Other, are really your own creation. And yet sometimes, in your own statements, it sounds as though they came from Sartre.

SdB: Oh! No, not at all! The ideas on woman are my own! Sartre has never been very interested in the woman question. As a matter of fact I had a dialogue with him published in *L'Arc*, two years ago, in which I asked him why he had not interested himself in the question [Beauvoir 1975] . . . No, these ideas are truly my own. I'm only saying that I am not a philosopher. That's all.

MS: But ideologically you were very creative.

SdB: That is not what you call ideological.

MS: So many critics, especially in America, among philosophers and even feminists refuse to acknowledge your own philosophical autonomy, which is very evident in your own consciousness. Why do they do it? I don't know why they do it . . . But sometimes I see in your own work . . . Am I mistaken? Do I see a problem in your own work . . . maybe it's a continuation . . . When you were young, just before you went to Marseilles, you had trouble finding your own autonomy; it was a difficulty finding your autonomy.

SdB: I think that's a problem for all adolescents!

MS: It hasn't continued? You don't consider that there is any problem in your mind in establishing your own autonomy? But you are so close, so close to Sartre. You have all these memories. Fifty years together, of memories; and sometimes you begin a sentence that he finishes.

SdB: We are very close. But that is not to say that he dictates to me what I write . . . That is a masculine point of view . . . Indeed there are men in France who always say that the woman is only a reflection of the man with whom she lives or close to whom she lives. That is a phallocratic prejudice.

MS: I agree. It is the same problem in America. Sometimes, I think it is a problem because very few intellectuals are couples, are close. Most people have a fight. You have someone who is a teacher and then the student has a big fight, and they have separate ideas, they are not close any longer. But you have maintained such a close relationship. Maybe it is a problem for other people to appreciate it. We do not have other models.

SdB: Perhaps.

JB: I think that the truth is that people are almost more fascinated by the fact that you could have a relationship with another person who was such a strong intellectual and not be overpowered than by any other fact. Obviously, you know that people in some way celebrate you, or they think that you are a model for them. And what astonishes them, what they cannot grasp is that you could have a relationship with such a powerful man and not be overpowered by him. I think that's what Peg is talking about. That's really what people wonder about when they wonder about you.

SdB: But, that's the way it is . . . (Laughter)

JB: There's really very little to say about it.

MS: Many times you have said that you have been very privileged in your life. That you have never been hampered by your feminine condition. But in some ways, I wonder if your experience of feminism in the last few years has made you reflect upon your life differently and maybe see your life in a different way, and in some ways affected by sexism. Jessica has suggested to me, for example, that your relationship with your mother, or with other women, has been negative in some ways. You were isolated very much from other women in the early years, when you were in school, and as an intellectual. How many women had this opportunity?

SdB: Yes, I was very, very privileged. That's certain. But I had very friendly relationships with a rather large number of women, which I speak about in my memoirs—Zaza, then Olga, and many others. Yes, I have had many very warm feminine friendships.

JB: In other words, it is not as though you really could not find anyone to support you in your identity as a woman.

SdB: Pardon?

JB: Well, there's a way in which you can feel yourself as a woman among other women that is different than when you are a woman with a man. Right?

SdB: No, it is not so different. I've had men as friends, I've had women as friends, and everything has worked out very well. I never asked myself questions like that, if you like.

JB: How would you put the difference between being alive in a world with a feminist movement and being in a world without a feminist movement? How does that seem different to you?

SdB: I know many feminists, I get on well with them. I like working with them very much, it brings me something . . . That doesn't make it a different world, because they are after all in the same world! Only, it is enriching, because many of these feminists are very conscious, very intelligent, very exacting women, who understand woman's situation very well . . . indeed, who have taught me many things from their experience. Because in fact, the great merit of feminists and the relations that women now have among themselves through feminism is that they speak to one another much more openly, much more sincerely, much more directly perhaps, than they did before, except with very intimate friends. Thus, it is, indeed, a great enrichment.

JB: So, in other words, with intimate friends it does not really make that much difference.

SdB: No, not at all.

MS: After you wrote *The Second Sex*, what an outcry! People were so negative.

SdB: Yes, especially the men!

MS: Now, in a feminist world, you have more support. There is more positive encouragement for your ideas and acceptance . . .

SdB: No, because the struggle is also very invigorating.

JB: I was going to ask you about another question that comes up a lot in your literary work and your autobiography. I loved your book *A Very Easy Death*. I thought it was beautiful and moving. And I think many people respond that way to that book. I am very interested in the question of death, in terms of feminist theory, etc. Because you say in *The Second Sex* that men resent women because women represent nature and mortality, and in that way, they represent death. Right?

SdB: Yes.

JB: Dinnerstein [1976], the book that I gave you, extends this idea; and she says that if men as well as women were parents, then people would not be able to blame this fact of mortality upon the women. And then they would have to face mortality without the ability to blame someone. And she argues that would keep people, as a species, as a society, from the self-destructive way that people use the fear of death. Do you still think that psychologically speaking, the hatred of women and the domination of women is based on this fear of death, and whether you think that it is really possible for human beings to accept death, to come to terms with the rage against the dying of the light?

SdB: That, I really do not know. One should not ask too many questions about the whole of humankind. I don't know how people face death, how they are able to cope with it, how they can accept or not accept it. I think that it is a very individual question. Everyone has their own relations with their own death and one cannot say, in a general manner, how one can bring people to accept death.

JB: Do you still believe that this has to do with the roots of the hatred of women?

SdB: No, but I think that one of the things, as revealed in their myths, that men detest about women is, in fact, that men are born and thus are mortal. But this is only one of the things, one of the myths, one of the hatreds. There are many other reasons, I think, for men's hatred of women. But this particular one, certainly, does exist for some men. There are many men who see in woman the face of death . . . That's certain!

JB: Do you think that in some way feminist politics can relate to this issue? I mean, do you think that there is some way in which politics could cease to exclude that? Or do you think that it can be only dealt with individually, this kind of hatred?

SdB: I believe that it is above all an individual matter. I do not see feminism being able to stop men from hating women, since she is their mother, consequently their death, in a manner of speaking . . . Some men, because it is a very individual thing.

JB: So, would you think that by changing motherhood, you could change that or not?

SdB: Oh, that! I don't know . . . You understand, I myself don't know about sociological questions . . . From my experience, I don't know what the world can become or how things are going to turn out.

MS: I read with great interest your interview with John Gerassi [1976], in which you said that to change the whole value system of society, to destroy the concept of motherhood, that is revolutionary. What does that mean? Do you remember?

SdB: Ah! Yes! I think that by changing the idea of maternity, by changing the idea of maternal instinct, of the feminine vocation, society would change completely. Because it is through the idea of feminine vocation that one enslaved women to the home, one enslaved them to their husband, one enslaved them to man, to housework, etc., etc. . . . . If one destroyed that concept, not maternity itself, but all the myths which are related to maternity, one would, obviously, change society completely.

MS: But you do not mean to completely destroy motherhood.

SdB: No! . . . Women want to have children and I, myself, have nothing against them. But I find that in today's world, in our Western civilization of today, maternity is a trap for women, because it enslaves them to man, to the home. It forces them back into the interior of this system that feminists want to destroy.

MS: And you reject very much a utopian vision of technology eliminating maternity. I am thinking of Shulamith Firestone and feminism that wants to eliminate motherhood, biologically, and end biological reproduction completely.

SdB: Well! . . . If one could change the conditions within which maternity is lived, one could keep maternity. I think that there are certain relations which can be very strong between a mother and her child, and, moreover, between a father and his child as well . . . Thus, if the world were made in a slightly different way and the woman were not enslaved as soon as she is a mother . . . then, why would one rule out maternity? But as maternity is today, the maternity-slave, as some feminists call it . . . indeed maternity turns today's women into slaves, and I believe that maternity is the most dangerous trap for all those women who want to be free and independent, to earn their living, think for themselves, and live for themselves. Conditions can change, perhaps . . . Let's hope so.

JB: Have you had a chance to see the work that has been done recently in America on this, like the work of Adrienne Rich on motherhood? Because I would say that now this topic is maybe the most important, the one that people talk about the most. Motherhood has really become very important, I think because so many feminists want to be able to unite being mothers and being active at the same time.

SdB: Yes.

JB: And so, one of the questions that many people ask when they look at what you said many years ago is "Is it still impossible for a woman to be a mother and also to be transcendent?"

SdB: It is perhaps not impossible. No! I think that there are some women who achieve it. But I think that it is very difficult. Very often women are actually split, because they feel that they are not good enough mothers, not good enough workers . . . But, there are successes, certainly! . . . There are women lawyers, women physicians, women who do loads of things, women engineers, women government ministers, etc., and who, at the same time, have children. Certainly, it is not impossible . . . But it is not possible for the majority, for the average woman, women without money, for women whose work is unrewarding. There are women who should stay at home . . . The double task of working at the factory and then being mother of a family, for example, is very hard . . .

JB: So you think that it has perhaps become easier for some women but not for all?

SdB: Yes! That's it! It is easier for certain women, the privileged women.

MS: There is a movement in American feminism which I think is a parallel to the movement in French feminism identified with the concept of *l'écriture féminine*. It takes the biological difference between woman and man and makes it an essential difference and takes an experience like maternity, like the woman's relationship with her body, and makes this biological being the center of her existence, of a woman's culture. It is a foundation for separatism, and it is very much opposed to the position from *The Second Sex*. How do you think about this now?

SdB: Well! I am against this opposition to *The Second Sex* . . . (Laughter) There are also in France some women who take this position, for example, Annie Leclerc in *Women's Speech*. There are a certain number of women who exalt menstruation, maternity, etc. and who believe that one can find a basis there for a different writing, etc. As for myself, I am absolutely against it because I find that it falls again into the masculine trap of wanting to enclose us in our differences. I think that one must not deny these differences, or despise them. It's good to demand that a woman could be . . . that she not feel degraded by, let's say, these monthly periods, that she could refuse to appear ridiculous because she is pregnant, that a woman could be proud of her body, as a feminine body, and of her feminine sexuality. But that's no reason to fall into a crazy narcissism and build, on the basis of these givens, what should be the entire culture and life of a woman. I don't think that woman should repress these givens. She has the perfect right to be proud of being a woman, just as man is also proud of his sex. After all, he has the right to be proud of it, as long as he does not deprive others of the right to their pride. Everyone can be happy with their body, but, even so, one should not make this body the center of the world! Thus, I refuse this separatism, if you will.

JB: Do you think that in other words the problem with separatism is that in a way it takes the biological fact as the social fact?

SdB: Yes! That's it! And that, basically, it's playing man's game to say that woman is essentially different! There is, in fact, a biological difference, but it is not the foundation of the sociological difference.

MS: In *The Second Sex*, you often equate masculine values with human values. But I think that you no longer agree with that view. When we first talked, in 1972, we were in disagreement about whether woman's situation leads her to have a perception of some experience that is valuable. You do see a value in women sharing and discussing their situation. Do you see any meaning in the idea of values from women's situation?

SdB: I think that there are certain masculine faults that women avoid, thanks to their situation. Women have less importance, less desire for emulation, and less of the ridiculous, in one sense, in their role. They are less comical, in the bad sense of the word, than men who take themselves so seriously. And I think that women escape, more or less, all of that. But the difficulty is that they escape it because they don't have power. As soon as they have it, they acquire all men's defects . . . But one cannot all the same wish for women to remain in a humiliating and inferior situation in order to keep certain qualities. However, one could wish for men to share also some of these feminine qualities that result from oppression, for example, patience, sympathy, irony, the somewhat ironic distance from things, the refusal of precisely the masculine values such as decorations, roles . . . that is, all this type of male tinware. Women can, perhaps, more than men, refuse all of that . . . But only to the extent that they are far from it.

MS: So you think that women, because of our situation of oppression, share experiences with other people who are oppressed, and it gives a unity. And instead of seeing feminism as isolated from other movements, you see a unity, because perhaps of this shared situation of oppression and so many experiences are very similar.

SdB: No! . . . I do not think that it suppresses isolation, unfortunately, precisely because they are not qualities which suppress isolation. But, I think that isolation may be, in itself, a source of certain qualities, because it leads a person to have recourse to herself, to have more of an interior life, of recourse to self, than men who seek recourse in such exterior things . . . but those qualities do not break down isolation.

JB: It doesn't break down their isolation to have this quality. This is a problem you talked about in *The Second Sex*, that woman's oppression is very peculiar because no one else is tied to their oppressor in that way.

SdB: Yes, that's it.

JB: The fact that many women think that if they are going to be a subject themselves they have to deny that men are subjects, so they make men into the Other. And in order for women to avoid doing that as feminists, they have to act as a subject in a way that men never acted, that is, they have to create a new subjectivity. Would you say that was true or not?

SdB: No! I believe that both parties must consider each other reciprocally as subjects. I do not think that women should take up power against men, to avoid what men did against women. I think that they must find a reciprocity.

MS: Exactly as you said in *The Second Sex*.

SdB: It is what I stated in *The Second Sex*.

JB: But in doing that they set themselves in opposition to the principle of nonreciprocity which men have invented. Then they argue that men are so much against reciprocity that you can't do this with them. I think that's what they would say.

SdB: In any case, it does not seem very realistic to me to think that women will be able to reduce men to objects. Nor do I think that it would be ideal. I think that nobody should reduce the Other to an object: neither women women, nor men men, nor women men, nor men women . . . (Laughter)

MS: Sometimes, I think that you have rejected *The Second Sex*, in some ways . . .

SdB: But not at all! . . . Absolutely not!

MS: So, do you think that *The Second Sex* still expresses a feminist position that is real today?

SdB: In my opinion, yes. There are some little outdated things in *The Second Sex* . . . The references may not be as applicable, that's all. But I am altogether in agreement with *The Second Sex*.

MS: Do you think there are other people . . . Do you think it defines . . . No, you're never worried about having other people agree with you.

SdB: No! I do not want everyone to be in agreement with me.

MS: No, you don't have to have a movement to believe that it exists.

JB: You said in your interview with Gerassi that you were going to give it a more materialistic basis?

SdB: Ah! Yes! A little bit.

JB: How would you do that? Have you thought about that?

SdB: But I already explained that in *All Said and Done*. That is to say that I think that with the Other, it is not simply an idealist relationship, it is a material relationship. It is a power relationship, based also on scarcity.

JB: So you would put it in relation to the exchange principle, in other words.

SdB: But that would not change the book as a whole. There, I believe that I've said quite a few things to you.

This interview, from the original transcription and translation by Veronique Zaytzeff, was published in an abridged version in *Feminist Studies* 5, no. 2 (Summer 1979): 330–45.

2

RACISM AND FEMINISM: A SCHISM
IN THE SISTERHOOD (1979)

F eminist theorists have often drawn extensively on an analogy with racism and with the struggle of minorities in America against racism, in developing theories of the women's liberation movement. These theorists have also customarily assumed that the struggle against sexism encompasses the struggle against racism. That minority women have not joined the women's liberation movement in large numbers has thus been a source of surprise for many feminists, and it has been a source of concern for a movement anxious to expand beyond its white, middle-class membership base and become an intercultural, international movement.

The explanation offered by many white feminists for the lack of minority members has, in the past, focused on what some have considered to be the low level of consciousness of minority women (Hole and Levine 1971, 150). According to Jo Delaplaine (1978, 12), for example, this has been a typical response to the political strategies and priorities of Latina women. Catherine Stimpson's excellent analysis in " 'Thy Neighbor's Wife, Thy Neighbor's Servants': Women's Liberation and Black Civil Rights" (1971) is an important, early exception. But the typical explanation by white feminists is simplistic and disparaging of the high level of political commitment of many minority women to social movements to combat racism and strengthen minority communities.

Minority women writers, such as Cotera (1977, 43), Wallace (1979, 46), Daniels-Eichelberger (1977), Lewis (1977), Beal (1970), and Ware (1970), analyze the roots of their oppression and provide more adequate explanations of the reluctance of many minority women to identify with the predominantly white women's movement. These explanations analyze factors within the minority community, such as the fear of dividing the community, lack of knowledge of feminism, the relationship of black and Latina women to the church, and, among black women, the focus on male liberation in the black social movement of the sixties and the idea of black matriarchy. But many minority women have also pointed out an additional factor inhibiting development of a feminist consciousness among minority women that arises within the feminist movement and community rather than within the minority community: racism. As Pauline Terrelonge Stone writes in "Feminist Consciousness and Black Women,"

> Racism is so ingrained in American culture, and so entrenched among white women, that black females have been reluctant to admit that anything affecting the white female could also affect them. Indeed, many black women have tended to see all whites regardless of sex, as sharing the same objective interest, and clearly the behavior of many white women vis-à-vis blacks has helped to validate this reaction. (Stone 1979, 583)

This important challenge for feminism, to confront the problem of racism and ethnocentrism in the movement, among its members, and within its theory, has not generally been accepted by white feminists. In an important recent article, "Race and Class: Beyond Personal Politics," Beverly Fisher (1977) reviews the experiences of minority women in various sectors of the women's movement and then cites the need for a more thorough analysis of bias in the central concepts of feminism. It is this task of critical analysis that defines the project of this chapter. In it I draw upon articles by black and Chicana feminists in exploring the issue of racism in several major works in feminist theory, including Simone de Beauvoir's classic, *The Second Sex* (1949); Robin Morgan's influential anthology *Sisterhood Is Powerful* (1970); Shulamith Firestone's *The Dialectic of Sex* (1970); Kate Millett's *Sexual Politics* (1971); and Mary Daly's *Beyond God the Father* (1973). A socialist-feminist perspective on racism is examined briefly in the anthology *Feminist Frameworks*, edited by Alison M. Jaggar and Paula Rothenberg Struhl (1978).

BEAUVOIR'S LEGACY TO CONTEMPORARY FEMINISM

In her 1949 classic, *The Second Sex*, Simone de Beauvoir relies upon a complex series of comparisons with racism and slavery in analyzing woman's oppression. In fact, the central question that defines Beauvoir's project in the book is posed in terms of the master/slave relationship described by Hegel in the *Phenomenology of Spirit* (Beauvoir 1949, 73). Hegel describes the dialectic in which a slave—a dependent, oppressed consciousness—comes to self-consciousness as an independent person, while the master, in the course of the same dialectic, realizes his dependency on the slave. In this way reciprocity is established in their relationship. Beauvoir recognizes woman's historical situation as analogous to the dependency of the slave on the master. But in woman's relationship to man the dialectic in which reciprocity is established has failed to operate. Why, Beauvoir asks, have women not contested male sovereignty? Her answer, sketched out in the introduction, emphasizes the many differences between sexism, racism, and class oppression. Living dispersed among men, attached to their oppressor with a bond like no other, and having no common religion, history, or culture, women have lacked both the concrete means to affirm their autonomy and, according to Beauvoir's analysis, the will to renounce the privileges and protection offered to them with dependency (Beauvoir 1949, xix–xxv).

Later, in a discussion of the historical genesis of woman's oppression, Beauvoir returns to a consideration of Hegel's master/slave relationship. But here, she argues that some aspects of Hegel's description are less applicable to slavery than to the man/woman relationship. Drawing on Levi-Strauss's analysis in *Elementary Structures of Kinship*, Beauvoir argues that women have never had power in any society and that they have never contributed to the shaping of culture through the productive labor that has historically defined man's experience. Woman's biological link to reproduction has always tied her more closely to a natural form of life than to the distinctly human form of man's existence. When his assertion of his individuality historically led him to emerge from the group identity of the clan, man established his autonomy by conquering Nature, which included woman. When he later instituted slavery, the woman remained more radically the "Other" than the slave who shared with his master work activities and engagement in battle. The master and slave, engaged in human activities, are, in Beauvoir's view, essentially similar and yet radically dissimilar to woman, who is confined to a lower, animal-like life. The male/female relationship thus forms a more radical opposition, in Beauvoir's view, than does the master/slave relationship, although women are offered privileges, denied to slaves, which mitigate the oppressiveness of their subordinate position (Beauvoir 1949, 70–71, 73, 83–88).

A major problem with this comparison between slavery and woman's oppression lies in Beauvoir's characterization of slavery. In the American slavery experience, which Beauvoir refers to extensively, justifications for slavery relied upon racist ideology espousing the animal-like character of the slaves. Instead of being seen as essentially similar to their masters, slaves were perceived as radically dissimilar. Slaves were thus confined to the category of the "Other" in racist ideology, as women were in sexist ideology. Beauvoir furthermore ignores, as does Hegel, the practically universal phenomenon of ethnocentrism in her analysis of oppression. This is perhaps a result of her emphasis on the historical emergence of the individual and the motivation of the individual in oppressing another person. The experience of a cultural, social identity is reduced to individual antagonisms. But ignoring the existence of ethnocentrism makes any explanation of racism, including slavery, inadequate. And, of major relevance to feminists, it fails to account for the factors that divide women of different races along with the discussion of those factors that unite us.

Another problem with Beauvoir's comparison of racism and slavery with woman's oppression lies in her description of women's lives. Her view reflects what some feminist anthropologists describe as an androcentric perspective (Martin and Voorhies 1975, 165). This perspective, which argues that the development of human societies has been the result of solely male innovation and production, was the predominant view at the time that Beauvoir wrote *The Second Sex*. Yet it reflects a distorted picture of male/female activities. Male activities are glorified as transcendent and distinctly human, while female activities are viewed as less significant and merely repetitive. Ironically enough, this view denies Beauvoir's own feminist heritage, in that it omits the historical struggle of Euro-American women to obtain their political rights. In Beauvoir's perspective, which might be described as reflecting an absolute notion of patriarchy, women have never acted historically.

Nor does Beauvoir's description of woman's historical experience reflect the activities of working-class Euro-American women. Its focus on female dependency and passivity reflects a class bias that is a serious problem in feminist theory, as pointed out, for example, by Riccio (1978). As a generalization from the Euro-American experience of middle-class woman's domestic role, this view also denies the experience of women in other cultures, including the experience of black women in America, most of whom have historically engaged in productive labor and whose families seem to be in some ways more egalitarian (Stone 1979, 578; Lewis 1977, 342; Hammond and Enoch 1976).

It should be noted that feminist anthropologists are far from agreement on the question of the universal subordination of women. The problem involves the definition of central terms, such as *power* and *subordination*, as well as the lack of conclusive research. My intention is not to prematurely take a stand on this complex issue, but merely to point out that Beauvoir and other feminist theorists have, in the past, unconditionally proclaimed the universal subordination of women with inadequate justification. This has effectively ignored the various economic, social, and political situations of women in different societies (Lamphere 1977; Jacobs and Hansen 1977, 86; Schlegal 1977, 355–56; Reiter 1975; Rosaldo and Lamphere 1974; Martin and Voorhies 1975). Beauvoir's conclusion that the man/woman relationship is more radical than the master/slave relationship is thus drawn into question by aspects of her characterizations of both slavery and women's experiences of oppression. But her comparison, although ultimately unconvincing, is nonetheless substantial and carefully argued. As we shall see below, in contemporary feminist theory a claim of the primacy of sexism is often made with little argument, with the resulting impression that the assumption is merely the result of political expediency.

The ethnocentrism of Beauvoir's perspective, with its tendency to generalize from her own cultural viewpoint, shows an insensitivity to the experiences of women in other cultures, which has continued to be a problem in feminist theory. Analyses by white feminists often deemphasize the differences in women's situations in an effort to point out the shared experiences of sexism. But the result is a lack of sensitivity to the situations of minority women and a failure to understand their reluctance to identify with a predominantly white organization (*see* Fisher 1977, 190).

Perhaps most importantly, in the context of a dialogue between minority and white feminists, the notion of an absolute patriarchy can obscure the reality, all too familiar to minority women, that some white women have historically had access to power that they have at times wielded against both minority men and women. Beauvoir's comparison of racism and slavery with sexism does show an awareness of the privileges, prestige, and status accorded to many middle-class and upper-class white women that have urged them to comply with their social role (Beauvoir 1949, 159, 335). But while many minority women refer to this problem, few white feminists have shared their insight.

INVISIBILITY OF MINORITY WOMEN

In reviewing the work of feminist theorists one is struck by the relative lack of attention given to racism and the oppression of minority women, a problem Mae C. King (1973) terms the "invisible orientation" toward black women. In Beauvoir's comparison of slavery and women's oppression, the experience of the enslaved woman is ignored (as it is in the Hegelian analysis of slavery). Yet why should the male's experience be considered typical? Surely a comparison between enslaved women and "free" women would provide the basis for an analysis of oppression as well as highlight the differences in their situations.

There is evidence of the "invisibility" of minority women across the political spectrum of contemporary feminist theory, including socialist and radical feminism. *Feminist Frameworks*, edited by the socialist-feminist philosopher Alison Jaggar, with Paula Rothenberg Struhl (1978), is a case in point. Discussions of racism and the situation of black women are included in a pretheoretical presentation of concrete problems, in spite of the statements by some minority feminists that affirm their autonomy from the white women's liberation movement and offer theoretical analyses that differ profoundly from those of other feminist theorists. The socialist-feminist anthropologist Gayle Rubin does criticize the absolute notion of patriarchy in her article in *Feminist Frameworks* "The Traffic in Women" (Jaggar and Struhl 1978, 155–57). However, she does not discuss racist oppression.

That socialist-feminist sensitivity to class differences does not entail a corresponding awareness of cultural differences is evident in a socialist-feminist article from *Feminist Frameworks* on the extended family, which assumes that all Americans live in the same sort of isolated, nuclear family (Jaggar and Struhl 1978, 263). This ignores the experience of extended families and "domestic networks" in many American minority communities, detailed by Carol Stack (1974). Historically, of course, the difficult questions confronting socialist-feminists have come in their struggle to define a feminist politics without forfeiting their socialist analysis of capitalist society. Thus the problem of socialist-feminists has been recognizing a sisterhood at all, whereas the tendency of radical feminists is to ignore class divisions among women.

That radical feminism, as well as socialist-feminist theory, is also marked by the invisibility of minority women is evident in two early collections of articles. *Notes from the Second Year* (Firestone 1970), an anthology of radical feminism, contains no articles by or about minority women. In *Notes from the Third Year* (Koedt 1971), the discussion of minority women is relegated to an early section on concrete problems and ignored in the section on theoretical analysis. The sense of a dialogue, in which the personal experiences of minority women contribute to the shaping of the political theory of feminism, is missing. In fact, dialogue itself was seldom present in the early seventies, with white feminists and minority women more often talking past each other than actually communicating. Two important exceptions to this trend are Leslie Tanner's *Voices from Women's Liberation* and Vivian Gornick and Barbara Moran's *Woman in Sexist Society,* which contain several articles by and about women in non-Euro-American cultures. But since the insights offered by these authors seldom seem to be accepted by other feminists, the sense of cultural isolation continues.

This problem is also apparent in Robin Morgan's influential 1970 anthology, *Sisterhood Is Powerful*, which contains several articles on the oppression of minority women and is one of the best feminist anthologies from that standpoint. However, the sense of theoretical isolation of these articles remains, in part because of the authors' emphatic proclamation of the importance of combating racism and capitalism along with sexism and because of their sense of solidarity with the men of their oppressed communities. These women emphasize the importance of building and maintaining their families as part of the defense against our racist society. Their analyses thus place them at odds with the theoretical orientations of many of the other feminist writers included in this volume.

An article by Enriqueta Vasquez (1970), "The Mexican-American Woman," is the only article in *Sisterhood Is Powerful* to be given an introduction. This sympathetic, sincere effort is intended to help white middle-class women understand Vasquez's perspective. The author, Elizabeth Sutherland Martinez, is obviously aware of the difficulties involved in bridging the communication gap between cultures and classes that separates American women. She warns that for many feminists the comments by Vasquez might "seem like a cop-out or 'Tommish.'" White middle-class feminists "have little gut understanding of the position of women from a colonized—not merely oppressed—group," Martinez writes. "Enriqueta Vasquez is a revolutionary, with her own tone of voice. Let Anglo women listen for her voice, not merely for echoes of their own" (Martinez 1970, 423, 426).

The entire section of *Sisterhood Is Powerful* containing the articles by minority women (as well as an article on high school women) is also given an introduction, but one of a markedly different character. This section, entitled "Go Tell It in the Valley: Changing Consciousness," is introduced with an article on "Resistances to Consciousness." The implication seems clear: this group of writers and/or their constituencies are operating at a low level of consciousness. It is a patronizing rejection of the historical and cultural uniqueness of minority communities in America, marginalizing the efforts of minority women to articulate a politics based on their own experiences. That this all too common reaction to their political analysis does not go unnoticed and unchallenged by minority women is obvious from the tone of Martinez's remarks:

> The middle-class Anglo woman must therefore beware of telling her black or brown sisters to throw off their chains—without at least first understanding the origins and reasons for those "chains." And also without first asking themselves: are there perhaps some aspects of these other life-styles from which we, with our advanced ideas, might still learn? (Martinez 1970, 425)

KATE MILLETT'S *SEXUAL POLITICS*

In *Sexual Politics* (1971), Kate Millett's debt to Beauvoir is enormous and largely unacknowledged, reflecting much of the ethnocentrism that mars Beauvoir's analysis. These shortcomings are all the more pronounced coming some thirty years later, long after the civil rights movement had begun to force white America to recognize the existence of minority cultures within its boundaries. Millett draws extensively on an analogy with slavery and racism in her analysis of sexual politics, misrepresenting the slavery experience, ignoring the experiences of minority women in her analysis of oppression, and masking the differences between the situations of white and minority women. Her theory relies upon an ethnocentric view of women's power, the character of sex roles, and the meaning of the family.

Millett's analogy with racism and slavery distorts the slavery experience by ignoring the history of slave resistance and repeating the stereotype of the passive slave. Women's "marginal life frequently renders them conservative, for like all persons in their situations (slaves are a classic example here) they identify their own survival with the prosperity of those who feed them." And, in spite of her frequent reliance upon an analogy with the black experience, Millett's direct discussion of racism is perfunctory. She deigns to "devote a few words to it as well" (Millett 1971, 38).

Her description of the experience of oppression, furthermore, ignores the experience of minority women. In her description of the family as the unit of patriarchal government effecting "control and conformity where political and other authorities are insufficient" (Millett 1971, 33), Millett omits the experience of minority communities where the family serves as a bastion against racist society or where the family has been systematically destroyed, as in slavery. In these cases, the building and strengthening of the family is an important aspect of the survival of the community. As Norton (1970, 403), Daniels-Eichelberger (1977, 23), and Delaplaine (1978, 11–12) argue, for minority women, the family is far from being experienced as a unit in the government of the racist state.

Unlike Beauvoir, Millett denies the differences in the situations of minority and white women, dismissing the power and privileges accorded to white women as mere mystifications.

> In a society where status is dependent upon the economic, social, and educational circumstances of class, it is possible for certain females to appear to stand higher than some males. Yet not when one looks more closely at the subject. (Millett 1971, 36)

Her analysis of women's economic position as essentially one of dependency ignores the independent economic role played by many minority women, just as the stereotypes of passivity and fragility misrepresent the sex roles of women in the black community.

The practice of feminist theorists, including Millett, of drawing analogies between the situations of oppressed minorities and white women, without sufficient attention to the dissimilarities in those situations is a serious problem, as noted by Catherine Stimpson.

> I believe that women's liberation would be much stronger, much more honest, and ultimately more secure if it stopped comparing white women to blacks so freely. The analogy exploits the passion, ambition, and vigor of the black movement. It perpetuates the depressing habit white people have of first defining the black experience and then making it their own. . . . Perhaps more dangerous, the analogy evades, in the rhetorical haze, the harsh fact of white women's racism. (Stimpson 1971, 650)

Another serious difficulty in Millett's theory comes in her views of the primacy of sexism as a form of oppression and of patriarchy as an absolute, universal phenomenon. Although most minority women experience racism as a more fundamental form of oppression, or at least as equally fundamental as sexism, Millett asserts that sexism is "perhaps the most pervasive ideology of our culture and it provides its most fundamental concept of power." Apart from a comment that Jean Genet's experiences taught him "how sexual caste supersedes all other forms of inegalitarianism: racial, political, or economic," Millett's conclusion rests on her problematic notion of absolute patriarchy (Millett 1971, 25, 39, 20). Millett's claim that patriarchy is "universal" throughout all cultures and times is a generalization from her own cultural experience that "every avenue of power within the society, including the coercive force of the police, is entirely in male hands." This claim denies that societies exist in which women do have power in some areas, such as the economy, although their power may not be as equally extensive as man's. Millett realizes that exceptions exist to her description of patriarchy, without altering the reality of patriarchy as a "social constant." In her view patriarchy is an absolute and idealized notion, inaccessible to counterexamples (Millett 1971, 25). Her interest is not with accurately representing the experiences of women in other cultures, but with describing and analyzing her own cultural experience, as was Beauvoir's in

The Second Sex. Her treatment of women's experiences in other cultures is cursory, and her generalizations appear hasty and ethnocentric.

SHULAMITH FIRESTONE'S *THE DIALECTIC OF SEX*

Perhaps the most influential radical feminist theorist, Shulamith Firestone, and her ethnocentrism, has been fundamental in shaping contemporary feminism. Although Firestone devotes more attention to the discussion of racism than does either Beauvoir or Millett, her analysis is, in many ways, much less satisfactory. In her reduction of racism to sexism, she relies upon an overextended and distorted metaphor of the "Family of Man." Her discussion is marked by racist stereotypes and an insensitivity to the oppression of black women. Firestone also espouses the notion of absolute patriarchy, claiming without substantiation that "throughout history, in all stages and types of culture, women have been oppressed due to their biological function." She openly expresses contempt for the efforts of anthropologists to improve our perceptions of women's roles in other cultures: "These biological contingencies in the human family cannot be covered over with anthropological sophistries" (Firestone 1970, 74, 9).

But a most serious shortcoming in her analysis rests, as mentioned above, in her comparison between racism and sexism. Her conclusion that "racism is sexism extended" rests on her metaphor of the "Family of Man." This metaphor is stretched to the breaking point and filled with ironies and racist stereotypes. Whites are pictured as the parents of the "Family," when in the actual evolution of human society Euro-Americans are the descendants of their African ancestors. The Mother is represented as the white woman, which is particularly ironic in the context of American history where black women mothered children of whites along with their own children and bore the children of white men as well.

In describing the relationships between white women and black men, Firestone takes the absurd position that the racism of white women is "inauthentic" as though there could be an "authentic," i.e., ethical in Beauvoir's sense, form of racism. The racist stereotypes are numerous: black people are pictured as children in Firestone's "Family"; the black woman is described as a seductress of white men, "the black sexpot" who has "freedom from the marriage bind" (Firestone 1970, 114). These characterizations stereotype and deny the reality of black people's oppression and their cultural autonomy, their status as objects of possession under slavery and their historic resistance, the sexual abuse of slave women, and the tragedy of the assault on the black family.

Firestone's argument for the primacy of sexism from the metaphor of the racial "Family of Man" begins with an appeal to her own cultural heritage: "In the Biblical sense the races are no more than the various parents and siblings of the Family of Man" (Firestone 1970, 108). Ironically, Firestone uses a part of her own culture to describe the relationship between cultures, unaware of the ethnocentrism that such a description expresses. It is not possible to arrive at any conclusive position concerning the relative primacy of sexism or racism on the basis of either historical or anthropological research. The era of the beginnings of human society is simply inaccessible to all but the most superficial archaeological study.

The assertion of the primacy of sexist oppression is also not justifiable on experiential or political grounds. Sexism may be a primary form of oppression experienced by many women in America, but the conclusion that the elimination of sexism would necessarily entail the end of racist oppression, without direct efforts at combating racism, does not follow. Nor is there any argument in support of that conclusion, other than untenable arguments based on androcentric views of women's roles, misconceptions about slavery, and racist metaphors.

Whatever the prehistoric origins of oppression, it should be clear to contemporary feminists that any liberation movement must be dedicated to a direct struggle against racial and class oppression as well as sexism. Minority feminists cannot be expected to identify with feminist organizations that confine their opposition to racism to the expression of empty platitudes and shaky theorizing. If white feminists are to work successfully toward the goal of true human liberation, they must also refute such positions and confront the realities of racism and class oppression in the women's movement and in the society as a whole.

MARY DALY'S *BEYOND GOD THE FATHER*

Mary Daly's work is an exciting addition to feminist philosophy and deserves careful study. However, her analysis of racism and sexism is no less problematic than the other theories discussed above. Daly's theory is ethnocentric in its view of woman's power. She offers no adequate support for her position that sexism is the primary form of oppression, and her approach to racism is abstract and suffers from some of the same myopia she attacks in critics of feminism.

Although recognizing what she terms the "derivative status" some women have as a consequence of their relationships with men, Daly dismisses any power that might be available to women as merely illusory. Sexual caste is "masked, hidden" by derivative status that "divides us against each other and encourages identification with patriarchal institutions which serve the interests of men at the expense of women." Daly's belief in an absolute patriarchy remains unshaken by this phenomenon of derivative status. Actually, according to Daly, there is a "basic sameness of our situation as women." "The bonding is born out of shared recognition that there exists a worldwide phenomenon of sexual caste, basically the same whether one lives in Saudi Arabia or in Sweden" (Daly 1973, 3, 2). This is her only reference to the experiences of women in other cultures, and it obliterates any differences in our situations. Thus, the development of autonomous minority women's feminist organizations must remain completely inexplicable in Daly's analysis, unless one resorts to the patronizing charge of false consciousness.

Along with her stance on absolute patriarchy, Daly's argument for the primacy of sexism as a form of oppression lacks adequate support. "Only radical feminism, of all revolutionary causes, opens up human consciousness adequately to the desire for nonhierarchical, nonoppressive society, revealing sexism as the basic model and source of oppression." While it is certainly true that feminism is radically nonhierarchical, a continued insensitivity to racial oppression contradicts this characterization and thus undermines Daly's conclusion as well. Sexism is certainly an important model and source of oppression, but not the only one. Sexism alone does also not provide an adequate explanation for genocide and war, as Daly asserts (Daly 1973, 190, 163, 118).

Daly criticizes the trivialization of sexism and the general pattern of "unseeing" common to opponents of feminism. The same criticisms, however, could be applied to her own analysis of racism. When she writes that "black feminists are voices crying in the desert" (Daly 1973, 164), she is referring to the black community as the desert. But the same metaphor could be used to describe the lack of sensitivity and receptivity shown by some white feminists when confronted with black feminist views.

CONCLUSION

My critique of an absolute notion of patriarchy does not imply a denial of some forms of sexist oppression in practically all contemporary societies. Nor does my criticism of analyses that ignore the class differences between many white and minority women in America imply that most white women have historically held positions of power either through personal achievement or through their derivative status. It is clearly a mistake to glorify the powers accessible to the wife in marriage, historically, as antifeminists are prone to do and as Mae C. King seems to do in "The Politics of Sexual Stereotypes" (King 1973, 17–19). But the error to which feminist theorists have shown themselves so consistently susceptible is equally serious, because it obliterates an historical root of animosity between white and minority women. As well as having higher status as whites in America and access to better education and employment, some white women have historically had access to power and authority, derived from family ties, denied to minorities.

If the feminist movement is to realize its dream of becoming an intercultural, international movement, it will have to confront the ethnocentrism and racism within feminism on both the theoretical and the personal/practical level. In theory, this would generally entail relinquishing the ethnocentric assumption that the Euro-American experience is a typical or model one. Specifically, it means refusing to rely on simplistic analogies of sexism with slavery and racism that ignore differences in these situations. It means at least recognizing that the subordination of women may not be a universal phenomenon and that the concept of absolute patriarchy, as it is found in much of feminist theory, is a distortion of the experiences of women in many cultures. We must further recognize that the sex-role stereotypes of our culture are not universal cross-culturally; the experience of the family differs between communities according to their different histories. Overcoming the ethnocentrism in feminist theoretical perspectives also entails relinquishing the assumption of the primacy of sexism as a form of oppression. For feminists whose commitment is to the elimination of classism and racism as well as sexism, this requires the recognition that all forms of oppression must be subjected to exposure, analysis, and confrontation. There is an urgent need for more theoretical discussion of the character and interrelatedness of these various forms of oppression.

But efforts on a theoretical level are not sufficient. Our efforts must extend to a personal and practical level as well. White feminists must confront racism and classism within their organizations and selves and strive to establish working coalitions with minority feminists. But to effectively define strategies for combating racism, classism, and sexism, minority and white women must first stop talking past each other and establish communication. Drawing on the experience of a 1976 interracial conference on sexism and racism, cosponsored by the Sagaris Collective and the National Black Feminist Organization, a first practical step to combat racism within feminism should be a discussion of racism on a personal level. The facilitators of the conference noted resistances on the part of white women to discussing racism, resistances no doubt of many feminists around the country. Of their initial efforts to have separate groups of white and black women identify their "bottom line," their personal limits in interracial relationships, a white facilitator, Ginny Apuzzo, noted the following problem.

> The big discussion was around the definition, what was meant by "bottom line." I've found that one of the most common tactics used in the beginning of any significant dialogue is to debate the validity of the question. The white women in my group all started to debate that definition. When you don't want to deal with something you tend to make believe that you don't completely understand the question. So before we could get down to the nitty-gritty of what each of us meant by the bottom line, an enormous amount of time was wasted on semantics. The women were conscious of what that question would bring out. There was great difficulty in recognizing that no matter how much we want to respond out of a growing consciousness, we have been here for too many years and are still encumbered with prejudice. (Apuzzo and Powell 1977, 13)

A second difficult step in overcoming racism within the feminist movement and developing strategies to combat racism and sexism in the general community involves establishing an interracial dialogue. On a practical level, reaching out to minority women can mean providing a

Spanish edition of a rape prevention pamphlet for a Latin community, as the District of Columbia Rape Crisis Center did several years ago (Delaplaine 1978, 13). Or it can mean including images of minority women in films and other outreach material. A teacher can include material on minority women, being prepared to respond to the all-too-often-heard complaints of white students that discussions of racism and the experiences of minority women are irrelevant to feminism.

For white feminists, participating in an interracial dialogue also means being willing to listen to minority women without censorship, as Elizabeth Sutherland Martinez urged in *Sisterhood Is Powerful*. Minority feminists, in writing on the effects of racism and sexism in their lives, have taken the first step in establishing a dialogue on these issues. More white feminists must respond positively to this initiative, addressing the issues that have been raised and contributing their own perspectives. Too often in the past, white feminists have seemed reluctant to listen to minority women without censure. One recent example is of a women's studies committee at a midwestern university that attempted to censure a course on black women and their cultural heritage that was being proposed by black women faculty. The committee's criticism was that the course was not reflective of a radical feminist critique of the practice of clitorectomy, which is found in some African cultures. But, as we have seen, feminist ideology has generally failed to reflect the experiences of women in other cultures. Rather than attempting to control the content and ideological orientation of courses taught by minority women, white feminists should recognize the right of minority women to articulate a politics based on their own experiences.

Another example of this problem can be seen in the response of the editors of a feminist newspaper to a series of articles by black feminist writer Brenda Daniels-Eichelberger, analyzing the feelings of enmity that black women often have toward white women (Daniels-Eichelberger 1977/78). Daniels-Eichelberger discusses, among other attitudes of black women, the ideas that white women appear to feel superior to black women, seem to exploit black women politically while shunning them socially and personally, and represent the institutionalized standard of beauty, and pursue relationships with black men to the detriment of relationships between black men and women. Daniels-Eichelberger emphasizes the important point that racial stereotypes, whether held by black women or white women, must be confronted and the source of animosity resolved, not simply hidden from view, if a viable sisterhood is to result. Unfortunately, the editors did not find Daniels-Eichelberger's articles appropriate and cut the series short.

Feminists must not avoid, but invite dialogue and confront racism and classism, as well as sexism, on both a personal and a theoretical level, to achieve the coalitions enabling feminism to become a truly international and intercultural movement.

Reprinted, with changes, from *Feminist Studies* 5, no. 2 (Summer 1979): 384–401.

3

BEAUVOIR AND SARTRE: THE QUESTION OF INFLUENCE (1981)

The question of the influence that Simone de Beauvoir and Jean-Paul Sartre had on one another's work during the fifty years of their relationship has seldom been posed in a rigorous fashion. Most writers analyzing Sartre's work have been content to refer to Beauvoir solely for biographical information concerning Sartre's life, assuming, often because of a sexist bias, that the question of influence has been settled, with Beauvoir's work having been found to have been written entirely within a Sartrean perspective even though the reality of the differences in their work challenges this assumption. One occasionally hears professors of philosophy who are teaching Beauvoir's *Ethics of Ambiguity* (1947) complain that it fails to be consistent with Sartre's philosophy. Irritated by this evidence of philosophical difference, they charge Beauvoir with deviating from the perspective of *Being and Nothingness* (1943) as though her philosophic autonomy were a fault. And feminist philosophers who consider *The Second Sex* (1949) to be merely an application of Sartre's perspective are similarly reminded of Beauvoir's philosophic differences from Sartre when their analyses confront the sexism and limitations of Sartre's understanding of woman's situation obvious in *Being and Nothingness* and his other writings. The fact that Beauvoir's works have often been translated into English with a casual disregard for either accuracy or consistency in the rendering of her ideas may have contributed to the failure to take Beauvoir seriously as a philosophic writer. One of her most important essays, *The Second Sex*, has been edited radically, with no indications of the deletions in the text, thus further disrupting the coherence of her ideas.

Once a closer study of the actual differences in the perspectives reflected in the works of Beauvoir and Sartre is undertaken, it soon becomes clear that the simplistic view that reduces Beauvoir's work and philosophical orientation to that of Sartre is inadequate for a full comprehension of her work. And such a view, by ignoring the considerable influence that Beauvoir had on Sartre's work, is inadequate for a comprehensive understanding of Sartre's work as well. The question of their mutual influence during the course of an intensely intellectual and personal relationship, perhaps unique in the philosophic tradition and far from being settled, must be addressed rigorously.

But the undertaking is not without difficulties, one of the most serious of which concerns Beauvoir's attitude toward her own work and that of Sartre. In her autobiographical texts, Beauvoir writes that in the early years of their relationship, she played a subordinate role to Sartre. He was content to use Beauvoir as a sounding board for his own ideas, and she to respond to his theories. But her role of critic did not challenge her to define her own philosophical perspective. Her approach remained negative rather than the positive articulation of her own theoretical perspective. In writing of those first postgraduate years, Beauvoir remarks that she felt, like most women of her generation, that she lacked the requisite audacity for bringing the world fundamentally into question, as philosophy demands (Beauvoir 1960, 228–29, 46). Even in the years immediately following World War II, when her sense of direction as a writer had matured, she could still feel embarrassed, excessive modesty when requested to submit an article explaining her own philosophical position. It was during this same period that she found herself giving lip service to an idea of Sartre's concerning one's freedom in "situation" because she still felt unable to define her own position clearly (Beauvoir 1960, 448). This attitude presents a problem for any commentator on the works of Beauvoir and Sartre who is interested in clearly defining their perspectives on various issues. In addition, Beauvoir has written relatively few philosophical essays and has, on occasion, explicitly defended Sartre's position for him. The commentator must be careful not to assume that Beauvoir is always doing so, in order to not miss the originality in Beauvoir's autobiographies and literary works and indications of the development of Beauvoir's own philosophical perspective.

Perhaps most disarming for the commentator is Beauvoir's claim that while her literary works were created out of her own life experience, and are thus entirely free from Sartrean influence, her philosophi-

cal perspective was completely influenced by Sartre, on whose philosophical stance she had no influence at all since she was not herself a
philosopher. Both elements of this claim are suspect. Many of her works,
as well as his, are literary as well as philosophical. Nor must one be a
philosopher in order to influence a philosopher. But since Beauvoir admitted that she may have influenced Sartre by introducing him to certain
important ideas or by changing his perspective on reality in some ways,
our disagreement over whether this constitutes a philosophical influence
might be a verbal one. In fact, Beauvoir's own reports of her often
heated arguments with Sartre (recorded in her autobiographies) provide
the commentator with some of the best indications of the direction of
their mutual philosophical influence. It should be noted that Sartre himself offers little help to the commentator in this regard, having seldom
acknowledged or discussed Beauvoir's influence on his work or on the
development of his ideas over the years.

But in spite of the difficulties inherent in a study of these writers
and their mutual influence, the approach to bring to the problem seems
obvious. One must begin with a discussion of their earliest writings and
the positions reflected in those writings and continue forward, tracing
the developments in their perspectives, determining their differences on
significant issues, and looking for evidence that the perspective of one
might have been taken up, even in part, by the other. My study begins
in just such a way, referring extensively to Beauvoir's autobiographies,
which have provided such important biographical information to students of Sartre's work in the past, for information on their earliest differences in perspective and then proceeding through the years of the war
when they both struggled to come to grips with social, political reality
in their writings. My discussion leaves them in the early 1950s, making
only brief suggestions concerning later directions in the development of
their work. My focus is more often on Beauvoir's writings, and on the
question of her influence on Sartre's work, since I assume that most of
Sartre's works are more familiar and require less exposition and that the
influence that Sartre had on Beauvoir is perhaps more obvious than is
the influence that extended from Beauvoir to Sartre. My intention, then,
is to correct a picture that has tended in the past to be too one-sided.

This study has confirmed my initial impression that Beauvoir's writings have expressed concerns and perspectives different from those of
Sartre, but at least in part, adopted by Sartre in later works of his own.

Broadly defined, an important area of Beauvoir's originality and influence on Sartre concerns the relationship of the individual to the social, historical context of the individual's action. Beauvoir, for example, was the first to address herself to the problem of the relationship with the Other, which was a problem Sartre was later to address himself, occasionally taking a very Beauvoirian perspective.

Beauvoir also recognized earlier than Sartre the limiting effects of the social-historical context, including one's personal history and childhood, on an individual's choice; she consequently found Sartre's early voluntarism exaggerated. Perhaps more so than in the first example, Sartre's perspective shifted over the years, often seemingly in response to Beauvoir's work, bringing him closer to her position. Both of these examples, as we shall see, suggest the obvious explanation that Sartre's perspective was in fact significantly influenced by that of Beauvoir.

THE PROBLEM OF THE OTHER

Sartre is well known for his study of the relationship with the Other in *Being and Nothingness* and in literary works such as *No Exit* (1945). But it is seldom acknowledged that Beauvoir, in her earliest works, focuses on the relation with the Other, writing prior to Sartre's work in this area and defining her description of the structures of this relationship on the basis of her own experience. For Beauvoir, the problem of the Other is multifaceted. One important aspect is the difficulty of retaining one's sense of individual autonomy while experiencing a longing, a yearning for complete union with the Other. This problem, which Beauvoir experienced first in her deep friendship with her childhood friend, Zaza, took on dramatic dimensions in the early years of her relationship with Sartre. This was a time when her own sense of direction was confused, as she began her adult life definitively separated from the restrictive confines of her family and school, outside the established social roles for a woman. She experienced a profound moral crisis in which she felt loss of her sense of self in her love for the Other. But along with her search for union with the Other, she also felt the profound moral necessity of assuming responsibility for her own life by firmly establishing her sense of individual autonomy. It was within the tension of these two often conflicting demands that Beauvoir conceived the possibility and challenge of an authentic relationship. It is a delicate balancing act few of the women in her writings, from *She Came to Stay* (1943) to *The Second Sex* (1949), *The Mandarins* (1954), and *The Woman Destroyed* (1968), are able to carry out successfully. For all its elusiveness, this authentic relationship remains a central value in Beauvoir's social philosophy, offering the individual an opportunity for authentic justification unobtainable in solitude.

This element of Beauvoir's perspective differs decisively from the early individualism she shared with Sartre. And her divergence on this point is partially responsible for the tension that characterizes the perspective of *Ethics of Ambiguity*. This tension, resulting from the strain of moving from individualism to a social perception of human reality, only becomes comprehensible when both her hesitations about defining her own philosophical perspective and her profound belief in individual freedom and the ultimate limitations of solitary individualism are understood.

Another aspect of the problem of the Other addressed by Beauvoir in her earliest writings that is also found in Sartre's writings is the threat posed by the image of one's self in the eyes of the Other. Beauvoir explains the genesis of her perspective on this problem once again in terms of her own life experience. During the period of great uncertainty in her life when she first began living independently of her family, she felt threatened by the presence of other persons whose values differed radically from her own but were forced upon her. In the eyes of these other persons, she felt her own values negated. *She Came to Stay*, the novel in which Beauvoir first addressed this question, ends with the annihilation of the threatening person, the radical overcoming of this negating of one's self. The novel's Hegelean epigraph "Each consciousness seeks the death of the other," often assumed to be evidence of the Hegelean influence on the novel, came to Beauvoir's attention only in 1940, after the book had been written (Beauvoir 1960, 324).

Beauvoir's novel, which was written from 1937 to 1941, anticipates the writings of Sartre on confrontations with the Other, including the section on the "Look" in *Being and Nothingness*. The entire section on the existence of others has a strange, tacked-on quality in *Being and Nothingness* and a secondary, derivative status ontologically, which might seem comprehensible if it were seen as a problem Sartre took up only as a later addition to his theory. Casual critics of Beauvoir's work, thinking of the famous line from *No Exit*, "Hell is other people," have concluded that Beauvoir's works, such as *She Came to Stay* in which the problem of the Other plays a mayor role, reflect the influence of Sartre. But as we have seen, the reverse would be a more plausible interpretation.

Beauvoir's most well-known application of the concept of the Other is, of course, in *The Second Sex*, written in 1948–49. Since Sartre had only a short time before, in 1944, written *Anti-Semite and Jew* (1946), in which a phenomenon very similar to sexism and the oppression of women is studied, one might expect Beauvoir's perspective to be profoundly influenced by Sartre. In fact, their perspectives do share certain common elements, especially an analysis of the psychological dynamics of self-justification and the search by both the sexist and the racist for security in superiority. But one thing the two works do not share is the use of the concept of the Other.

Sartre never writes of the anti-Semite seeing the Jew as Other, although he certainly might have done so. It is only in a work that followed the publication of *The Second Sex*, *Saint Genet* (1952), a pivotal but too often ignored work written from 1950 to 1952, that Sartre utilizes the concept of the Other in the analysis of social oppression, in this case, society's labeling of the boy Genet as a thief. Sartre describes the process by which Genet came to see himself [as the Other], which is the effect that Beauvoir had noted as resulting from a sexist socialization of a young girl. Here is an even more striking example of the introduction of a concept first found in a work by Beauvoir into Sartre's perspective.

In *Saint Genet* Sartre first utilizes the concept of fraternity and links freedom with reciprocity, as Beauvoir had done earlier in *Ethics of Ambiguity* and *The Second Sex*. The complex issue of whether Sartre's philosophical perspective ever encompassed an entirely adequate concept of fraternity, of social identity, an issue hardly made less complicated by the publication of the final interviews with Benny Lévy, cannot be resolved in this chapter. But it should be clear that any such discussion cannot ignore either the importance of *Saint Genet* or the influence of *The Second Sex* on the development of Sartre's perspective (*see* Edwards 1980).

LIMITATIONS ON FREEDOM

The problem of the Other is not the only area in which Beauvoir's ideas on the relation of the individual to society differed from those of Sartre and, at least in part, were to influence him. A second significant area concerns the effect on an individual's freedom of the social-historical context, including the personal history of one's childhood. In her 1960 autobiographical text *The Prime of Life*, Beauvoir reports that in the early years of her relationship with Sartre, they both held a "rationalist-voluntarist" attitude toward reality and a belief in their radical freedom. As young teachers, Beauvoir comments, "circumstances permitted us a certain measure of detachment, free time, and lack of concern. It was tempting to confound them with sovereign freedom." "It was our conditioning as young petite bourgeois intellectuals that led us to believe ourselves free of conditioning" (Beauvoir 1960, 26, 19, 24, 25).

But while their profession as teachers gave them a shared perspective, their childhoods provided them with profoundly differing experiences with which they began adult life. At the onset of his teaching career, Sartre felt his freedom threatened by the end of his years of childhood irresponsibility, the approach of his military service, and the beginning of his career as a teacher, a civil servant, and a member of the dreaded establishment. While he and his closest male friends outlined the works they would write, challenging and undermining the status quo, Beauvoir was adrift, without a clear sense of direction, living outside the confinement of social roles and expectations. She celebrated her first teaching assignment as the fulfillment of her dreams of independence, her victory against the threats to her individual survival that had been posed by her family and teachers. She had experienced her adolescence as a struggle for freedom from the future of dependency to which she was destined as a young bourgeois woman. When her best friend Zaza died in the midst of a struggle with her mother to escape an arranged marriage, Beauvoir felt as though her own freedom had been won at the cost of her friend's life. Thus, while she had a profound belief in her own individual freedom, in her own capacity to determine and will her own destiny, she also had an immediate awareness of the power of social oppression, which Sartre's childhood experiences had not given him.

Their differing backgrounds also translated into different attitudes toward their work and extended to epistemological questions. Beauvoir admired Sartre's dedication to literature, which far exceeded her own commitment as a writer, a profession which she, like Sartre, had chosen at an early age. But she found her newly won freedom so exhilarating that her first commitment was to experiencing life in all its richness. That commitment set her at odds with Sartre, who assumed what Beauvoir felt to be an exaggerated subjectivist position. She asserted that the fundamental ambiguity of reality prevented it from ever being captured totally in a sentence or an essay; Sartre argued that reality coincided exactly with man's knowledge of it (Beauvoir 1960, 46, 151). Later in their relationship, Beauvoir's passions, which astonished her with their intensity, forced her to modify her psychological voluntarism, a position, however, which Sartre continued to hold. He argued that she had chosen to give in to her emotions, to the demands of the body, and that the will always retains its dominance. Thus, although both Beauvoir and Sartre had many attitudes in common in the early years of their relationship, Beauvoir's experiences provided a different perspective and led her eventually to modify her position in ways taking her further away from Sartre's perspective.

A critical problem for the commentator at this juncture is that Beauvoir began her career as a writer later than did Sartre and at first wrote exclusively fictional works, short stories, and novels, making the task of comparing their early philosophical perspectives difficult. But Beauvoir's differing perspective does emerge from a consideration of their early works, notably in her references to the childhoods and personal histories of her characters and in her efforts to come to grips with the experience of Zaza's death. Beauvoir explored the childhoods of her characters in almost all of her early writings, which focused on the problem of the relation with the Other. Her second novel, which is untitled and unpublished, is the story of a young woman's apprenticeship in life, in which she learns to accept another person without idolizing her and to consent to her own freedom without expecting the other person to support her existence (Beauvoir 1960, 108). Beauvoir writes that she also tried to tell the story of Zaza's death in this novel, where a character dies in a struggle to escape the bonds of bourgeois society. Beauvoir's third, unpublished novel, written in 1933–35, focuses on an oppressive childhood experience, the efforts of a young girl to avoid an arranged marriage and her subsequent difficulties in a relationship in which her independence and self-confidence are threatened by feelings driving her impetuously toward another person.

When Things of the Spirit Come First (1935–37), Beauvoir's collection of stories unpublished until 1979, describes the stifling effects of bourgeois society on the development of its children. In the manuscript of her next novel, *She Came to Stay* (1943), Beauvoir gave a lengthy account of the central figure's childhood, which she later deleted from the published version. She also drew heavily on an account of the central figure's childhood in *The Blood of Others* (1945), which again focuses on the problem of the Other and establishing a relation of freedom to freedom. Although Beauvoir also felt the necessity of describing the childhood of another central figure in the book, she decided to only indicate it through several brief allusions (Beauvoir 1960, 325, 556). Beauvoir's commitment to seeing the individual within the context of childhood experiences is evident in all of her novels and short stories from 1931 through 1945.

This concern, however, is in sharp contrast to Sartre's attitude at that time toward one's childhood and the past in general. The for-itself emerges full blown in *Being and Nothingness*, with birth and development, and possible hindrances to development, ignored. Nor are the childhoods of the characters in his novels often considered to be significant. In a 1945 interview with Dominique Aury, where Sartre discusses existentialism and the problem of freedom in a novel, he contrasts his approach to that of Zola saying,

> For Zola, everything obeys the narrowest determinism. Zola's novels are written in the past, while my characters have a future. . . . The childhood of Mathieu is of no importance. (Aury 1945; quoted in Contat and Rybalka 1970, 128)

And consider Sartre's essay *Baudelaire* (1946), where his interest is in both Baudelaire's life and writings. Even here, Sartre's treatment of Baudelaire's childhood is perfunctory. His descriptions seem less interested in the actual experiences than in providing an occasion for an "original choice" that would then be the theoretical starting point for the study of the adult and his writings.

Sartre did not write effectively about childhood until after Beauvoir had completed her monumental study of women's oppression, *The Second Sex*, which traces the inhibiting effects of childhood socialization on the development of the young girl's sense of personal autonomy and self-assertion. It was only in 1950 that Sartre began his essay on Jean Genet, where he first confronted the realities of childhood experience.

Although his approach to childhood, with its emphasis on the choice that gives childhood importance in the case of Genet, is certainly not identical to Beauvoir's, Sartre has definitely gained an awareness of the significance of the concrete experiences of an individual's past, the personal history that is one's childhood. In our 1979 interview, Beauvoir agreed with my suggestion that Sartre's appreciation of the experience of childhood might represent an area in which her influence is evidenced in his work.

Both Sartre and Beauvoir found their perspectives fundamentally altered by World War II, the defeat and occupation, and Sartre's imprisonment. Both writers struggled to come to grips with the social, political, and historical dimensions of reality that they had formerly kept at a distance. But their viewpoints, although they remained united in many respects, once again significantly differed. And that difference centered on the issue just discussed in relation to the analyses of childhood—the problem of choice.

In *The Prime of Life* Beauvoir describes how her perspective and that of Sartre changed during the years of the war. In 1940, Beauvoir writes, Sartre returned on military leave to present her with

> his new ethics based on the notion of authenticity—that everyone must "assume" their "situation"; everything else is a flight, an empty pretension, a masquerade founded on bad faith. . . . Assuming one's situation meant to transcend it and engage oneself in an action. . . . One could see that there had been a serious change in him and also in me, who rallied immediately to his idea, because formerly our first care had been to keep our situation at a distance by games, deceptions, and lies. (Beauvoir 1960, 442)

But later, after Sartre's return from a prison camp, they argued about the question of the relation of situation and freedom. Beauvoir maintained

> that, from the point of view of freedom, as Sartre defined it—not stoical resignation but active transcendence of the given—situations are not equivalent; what transcendence is possible for a woman enclosed in a harem? But, there are different ways of living this confinement, Sartre said to me. I stuck to my position for a long time, and only gave lip service to Sartre's. Basically, I was right. But in order to defend my position, it would have been necessary for me to aban-

don the terrain of the individualist, thus idealist, ethic, on which we were placed. (Beauvoir 1960, 448)

Beauvoir's reluctance to accept this theory of the fundamental equivalence of situations is evident in *Ethics of Ambiguity*, written in 1946–47, an essay I described earlier as marked by a profound tension. The stress evident in this provocative essay stems from Beauvoir's attempts to reconcile not only her individualism with her social ideal, but also her belief in human freedom with the reality of human oppression. Unwilling to simply consign them to mutually exclusive spheres of existence, for example, the ontological and the concrete, Beauvoir sought to describe human freedom as both a defining feature of human reality and a concrete experience of transcending the givens of reality, an experience that is thus capable of being denied under oppression. Sartre's essay on Baudelaire and his popular lecture "Existentialism is a Humanism," which is assuredly too superficial to give much indication of his ethical theory, are in many respects similar to *Ethics of Ambiguity*. But they lack this tension, the signs of the strain evident in Beauvoir's attempt to move beyond what she found to be the limitations of the notion of freedom she shared with Sartre.

Beauvoir's realization of the force of social conditioning and the limitations on human freedom suggested in *Ethics of Ambiguity* acquires depth and consistency in *The Second Sex*, where she describes the historical development of woman's oppression as being rooted in the biological reality of woman's reproductive function and physical weakness and the ontological reality of man's yearning for escape from freedom in the security of a given superiority, institutionalized in economic and political institutions, inculcated through oppressive techniques of socialization of sex roles, and justified historically in sexist ideology permeating every aspect of culture. Beauvoir asks whether a girl raised in a sexist society can be said to have ever been allowed the possibility of choosing her freedom, of assuming her existence (Beauvoir 1949, 566).

Ironically *The Second Sex* is often reduced by critics (and by Beauvoir herself on occasion) to merely an application of Sartre's perspective to a social problem. The limitations of this analysis are evident when the perspective of *The Second Sex* is contrasted with that of *Anti-Semite and Jew* and Sartre's 1946 essay on class oppression and the limitations of materialism, "Materialism and Revolution." These essays reveal the inability of Sartre's perspective to comprehend the complex historical and cultural dimensions of oppression and its concrete experience for the oppressed person, which Beauvoir describes so effectively in *The Second Sex*. In fact, Sartre only began to deal more adequately with these dimensions of existence after Beauvoir's work in *The Second Sex* was completed. Shortly thereafter, in 1950, Sartre began to realize, perhaps through the recognition of the theoretical advances represented by *The Second Sex*, the necessity of developing his understanding of historical materialism. He undertook a study of Marx and then began his work on Jean Genet, using a theoretical framework strikingly similar to that developed by Beauvoir in *The Second Sex*.

The aspects of *Anti-Semite and Jew* most anticipatory of *The Second Sex* are the descriptions of the psychology of the anti-Semite and his search for security of identity in a static racial superiority. One sentence, "If the Jew had not existed, the anti-Semite would have invented him" (Sartre 1946, 15), is taken up almost exactly in *The Second Sex* to describe the satisfaction a man can feel in a sexist society. It is the description of the experience of the Jew that is problematic in Sartre's essay and in sharp contrast with Beauvoir's description of women's experiences under sexism. Sartre lacks a framework for recognizing a Jewish historical, cultural identity (just as he refuses to consider any historical dimension in the practice of anti-Semitism, considering it in each instance as the unconditioned choice of a free individual). The only identity he can recognize as shared by Jews is their identity as victims, given to them by the anti-Semites. He ignores the cultural heritage maintained in their use of Hebrew, for example. He contemptuously dismisses the statement by an American observer that Jews in America do not seem to fundamentally desire assimilation and loss of their cultural identity. And yet Sartre calls inauthentic those Jews who take a traditional liberal stance and demand their universal human rights. Sartre wants to apply an analysis analogous to that of Marx, that Jews, like the members of the working class under capitalism who fight for rights as workers, must demand rights as Jews. But Sartre's total lack of historical perspective and his rejection of any sense of Jewish cultural self-identity results in an ethical condemnation of the behavior of individual Jews. Sartre ironically criticizes them for not acting as Jews while denying that an identity as Jew is possible outside of their role as victim, their stereotyped identity under oppression.

The individualism, insensitivity, and political naïveté of Sartre's perspective, which ignores the practical limitations in a political situation that might require a liberal approach, dramatically distinguish this work from *The Second Sex*. Beauvoir, like Sartre, is aware of the danger in liberalism of trying to gain freedom by conformity to a supposedly universal, abstract bourgeois notion. But unlike Sartre, Beauvoir defines in *The Second Sex* concrete realities and shared situations of women's experience on which liberation as women, not as victims, can be based (although her analysis is not without problems of a masculinist definition of human reality). Beauvoir is cognizant of the dangers of playing into the hands of the oppressor in telling the oppressed they are inauthentic if they deny their womanliness (their femininity?), if they try to be men, when men have excluded women from access to transcendent, human activity. Sartre's insights in *Anti-Semite and Jew* remain centered in his understanding of the flight from freedom inherent in the anti-Semite's attitudes, although here too his description is weakened by a lack of historical perspective. In "Materialism and Revolution," Sartre's strength lies in his recognition that freedom is implied in the revolt of the oppressed and in their coming to consciousness of their oppression, an experience assumed in the action of party organizers. But once again, Sartre fails to come to grips with the other experience, the experience of oppression that is the background of the struggle for liberation.

The fundamental insights into the historical experience of oppression are not found in any of Sartre's earlier writings, and his work certainly does not provide a foundation for understanding woman's oppression and struggle for liberation. But *Saint Genet*, begun after *The Second Sex* was completed, represents a major advance in Sartre's perspective. Although he emphasizes that it was Genet's choosing to take up the experience of his childhood in his work that gives those experiences significance, there is a richness of concrete detail that gives the study of Genet's life and writing a reality lacking from Sartre's earlier study of Baudelaire. Strikingly, Sartre utilizes some of the central structures of *The Second Sex* in his description of Genet's experience, for example, the immanence/transcendence distinction and most importantly, the identity of the Thief as an Other that becomes absolute. Both structures are used differently by Sartre than by Beauvoir, just as she utilized in a new way theoretical structures from *Anti-Semite and Jew*.

Sartre's stated purpose in *Saint Genet* is almost identical to that of

Beauvoir in *The Second Sex*. Indeed, his statement of intention reads like an outline of *The Second Sex:* he will "show the limits of psychoanalytic interpretation and Marxist explication and . . . show that only freedom can account for a person in his totality" (Sartre 1952, 536). *The Second Sex* begins with critiques of psychoanalytic theory and Marxist explanations of woman's oppression and argues that woman's situation can only be understood in the context of an existentialist ethics that restores to woman a degree of freedom impossible within the other theoretical perspectives. The primary difference in the two books is that Beauvoir is describing the history of a social group and their oppression and struggle for liberation, while Sartre is concerned with tracing the history of a single individual. In this focus on an individual, Sartre's work on Genet is actually a much more appropriate example than *The Second Sex* of the application, the extension of Sartre's perspective in *Being and Nothingness,* and thus highlights the non-Sartrean perspective of *The Second Sex*.

This chapter has emphasized some of the areas in which Beauvoir seems to have influenced the development of Sartre's theoretical perspective on questions concerning the relation of the individual and individual freedom, to the Other, and to the situations that shape and limit the possibilities of choice. In that sense, it is distorting, although, of course, it is meant to correct a distortion in the opposite direction, where Sartre's influence on Beauvoir's work is overemphasized. The result is a challenge to begin considering their work together, as each new work being in some sense a response to the work of the other, for that is how it was written. If it has been obvious in the past that Beauvoir's work cannot be adequately understood without reference to Sartre's writings, it should now be equally apparent that no completely adequate comprehension of the development of Sartre's perspective is possible without a consideration of Beauvoir's work, which influenced him greatly. The directions of these influences over the fifty years of their relationship have just begun to be analyzed in this study. More questions remain than have been answered concerning the interrelatedness of their writings; they must be addressed.

Reprinted, with changes, from *EROS* 8, no. 1 (1981): 25–42, with permission from the Department of Philosophy, Purdue University. A later version was published as "Beauvoir and Sartre: The Philosophical Relationship" in *Yale French Studies* 72 (1986).

4

BEAUVOIR INTERVIEW (1982)

PARIS, 11 MAY 1982

Margaret Simons: I have a question about Sartre's influence on *The Second Sex*. You wrote in *The Prime of Life* that Sartre's questions about your childhood, about the fact that you were raised as a girl, not a boy, are what gave you the idea for *The Second Sex*.

Simone de Beauvoir: No, not exactly. I had begun—well, he was the one who actually told me . . . I wanted to write about myself and he said, "Don't forget to explain first of all what it is to be a woman." And I told him, "But that never bothered me, I was always equal to men." And he said, "Yes, but even so, you were raised differently, with different myths and a different view of the world." And I told him, "That's true." And that's how I began to work on the myths. And then, he encouraged me by saying that in order to understand the myths, one had to understand the reality. So I had to come back to reality, all of it, physiological, historical, etc. Then afterwards, I continued on my own on woman's situation as I saw it.

MS: You wrote somewhere that you never suffered from being female in your childhood.

SdB: No, I never suffered.

MS: But, was not your childhood different from a boy's? When you did the research for *The Second Sex,* did that change your interpretation of your childhood?

SdB: Not of my own childhood, but I interpret differently other people's childhood. I see many women whose childhood was unfavorable compared to that of a boy. But for me my childhood was not unfavorable.

55

MS: I remember a passage from *Memoirs of a Dutiful Daughter.* You were walking past a [boy's] high school . . .

SdB: Ah yes, near the Collège Stanislas. And I thought that they had a superior education, that's true. But in the end, I adapted to mine because I thought that later on I would be able to go on to higher education. But at that moment, yes, I thought that there was something there that was more intellectual than our course of study.

MS: And this was the case?

SdB: Yes, it was true.

MS: In your autobiography, you wrote that there was a disagreement between you and Sartre concerning literature and philosophy, and life. He put one before the other, and you did the reverse?

SdB: Yes, that's right.

MS: And somewhere you described sexuality and passion as overwhelming you when you were young. He always thought that it was a question of will, an act of will. And you thought that the body, that passion, could overwhelm . . . That's a difference between the two of you.

SdB: Yes, Sartre was much more voluntarist. But he also thought that about seasickness. He thought if you got seasick, it was because you had let it happen and with willpower, you could conquer seasickness.

MS: I thought that perhaps that might be a problem in *The Second Sex.* You used Sartre's philosophy, which is voluntarist, but you studied the body, and passion, and the training of girls. And you questioned whether there is a choice . . .

SdB: All the same, there's a choice in the Sartrean sense, that is, choices are always made in a certain situation and, starting from the same situation, one can choose this or that. One can have different choices in a single situation. That is, granted, one is a girl with a certain physical training and a certain social training; but starting from that, one can choose to accept it or to escape it or to . . . Well, naturally, the choice itself depends upon a number of things. But after all, there is still some freedom or choice, even in resignation of course.

MS: But you didn't think that was a great problem for you, to reconcile the Sartrean philosophical foundation with your research in biology, on the body?

SdB: But Sartre was not so voluntarist. In *Being and Nothingness,* there was a lot of things about the body.

MS: And in 1949, he also changed his ideas.

SdB: Oh no, *Being and Nothingness*, which he wrote well before that, is full of texts about the body. The body always had a lot of importance for him.

MS: But not exactly the same importance as for you.

SdB: When, in *Being and Nothingness,* he speaks of masochism as well as sadism, of love, etc., the body plays a very great role for Sartre also. Yes, always.

MS: And that wasn't a problem for you?

SdB: No, not at all.

MS: And you don't think he changed his ideas at that time?

SdB: No.

MS: How did he react to your book [*The Second Sex*]?

SdB: He read it along the way, as I was writing it, as we always read each other's work. From time to time, after reading a chapter, he would tell me that there were corrections to make, as I would sometimes tell him. So that book too, he read it as I wrote it. So he was not at all surprised by the book. He was in complete agreement with me.

MS: Not long before you wrote *The Second Sex,* he wrote *Baudelaire,* mentioning very little about Baudelaire's childhood. And afterwards, in *Saint Genet* he wrote a lot about Genet's childhood. Perhaps your interest in childhood experience might have interested him in it as well.

SdB: No, I don't think so. I think that was a development. *Baudelaire* was written very quickly and for Genet he wanted to do something more extensive. And then, Genet himself speaks a lot about his childhood and about children, so it's the subject Genet which required that one speak a lot about childhood . . .

MS: I see differences between your perspective in *The Second Sex* and Sartre's perspective in *Being and Nothingness.* You have said that in social relations one ought to look for reciprocity. That's a kind of optimism that was not in *Being and Nothingness.* Do you agree? Is there a difference, at least in attitude, if not in philosophy?

SdB: Yes, in effect, I think that the idea of reciprocity came later for Sartre. He had it in the *Critique.* In *Being and Nothingness,* reciprocity is not his subject. But that doesn't mean that he didn't believe that reciprocity was the best way after all to live out human relationships. That *was* what he believed. It's just that it wasn't his subject in *Being and*

Nothingness, because in *Being and Nothingness* he's concerned with the individual and not so much with the relations among individuals . . .

That is, in *The Second Sex,* I place myself much more on a moral plane whereas Sartre dealt with morality later on. In fact, he never exactly dealt with morality. In *Being and Nothingness,* he's not looking for the moral, he's seeking a description of what existence is . . . It's more an ontology than a morality.

MS: Now a final question on motherhood. You opened your discussion of motherhood in *The Second Sex* with a study of abortion, and you described motherhood as something rather negative, as an inhuman activity.

SdB: No, I didn't say that exactly. I said that there could be a human relation, even a completely interesting and privileged relation between mother and child, but that in many cases it was on the order of narcissism or tyranny or something like that. But I didn't say that motherhood in itself was always something to be condemned; no, I didn't say that. No, something that has dangers, but obviously, any human adventure has its dangers, such as love or anything. I didn't say that motherhood was something negative.

MS: I thought that you said that it did not support human meaning.

SdB: No, oh no, I didn't say that motherhood does not support human meaning. No, I am sure that I never said that.

MS: Is this a question that interests you now?

SdB: Oh yes, of course, motherhood interests me a great deal, because one also discusses it a lot in feminist quarters. There are feminists who are mothers and, of course, just because one is for abortion—naturally, all feminists are for abortion—but that doesn't mean that there aren't some who have chosen to have children. And I find that that can be a completely valid choice, which is very dangerous today because all the responsibility falls on the shoulders of the woman, because in general it's enslaved motherhood. One of my friends has written a book called *Enslaved Motherhood* [Les Chimères 1975]. But motherhood in itself is not something negative or something inhuman.

No, I certainly didn't write that motherhood had no human meaning. I may have said that one had to give it one or that the embryo, as long as it is not yet considered human, as long as it is not a being with human relationships with its mother or its father, it's nothing, one can eliminate the embryo. But I never said that the relation to the child was not a human relation. No, no, reread the text, I don't have it here.

Listen, I'm very happy [that you are undertaking the new translation of *The Second Sex,* and correcting the mistranslation of *"la realité humaine"* as "the real nature of man"] since the base of existentialism is precisely that there is no human nature, and thus no "feminine nature." It's not something given. There is a presence to the world, which is the presence which defines man, who is defined by his presence to the world, his consciousness and not a nature that grants him a priori certain characteristics. That's a gross error to have translated it in that way.

MS: Woman-identity is an important issue in America, now, with many feminists searching for a feminine nature.

SdB: There are also women in France who do that, but I am completely against it, because in the end they come back to men's mythologies, that is, that woman is a being apart, and I find that completely in error. Better that she identify herself as a human being who happens to be a woman. It's a certain situation which is not the same as men's situation of course, but she shouldn't identify herself as a woman.

MS: In America the question of woman-identity is often connected with motherhood; a woman sometimes becomes pregnant when she is insecure of her identity. Was it rather difficult for you because almost all women of your generation, all of your friends were mothers?

SdB: No, in general, my friends are not mothers. Most of my friends don't have children. Of course, I have friends with children but I have many friends without children. My sister doesn't have any children; my friend Olga has no children; many, many women I know have no children. There are some who have a child, and it's no big deal. They don't consider themselves mothers. They work in addition. Almost all the women I'm connected with work. Either they're actresses, or they're lawyers. They do things besides having children.

This interview was transcribed and translated by Jane Marie Todd, and is reprinted from "Two Interviews with Simone de Beauvoir," *Hypatia: A Journal of Feminist Philosophy* 3, no. 3 (Winter 1989): 11–27, by permission of Indiana University Press.

5

THE SILENCING OF SIMONE DE BEAUVOIR: GUESS WHAT'S MISSING FROM *THE SECOND SEX* (1983)

Once past the "gatekeepers" controlling access to the major publishing houses, a feminist book that has been published and translated into other languages for worldwide distribution should have no problem reaching an audience, especially if it is the work of a famous writer like Simone de Beauvoir. Not so. No English edition of *The Second Sex* (Beauvoir's famous 1949 feminist masterpiece, the common ingredient in all of the early women's studies courses) contains everything she wrote or accurately translates her most basic philosophical ideas.

Both the 1968 Bantam paperback edition of *The Second Sex* (the one with the photograph of a naked woman on the cover—after all, this is a book about *sex*) and the more demure plain-labeled 1970 Bantam edition brazenly advertise themselves as "complete and unabridged," a statement that is less revealing than the cover photo, given the fact that more than 10 percent of the material in the original French edition is missing from the only English translation available.

Technically, both of these paperback Bantam editions of *The Second Sex* are unabridged since they contain the complete text of the original hardcover edition of the English translation. The cutting that the publishers fail to advertise took place in that original edition. Trying to determine what had been deleted was no simple task, since there are no ellipses indicating deletions in the text. So I had to locate them the hard way. I first counted all words on several pages that had been translated in full to determine the differences due to type and page size. Once

I had this ratio of French pages to English pages, I was able to predict the length of each chapter in English, had there been no deletions. When I found gross discrepancies, I went through each chapter, comparing the French and English texts to locate the deleted passages.

HIDDEN FROM HISTORY

The translator who made the cuts, Howard Parshley, a professor emeritus of zoology at Smith College and the author of a 1933 book on sex and reproduction lauding the merits of sexual complementarity à la Havelock Ellis, must have found women's history boring. He deleted fully one-half of one chapter on history, cut one-fourth of another, and eliminated the names of seventy-eight women. Politicians, military leaders, courtesans, saints, artists, poets, and an eighteenth-century writer, Mme de Ciray, in whom "we see a feminist economist timidly peeking through" (Beauvoir 1949, 1:182), are all missing from the English version of *The Second Sex*.

Have you ever read tales of the medieval chatelaines, noblewomen who lived around the time of Charlemagne? Their legends, which Beauvoir recounted in the French edition of *The Second Sex,* were deleted from the English (Beauvoir [1949] 1970, 112). But why? I certainly don't find them boring—a little gruesome, maybe, but not boring. Here they are; what do you think?

> The chatelaine Aubie, after having had a tower built that was higher than any donjon soon had the architect's head cut off so that his secret would be well guarded. She chased her husband from his domain; he returned in hiding and killed her. Mabille, the wife of Roger Montgomery, delighted in reducing the nobles of her domain to begging. They revenged themselves by beheading her. Julienne, the bastard daughter of England's Henry I, armed the castle at Breteuil against him and lured him into an ambush, for which he punished her harshly. (Beauvoir 1949, 1:159)

Parshley dispenses with the incredible women of the Italian Renaissance in two sentences (Beauvoir [1949] 1970, 118), eliminating all mention of specific women and their stories and distorting an important point in Beauvoir's analysis of women's historical oppression. Could it be the military exploits of these women that made the translator uncomfortable?

> We find there [in the Italian Renaissance] women who were powerful sovereigns, such as Jeanne d'Aragon, Jeanne de Naples, Isabelle d'Este; others were adventurous "condottieres" [mercenary leaders] who took up arms like the men. Thus the wife of Giralomo Riario fought for the liberty of Forli; Hippolita Fioramenti commanded the troops of the Duke of Milan and, during the siege of Pavie, led a company of noblewomen to the ramparts. In order to defend their city against Montluc, the women of Sienna formed themselves into three divisions of three thousand women each, commanded by women.
>
> Other Italian women were celebrated for their culture or their talents, such as Isara Nogara, Veronica Gambara, Gaspara Stampara, Vittoria Colonna, who was the friend of Michelangelo, and especially Lucrece Tornabuoni, mother of Laurent and Julien de Medicis, who wrote, among other things, some hymns, a life of Saint John the Baptist and the Virgin. . . .
>
> A majority of these distinguished women were courtesans who combined a free spirit with their freedom of morals, and assured their economic autonomy by the exercise of their trade. Many were treated with deferential admiration by men. They patronized the arts, took an interest in literature and philosophy, and often, themselves, wrote or painted. Isabelle de Luna, Caterina di San Celso, and Imperia, who was a poet and musician, revived the tradition of Aspasia and Phryne. However for many of them freedom could still only take the form of license. The orgies and crimes of the noblewomen and courtesans of Italy have become legendary. (Beauvoir 1949, 1:172–73)

Parshley cut all of these stories from the English edition of *The Second Sex* and destroyed Beauvoir's distinction between freedom and mere license. In Parshley's condensed version, freedom in spirit, manners, or finances is equated with sexual and criminal license, a serious distortion obscuring Beauvoir's point that never in history have women been allowed the combination of independence and concrete opportunity that defines real freedom. "As for positive accomplishments," Beauvoir continues, in a sentence Parshley deleted from a concluding paragraph, "they were still possible only for a very small number" (Beauvoir 1949, 1:173).

Limiting himself to no one particular period in history, Parshley deleted an ancient Assyrian-Babylonian legend of the fall of woman from power (Beauvoir 1949, 1:145) and hacked away at the section on nineteenth-century feminism. In his description of the French feminist movement, Parshley retained Beauvoir's reference to Léon Richier, the man who organized the International Congress on Women's Rights in 1869, while eliminating all reference to Hubertine Auclert, a woman who opened a suffrage campaign and created the French Women's Suffrage Organization and a newpaper, *La Citoyenne*. Parshley also deleted much of Beauvoir's description of the violent history of the women's rights struggle in England and muddied Beauvoir's reference to the first American women's rights convention at Seneca Falls, New York.

SO MUCH FOR SENECA FALLS

In the French edition of *The Second Sex*, Beauvoir writes,

> The antislavery congress held in 1840 in London having been closed to them, the Quakeress Lucretia Mott founded a feminist association. On July 18, 1840 [*sic*] in a Convention convened at Seneca Falls, they composed a manifesto of Quaker inspiration which set the tone for all American feminism. (Beauvoir 1949, 1:210)

Beauvoir then quotes several passages from the "Declaration of Sentiments" without identifying their source. Using some unfathomable logic, Parshley deleted the reference to the London antislavery congress, the words "Seneca Falls," and the correct month and day, while leaving intact, without comment, the wrong year (Beauvoir [1949] 1970: 140). Immediately following the mention of the convention and the quotations from the "Declaration of Sentiments" is a reference to Harriet Beecher Stowe writing *Uncle Tom's Cabin* three years later. This should have alerted a conscientious (or even interested) translator that the 1840 date was a misprint, since Stowe's well-known book first appeared in 1851, three years after the Seneca Falls convention of 1848.

Parshley did make an effort to locate all of the passages from English works quoted by Beauvoir in order to provide the page numbers in English editions. This was no easy task, since Beauvoir neglects in many cases, as in the quotations from the "Declaration of Sentiments," to give even the title of the book from which the passages are taken. But in this particular instance, not only did Parshley fail to provide the title of the "Declaration of Sentiments" while including the quotations, he actually contributed to their obscurity by failing to correct the misprinted date and deleting the vital reference to Seneca Falls. History—or rather women's history—was not Parshley's strong point.

FEMINIST ANGER AND LESBIAN LOVE

Women writers and poets fared no better in Parshley's translation of *The Second Sex* than did the medieval chatelaines or the leaders of the suffrage movement. Perhaps the anger in the writings of Lady Winhilsea and the duchess of Newcastle offended him. For whatever reason, he deleted the following passages describing them and their poems from *The Second Sex*.

> Towards the end of the seventeenth century, Lady Winhilsea, a noble-woman without children, attempted the adventure of writing. Certain passages from her work show that she had a sensitive, poetic nature; but she was consumed by hate, anger and fear: "Alas! a woman who takes up a pen is considered to be a creature so presumptuous that she has no means of atoning for her crime!" Almost all of her work is consecrated to indignation at the condition of women.
> The case of the duchess of Newcastle is analogous. Also a noble-woman, her writing provoked a scandal. "Women live like cock-roaches or poodles; they die like worms." Insulted and ridiculed, she had to shut herself away on her estate; and in spite of a generous spirit, she became half crazy producing only extravagant fantasies. (Beauvoir 1949, 1:177–78)

In volume two of *The Second Sex*, unlike the history chapters of volume one, Parshley deleted primarily quotations cited by Beauvoir. (But they add up to quite a sum; he cut approximately sixty pages, or 12 percent from volume two, thirty-five pages coming from the chapter on "The Married Women," cutting it almost in half.) Some of the quotations in the French edition are certainly too long. But the deletion, or condensation, of others is a great loss. How much did the publisher save on the printing bill by chopping up the love poems of Renée Vivien, quoted in the chapter on "The Lesbian," or by deleting the title of one of her poems? Look what Parshley's deletions did to Vivien's poem "Sortilèges" [magic spells], which appears in its entirety in the French edition. First the original.

> Our heart is similar in our woman's breast
> Dearest! Our body is made alike
> A same heavy destiny weighs on our soul
> I express your smile and the shadow on your face
> My gentleness is equal to your great gentleness
> Sometimes it even seems that we are of the same race
> In you I love my child, my friend and my sister.
> (Beauvoir 1949, 2:184)

In Parshley's version the dramatic sense, indeed the poem itself is gone: "Our bodies are made alike . . . Our destiny is the same . . . In you I love my child, my darling, and my sister" (Beauvoir [1949] 1970, 465).

SEXIST SELECTING

The pattern of some of his other deletions adds to the evidence of his sexism. *The Second Sex* is a long and difficult book, with lots of repetition of Beauvoir's central ideas and detailed examples from literature. Any translator anxious to please a publisher whose eye is on the printing bill might be tempted to hack away with abandon, especially in those sections that bored or irritated him. Parshley obviously found women's history boring, but he apparently found some sections more irritating than others. He did not care to have discussions of women's oppression belabored, although he was quite content to allow Beauvoir to go on at length about the superior advantages of man's situation and achievements, as the pattern of deletions in the first history chapter shows.

In the chapter on "The Married Woman," Parshley threw out entire pages from Beauvoir's description of the tedious work comprising a housewife's day. He eliminated most of Beauvoir's quotations from the journals of Sophie Tolstoy, which provide her primary source of illustration for the "annihilation" of woman in marriage. But Parshley chose to include the entire quotation from an Edith Wharton novel about a young *man's* misgivings on the eve of marriage (Beauvoir [1949] 1970, 513–14), one of the few quotations he found sufficiently interesting to retain in its entirety.

Parshley apparently found evidence of woman's oppression and genuine struggle between the sexes irritating. He systematically deleted misogynist diatribes and feminist arguments from the writers of ancient Greece, like Simonide d'Amorga who wrote, "Women are the greatest evil that God has ever created" (Beauvoir 1949, 1:146), to the historic fifteenth-century *querelle des femmes* and the later debate on women's nature during the French Renaissance. He deleted not only references to a work by Cornelius Agrippa defending woman's superiority and the misogynist works it elicited in response, but also all mention of two works by women authors, *Docte et subtil discours* by Marguerite de Valois and *L'Egalité des hommes et des femmes* by Mlle de Gournay (Beauvoir 1949, 1:170, 178–81). These deletions often create confusion, especially when later references to earlier passages that have been deleted are left intact. Such is the case in Beauvoir's discussion of socialist feminism.

SO MUCH FOR SOCIALIST FEMINISM

The damage done by Parshley's random deletions to Beauvoir's historical accounts of the utopian Saint-Simonian movement and socialist feminism would be serious enough problems for any historical study of feminism. They are particularly devastating in *The Second Sex*, given that Beauvoir, in building her own theory, relies on a critical appropriation of socialist feminism.

Through a dexterous juggling of deletions and the addition of a few words, such as "for example," Parshley managed to transform the nineteenth-century utopian socialists Charles Fourier and Etienne Cabet into members of the slightly bizarre Saint-Simonian movement (Beauvoir [1949] 1970, 126), which would have been news to Fourier and Cabet, and a shock to the residents of the utopian communities they established in New Jersey and Illinois, had they been around to hear it. Parshley deleted Beauvoir's fairly detailed analysis of the movement, including the entire reference to Enfantin's religious cult of the Woman-

Messiah for which Saint-Simonianism is known, as well as a description of women's newspapers such as *Voix des femmes* [women's voice].

References to Jeanne Decoin's electoral campaign of 1849, the socialist Flora Tristan's "belief in the redemption of the people by woman" (Beauvoir 1949, 1:190), and a lengthy analysis of Proudhon's rupture of the alliance between feminism and socialism are all gone. Lost as well is the following passage giving Beauvoir's analysis of the class division within feminism and her only explanation of the phrase *revolutionary feminism,* which causes great confusion when it appears later, without explanation, in Parshley's translation.

> This weakness of feminism had its source in its internal division; in truth, as one has already indicated, women lacked solidarity as a sex. Their first tie was to their class. The interests of the bourgeois women and those of the proletarian women didn't intersect. Revolutionary feminism took up the Saint-Simonian and Marxist tradition. It should be noted, moreover, that a Louise Michel declared herself against feminism because this movement merely diverts forces which ought to be entirely employed in the class struggle; woman's fate will be determined by the abolition of capital. (Beauvoir 1949, 1:205)

By the time Beauvoir arrives at the feminist movement at the turn of the twentieth century, socialist feminism has pretty much disappeared from the English edition. When Parshley finally leaves in a slightly obscure reference to socialist feminism fairly late in the discussion, "The situation was complicated: to revolutionary feminism and the 'independent' feminism of Mme Brunschvicg was added a Christian feminism" (Beauvoir [1949] 1970, 138), the reader is hopelessly lost. What is revolutionary feminism? Parshley has left no answer.

PHILOSOPHICAL MISINTERPRETATION

Deletions can destroy the continuity of an author's thought, as they do in the history chapter of *The Second Sex,* or mask an author's debt to other writers and their works, as the massive cuts from volume two obscure the influence on Beauvoir of writers such as Hegel, Kierkegaard, Colette, Virginia Woolf, Colette Audry, Bachelard, and Violette Leduc. But inaccurate or inconsistent translations of key philosophical terminol-

ogy can do as much, if not more, damage to an author by misrepresenting her ideas and obscuring her links to a philosophical tradition. For
instance, Beauvoir is careful in *The Second* Sex to use the Heideggerian
phrase, *la réalité humaine* (human reality), when describing human existence in order to differentiate it from the life of lower beings who are
defined by their "nature." Human existence has at least the potential to
transcend nature and define itself through creative action. But Parshley
translated *la réalité humaine* as "the real nature of man" (Beauvoir 1949,
1:40; [1949] 1970, 7), which, as Beauvoir has remarked to me, is exactly
its opposite meaning.

Parshley also reversed the meaning of another distinctive phrase
from existentialism, "being for-itself" (*pour-soi*), which refers to human
consciousness, once again in contrast to those beings who lack consciousness and, following the dictates of nature, live at the level of the
"in-itself" (*en-soi*). In her phenomenological description of woman's
oppression, Beauvoir writes that "woman knows and chooses herself not
so much as she exists for herself [*pour soi*] but as man defines her" (Beauvoir 1949, 1:228). In his translation Parshley not only reversed the
meaning of "for-itself," equating it with nature, he actually replaced it
with the technical phrase "in itself," with the opposite meaning:
"woman sees herself and makes her choices not in accordance with her
true nature in itself, but as man defines her" (Beauvoir [1949] 1970,
155).

In another passage Parshley once again misses (and destroys) a philosophical point in a mistranslation. Explaining that a boy, like a girl, is
conscious of how he appears in the eyes of another person, Beauvoir
writes, "Certainly, he also experiences himself as 'for-others' [*pour autrui*]" (Beauvoir 1949, 2:27). Parshley's translation eliminated the distinctive phrase, "for-others," and rendered the sentence as "Certainly
he tests himself also as if he were another" (Beauvoir [1949] 1970, 315).
Just how the boy does that or what in fact it is, certainly isn't clear to
the reader (nor, I think, to Parshley). Parshley's translations do not eliminate the hyphens that plague phenomenological writings; consider the
following example. Parshley translated Beauvoir's phrase "her being-
for-men," as "what-in-men's-eyes-she-seems-to-be" (Beauvoir 1949,
1:228; [1949] 1970, 155).

Expressions like "being for-itself," "in-itself," or "for-others" may
not be immediately obvious in their meaning; but an interested reader

could find an explanation of these technical expressions because they belong to the accepted vocabulary of existential phenomenology. Far from simplifying Beauvoir's language in a way that would make her ideas clearer, and more accessible to an American audience, which was evidently the translator's intention, these mistranslations have the opposite effect. They make Beauvoir's ideas less accessible and unfortunately give the impression to the English-speaking audience that she is a sloppy writer and thinker. They often have the additional consequence of obscuring the philosophical context of her work. As William McBride (1981, 88–89) notes, Parshley's translation of volume two, *L'expérience vécue*, as "Woman's Life Today" rather than, more accurately, as "Lived Experience" effectively masks the significance of the work as a phenomenological description. Together these factors might help account for the nearly universal failure of contemporary American phenomenologists to acknowledge Beauvoir's contribution in *The Second Sex* to the articulation of a phenomenological analysis of the social world.

Beauvoir's use of Marxist and existentialist concepts that identify her philosophical orientation is further obscured by Parshley's practice of translating important terms one way in one location and another way elsewhere. For example, Beauvoir uses the Marxian concept of "mystification" quite often in the French edition; in the English edition, Parshley variously translates it as "hoax" (Beauvoir 1949, 1:228; [1949] 1970, 154), "mockery" (Beauvoir 1949, 1:222; [1949] 1970, 149), or even "mystification." Alienation is an Hegelian concept important to both Marxism and existentialism. Parshley inconsistently translates it as "projection" (Beauvoir 1949, 2:25; [1949] 1970, 313) or "identification" (Beauvoir 1949, 2:24; [1949] 1970, 313). Mistaking alienation for identification is particularly misleading since existentialists like Sartre and Beauvoir use the concept of identification, and especially that of self-identity, very critically.

Were these deletions and mistranslations the result of some kind of sexist plot to undermine Beauvoir's work? Probably not. Parshley may have been bored by history, and no philosopher, but his preface to *The Second Sex* reveals his warm and genuine appreciation for Beauvoir's book. We owe him and Alfred A. Knopf, the publisher, a debt of gratitude for bringing out the first English translation of *The Second Sex* so soon after its publication in France. But neither the publisher, who apparently insisted on the deletions, nor Parshley, who considered a careful study of existentialism unnecessary ("Mlle de Beauvoir's book is, after all on woman, not on philosophy," he tells us in his preface) (Beauvoir [1949] 1970, vi), anticipated the women's studies movement and the seriousness with which women would study feminist philosophy.

Parshley remarks, almost casually, in his preface that he has "done some cutting and condensation here and there with a view to brevity." He was apparently equally as casual in seeking Beauvoir's permission. "Practically all such modifications," he writes, "have been made with the author's express permission" (Beauvoir [1949] 1970, x). That Beauvoir did not realize the dimensions of the problems in the English translation until much later is evident from a letter she wrote me in response to this chapter (which first appeared as an article in a women's studies journal): "I was dismayed to learn the extent to which Mr. Parshley misrepresented me. I wish with all my heart that you will be able to publish a new translation of it." Publishing a new, authoritative translation of Beauvoir's most influential work would be a wonderful way to honor her for her contribution to American women and feminist history.

NOTES

Reprinted from *Women's Studies International Forum* 6, no. (5: 559–64, copyright 1983, with permission from Elsevier Science). As noted above in the preface, passages from the synopsis originally published with this article appear without acknowledgment in Bair's introduction to the 1989 Vintage Books edition of *The Second Sex*, p. xxii.

6

MOTHERHOOD, FEMINISM, AND IDENTITY (1984)

Along with other members of "the baby boom generation" who have reached their thirties I have begun to hear my biological clock ticking away the remaining minutes of my life as a "fertile" woman, a potential mother. For those women who, like me, felt themselves at twenty drawn to the pursuit of a career that seemed to exclude motherhood, this can be a time of reflection on that earlier choice. It's not an easy decision, I'm sure, for any of us and is especially difficult for those women whose tenuous hold on a middle-class identity has been seriously shaken by financial realities.

But I am talking about a choice. This in itself might strike some people as odd, since motherhood is very often experienced as a fact of life over which we have little control. Some seem to feel we should not have any control in this matter, fearing that if actually given the choice, women would never have any more babies. One of my colleagues, an ardent male socialist with a perhaps not unexpectedly conservative social philosophy, seems to hold this view. In response to my (somewhat hesitant) revelation that I seemed to be deciding not to have any children, he angrily replied that it was another instance of privileged feminists casting off their burdens onto the backs of the poor.

This strikes me as a strangely ahistorical response; not since slavery have the policies of the United States encouraged the poor, black, Native American, or Hispanic women of this country to bear children at all. The racist ideology that has too often defined those policies has, instead, been designed to discourage people of color from reproducing themselves. Programs of forced sterilization have threatened the survival of entire communities and made the struggle to give birth a social and

73

political as well as a personal and economic choice, for many American women. These women have had to assert their right to have children, as well as their right to decide not to (*see* Davis 1981).

My colleague's remark reveals some of the complexities that surround motherhood as a moral issue. It can present a woman with one of the most profound decisions of her life, requiring tremendous emotional as well as intellectual effort to resolve. Motherhood has thus become an apt candidate for philosophical inquiry. Its absence from the traditional philosophical literature is due, no doubt in large part, to the men who have claimed the discipline of philosophy as their own to the exclusion of women. Male philosophers have lacked the experiential knowledge that poses motherhood as an issue and defines its content. At best (or rather, worst) they have shared in defining its context, which Adrienne Rich (1976) has called the oppressive "institution" of motherhood. My own interest is in providing a philosophical justification for the choice not to be a mother. It's my belief that for feminism to be really prochoice, a woman must be able to choose not to be a mother without losing her self-respect or identity as a woman.

I remember watching a television special on women who hoped to become pregnant with the aid of fertility clinics. The interviewer asked some of the women why they were spending so much time and money trying to have children. I'll never forget the response of the woman who first glanced shamefully across at her husband and then answered that the future of her marriage depended on it, that her husband felt that without children there would be no family, no reason to stay married. At some basic emotional level, women's liberation from oppressive roles has had no effect at all if a woman is thought to have no value outside of her role as wife-and-mother.

This husband's and my male colleague's responses to the motherhood issue point out the necessity for men to explore the complexities of their own feelings about parenthood and their own need for children, and how it's related to their feelings about women, whom they need in order to have children. They, like women, seem to be ambivalent: wanting an "heir," yet resenting the power this gives women over them or, thanks to the early pregnancies of young, nurturing wives-and-mothers, being able to leave their own feelings unexamined and unacknowledged until late in their own middle-age crises. I have a suspicion that many men are being forced by their thirty-year-old career-oriented wives to become involved in this decision. If so, this gives them an opportunity that was available to few of their fathers, making parenthood a topic of philosophical interest and exploration for male as well as female philosophers of my generation.

That I feel the need to defend the choice not to be a mother also reflects an important historical development in feminism: the rebirth of mothering as a respectable feminist experience. In the 1960s and 1970s many feminists felt forced to defend their decision to have children, as though it were a sign of their lack of radical commitment to the feminist cause. Feminism had reached an apparent impasse. Women inside and outside the movement were alienated by what they saw as the feminist demand that they choose between their families and their individuality. They felt that equality could only be gained at the cost of their mothering; for many women this price was too high (*see* Ehrenreich and English 1978; Friedan 1981). Providing a feminist justification for the choice to become or not to become a mother necessitates finding a way out of this predicament. My suggestion is that we search the feminist movement itself for a way to integrate an appreciation of the values of life, family, and community into feminism.

HAS FEMINISM REACHED AN IMPASSE?

My own experience in a university-based women's liberation movement from 1969 to 1973 was that practical activities such as cooperative day care centers designed to help mothers and their children existed side by side with efforts to open up career opportunities by combating employment discrimination. Some feminists, of course, rejected the validity of any activities that supported women in the oppressive roles of wife and/or mother. But there have always been integrators who saw the relationship between activities such as work in a day care center, projects to combat violence against women, and legal efforts to end employment discrimination and secure health benefits for women.

Integrative theory of that era also supported the equality of women and their rights as individuals, while respecting mothers and fighting for their right to make motherhood a positive, enriching experience rather than an alienating one. *Our Bodies, Ourselves* (Boston Women's Health Collective, 1973) is representative of these efforts. Shirley Chisholm is an example of a feminist political leader who, although not herself a mother, fought for an integrative solution to racism, sexism, and class oppression, fired by her profound belief that motherhood gives women a unique sense of social value that is desperately needed in public life. Adrienne Rich's 1976 classic *Of Woman Born* provides an eloquent analysis and defense of mothering and distinguishes between the oppressive institution of motherhood and the experience itself, which has so much capacity for beauty. For a deeper historical foundation, we could go back to the eighteenth-century feminist Mary Wollstonecraft, who argued for equality and motherhood in practically the same breath.

It takes a sympathetic observer to find this tradition in feminism. There's no denying the existence of a militant, angry feminist attack on woman's traditional role. It certainly received much more press coverage than moderate feminism and even intimidated some moderate feminists into silence. The emphasis on more-radical-than-thouism within the feminist movement and in the media coverage of the movement may have masked the historical presence and contemporary endurance of integrative traditions in feminist theory and practice. These traditions should provide encouragement that integrative solutions are part of the ongoing reality of feminism, rather than impossible or even unusual. Can our quest for an integrative tradition shed new light on Simone de Beauvoir's classic work *The Second* Sex, a major theoretical source for the radical feminist attack on motherhood and woman's traditional role?

BEAUVOIR'S PHILOSOPHY OF MOTHERHOOD

The French bourgeois society in which Simone de Beauvoir grew up was radically divided into male and female spheres, which presented almost insurmountable obstacles for a woman aspiring to a career. Beauvoir's analysis of motherhood reflects this reality. In a concluding chapter of *The Second Sex* on the independent woman, Beauvoir remarks that "there is one feminine function that it is actually almost impossible to perform in complete liberty: that is maternity . . . [The independent woman] is forced to choose between sterility, which is often felt as a painful frustration, and burdens hardly compatible with a career" (Beauvoir [1949] 1952, 774).

The absence of women who successfully combined a professional career with motherhood and Beauvoir's own profound alienation from woman's traditional role of wife and mother can provide insight into her angry, sometimes ambivalent but largely negative view of motherhood in *The Second Sex*. The philosophical challenge that Beauvoir faced in her analysis was twofold. She had to provide a serious philosophical description and analysis of women's experience, which other, male, phenomenologists such as Jean-Paul Sartre had failed to do. She also had to combat the conservative position exemplified by Hegel's philosophy, that woman's differences from man define/confine her to the limited sphere she then occupied.

Beauvoir's response was to make some philosophical distinctions—between necessary and contingent aspects of human existence, for example. The effect of this distinction was to make sexual differentiation not definitional, that is, not essential to our experience. It was an unfortunate position to take since it both undercut her phenomenological commitment to describe experience without preconceptions and left her own work describing women's experience without adequate philosophical foundation.

When she felt forced, in the context of a discussion of various male phenomenological analyses of biology, to see the phenomenon of reproduction as ontologically founded, she projected her own struggle against the oppressive institution of woman's traditional role onto her interpretation of biological reproduction. In her chapter on the biological givens of experience, Beauvoir sees woman as engaged in a struggle to assert her individuality against the efforts of nature to enslave her to the species. Nature condemns woman to an animal-like maintenance of biological life and prevents her from engaging in the truly creative, human, transcendent work of producing culture, for which nature rewards individual men.

In a chapter on history that is much indebted to Hegel, she writes that the male activity of warfare is superior to giving birth. In risking life for human ends, war creates human values that the mere reproduction of life does not. The values of women's traditional sphere are the creation of men anxious to justify woman's dependent, subordinate status. Women accept this role, because men have denied them any other alternatives and because of an inauthentic desire to evade the anxieties of their own autonomy. Beauvoir had herself experienced the desire for social identification and dependence as an inauthentic temptation to abdicate her responsibility for her own life by seeking to identify with and live her life through an Other. This problematic relationship with the Other is a major theme in Beauvoir's work.

Later in *The Second Sex,* in the chapter on motherhood, where her descriptions of women's lived experience come not from arguments with male philosophers, but from writings by women, her portrayal of motherhood is much less negative. Beauvoir is there able to recognize that motherhood can be the source of authentic experience for women, for it confronts the mother with the profound human realities of identification and separation from another person and provides her with the opportunity to develop the authentic human value of generosity. But these later insights on motherhood are not incorporated into the fundamental philosophical position defined in *The Second Sex*'s opening chapters. This philosophical position does go beyond Sartre's radical individualism in acknowledging the interconnectedness of individual freedoms. Beauvoir defines a social ethic that condemns oppression and establishes generosity as a defining element in moral authenticity. But this acknowledgment of moral obligations between individuals leaves unaddressed the moral values entailed, for example, in the nurturing of a helpless infant. Social identification and loving devotion are not positive values in Beauvoir's philosophy; they are evidence of an inauthentic evasion, the mystification of oppression, or an undeveloped, immature consciousness.

Beauvoir's mistake was in thinking that the desire to nurture another person, to accept a relationship of social identification and dependency, was only a temptation, rather than the expression of a positive human value and activity. What she was unable to realize fully was the limitations of an ethos defined solely by the individual pursuit of transcendence over nature. But now, for many American women who have sought their personal success in a society defined by individual mobility, the avoidance of personal commitment and social identity can seem, at thirty, just as immature and inauthentic as getting married and/or pregnant to escape future uncertainties did ten years earlier. The question is how feminism can integrate the changing values in women's lives in both the private and public spheres.

What we need, and Beauvoir isn't able to provide, is a philosophical appreciation of the social values engaged by mothering as well as the value of individual autonomy. It's possible though, and important, for a feminist philosophy to acknowledge the value of nurturant relationships between adults and to describe the unique relationship between child and mother. They are, after all, connected. We often emotionally reenact that first intimate relationship of our childhood in our adult relationships, but the fundamental significance of this relationship for moral philosophy has only recently begun to be explored philosophically, as for example in the work of Sara Ruddick (1982).

A FEMINIST MATERNAL ETHIC

Ruddick's objective in "Maternal Thinking" is to define the moral structures of maternal thinking and the temptations and virtues conceived through the social practice of mothering. "Interests in preservation, growth, and acceptability of the child govern maternal practices in general" (Ruddick 1982, 79). Each of these interests defines its own set of temptations and virtues. The mother's interest in preservation, for example, makes her liable to the temptations of fearfulness and excessive control, just as it defines the virtues of humility and resilient cheerfulness, according to Ruddick. Ruddick implies that her description of maternal thinking is generally applicable to both men and women outside of biological or adoptive parenting practices (Ruddick 1982, 89). However, women who choose not to give birth appear as either disabled or moral failures in her analysis (Ruddick 1982, 79, 89). We must define a feminist maternal ethic that supports a woman's right not to have children. We must also recognize the problems and difficulties created by the institution of mothering that would lead some women to decide that they ought not to become mothers.

One such problem not fully discussed in Ruddick's article is child abuse. As Chinese mothers once bound their daughters' feet, contemporary American mothers can pass on to their children the physical and emotional abuse they themselves suffered in childhood. No description of maternal thinking can be complete without a recognition of the rage and bitterness hidden in the heart of an abused child/mother. Carol Conger's courageous analysis of the long-term effects of the abuse she suffered as a child (1983) suggests some of the shortcomings of Ruddick's analysis and possible directions for developing a more adequate feminist maternal ethic. Ruddick describes the daily expression of the maternal virtue of cheerfulness as "a matter-of-fact willingness to continue, to give birth and to accept having given birth, to welcome life despite its conditions" (Ruddick 1982, 81). Consider a possible effect of such a morality on a victim/survivor of child abuse. Such an attitude of cheerfulness might well seem utterly inauthentic, emotionally inconceivable. The imperative to be cheerful becomes, in fact, what Ruddick terms its degenerative form: denial. In the light of such a woman's experience, Ruddick's list of moral virtues evokes the very sentimentalized concept of motherhood that she wants to avoid.

When cheerfulness is a moral virtue, not being cheerful becomes another instance of a mother's failure, feeding into the patriarchal attack on mothers that both Adrienne Rich (1976) and Conger (1983) describe. One of the factors that leads to child abuse, according to Conger, is the "rage and guilt at not being able to fulfill the romantic ideals of motherhood and childhood" (Conger 1983, 21). The danger in defining idealized virtues as central to the maternal experience, as Ruddick has done, is that such an approach takes an emotionally privileged maternal practice as the norm. It can thus compound the suffering of women who are still striving to overcome the effects of their victimization. Conger writes, "The scars left on me will *always* impair my ability to love and respect myself and others" (Conger 1983, 21). In not evidencing a caring attitude toward the suffering of those women, such an ethic fails to reflect what must be a central value of feminist maternal ethic: a caring and nurturing of all women, along with their children. Conger's analysis provides insight into an alternative conception of a feminist maternal ethic. Instead of accepting the maternal role, and defining its moral dimensions from within its present oppressive structures, her own work in "reinventing child rearing" to eliminate the possibilities for abuse involves radically transforming the entire institution of motherhood. Her radical approach involves bringing "more women to mother children, trying to do away with acting out of the mother role/child role, teaching them to recognize and defend themselves against abuse, taking the issue out of the closet" (Conger 1983, 20).

In order to encompass experiences as disparate as Ruddick's and Conger's, a feminist maternal ethic must be context dependent. We could thus recognize that the opportunities and obstacles present for mothers and their children differ radically. Rather than offering a set of ideals reflective of a given idealized maternal practice, such an ethic could be based upon feelings of nurturance and compassion for others as well as the rights to be assertive and to pursue one's own goals. Since one can use such values not merely in relationships with one's own children, but in one's social life, the ethic would be applicable to non-mothers as well. Since some people, furthermore, are more successful at nurturing others than their own children, some women not only have a right not to mother but perhaps ought not to do so.

This framework for a feminist maternal ethic may enable us to proceed further in our project of integrating the apparently conflicting experiences of motherhood present in feminism. One starting point for this project is the critique of the individualist feminist tradition by Ehrenreich and English (1978, 269–313). They charge that this tradition, originating with Beauvoir, is selfish and masculinist. This is a tough criticism for a woman professional to face, because there's more than a grain of truth in it. But a consideration of its implications can reveal much about the problems in defining a feminist analysis of mothering and a maternal ethic.

FEMINISM AND SELFISHNESS

My own experience confirms the insight that being totally caught up with one's self and success in a career insulates a person (traditionally, men) from another important aspect of human reality: the experience of true generosity and nurturing. I remember responding to a questionnaire a couple of years back about my anticipated future activities as a professor. At the time I couldn't imagine acting as a mentor for younger people in the field—"Who could I possibly help?" I remember asking myself, "I'm the most junior member." The challenge for women who choose not to have children is to overcome the temptation to evade relationships involving commitment and love. A woman professional may fear, as Beauvoir described, that once she admits her vulnerabilities, she may dump her entire self onto the Other. But in my experience, only when a woman can admit her own feelings of vulnerability and dependency can she really accept herself, be receptive to other people, and be cognizant of their needs.

For those of us who are not mothers the challenge is to find other ways of expressing the social values that find their existential origins in the experience of motherhood. We can start by trying to understand the experience that was our daughterhood. This will help us come to terms with those feelings that draw us into nurturing relationships. These are relationships in which we are genuinely concerned with the life and happiness of another person, in which competitiveness is not a defining feature, and in which we no longer fear our own individual obliteration in opening up to another person and giving ourselves to them. For a woman professional, it can mean learning to help a younger colleague, for example, and to accept one's limitations without feeling threatened.

We can find opportunities for caring, nurturant relationships in many of our social relationships, with our clients, students, coworkers, friends, and family members. A woman professional can feel a tremendous social responsibility to her aging parents or to young women in need of role models and mentors. Claiming that a woman is selfish because she doesn't bear a child is a non sequitur; instead, one should look at all of her social relations to see whether she is practicing a maternal ethic. *The Second Sex* reflects Beauvoir's profound concern for the fate of women, few of whom had access to the educational opportunities that enabled her to write so eloquently in defense of their liberation. A woman who is not a mother can devote herself, as Shirley Chisholm has done, to the struggle for social justice and opportunities for the children born of other women.

We should remember also that a feminist maternal ethic includes a recognition and affirmation of the rights to be assertive and to pursue one's own goals. It thus incorporates the values of individualist feminism, rather than rejecting them. The charge that pursuing one's individual goals is selfish can ignore the reality that respecting ourselves and our interests is part of a feminist maternal ethic. It is not something that society has made easy; it can discourage women in nurturing roles from facing the moral challenges of self-affirmation. Indeed, learning how to be "selfish" without feeling guilty can be as profound a challenge for a full-time nurturer as learning to nurture can be for a woman used to the competitive environment of the public arena.

IS FEMINISM MASCULINIST?

The charge that feminism is masculinist is a troubling criticism, implying that women who honestly prefer a career over motherhood are male-identified in their rejection of woman's traditional role. It raises important questions about who we are as women, who we will become as our roles change, and what will happen to our woman-identity in the process. It would be hard to imagine anything more closely tied to a daughter's sense of being a woman than being a mother, since she gets so much of her emotional concept of what a woman is by relating to real women; for most of us, the woman who was most present in our earliest, impressionable years was the woman (or women) who mothered us. But many women professionals, in fact, share the experience of having been treated in some respects as a son by their father. Our fathers often identified with us, giving us many of the pressures to achieve, if few of the privileges of freedom of movement, that they would have given a son. My father was demanding and harshly critical of my performance at school but wouldn't allow me to start the lawn mower or run the power saw. I could get hurt.

I remember criticizing Beauvoir's perspective for being masculinist in my dissertation on *The Second Sex* in 1976. There is an element of truth in that criticism. She does accept some of what she terms masculine values, but not all of them. She only recognizes those values of self-assertion and individual achievement necessary for productive, creative work in the public sphere. She rejects those male values that denigrate women and consign them to a subordinate social sphere. She also criticizes male values that make relationships into battlegrounds.

Beauvoir's father was ambivalent about his eldest daughter's academic success. Her mother was a very traditional, religious woman who identified with the role of a wife and mother and considered her daughter a lost soul. Beauvoir knew of few independent women in the professions, and none of them had children. Now more and more women, like me, have mothers who have also held full-time jobs. One result we might expect from this change is that women will increasingly come to experience a job or career as part of their identity as women rather than as something opposed to it, as Beauvoir did. It's interesting to note, in this regard, that in *The Second Sex* Beauvoir does not disclaim her identity as a woman while accepting the male values of individual accomplishment. She just locates that identity elsewhere than in the values implicit in the role of wife-and-mother. She draws extensively on the work of women writers such as Virginia Woolf and acknowledges their insights into the difficulties and ambivalence experienced by women trying to escape the confines of their traditional role. She identifies with them both as women and as writers and finds confirmation of her own experiences in their work. Sexuality was another aspect of her experience that expressed her identity as a woman. One of the few instances in which she criticizes man's values and experience in the name of woman's experience comes in her description of sexuality. Woman has a more authentic erotic experience, she argues, than does man, who uses his aggressive posture to avoid seeing himself fully as flesh (Beauvoir [1949] 1952, 450).

In a sense *The Second Sex* is a reflection and analysis of Beauvoir's woman-identity; it is out of her experience that she feels so threatened by motherhood, so rejecting of the role that bourgeois society would force on her that she saw as causing the death of her best friend Zaza. This is a woman's experience of oppression. I wonder now about the validity of charging Beauvoir with being masculinist. The connotations of the term are wholly negative in a feminist context. A simplistic charge, it ignores the importance of traditional "masculine" values of economic, political, and literary achievement in contemporary feminist practice.

Women professionals have unique experiences from which all women can learn. Women professionals extend the limitations of woman's traditional role, making inroads into male territory. The challenge, like Beauvoir's, is not to end up like men in the process. This means several things: first, one must make special efforts to tie into woman-identified activities. Secondly, heterosexual women need to overcome alienation by the early lesbian-feminist definition of the woman-identified-woman and rediscover the pleasures and love of women friends. Another difficult step is learning to be woman-identified in a male-dominated career. This means learning loyalty to women who are trying to break into the field and trying to make it easier for them, those women who come after, by forcing the criteria of excellence in all fields to accommodate women's lives. It means overcoming feelings of resentment and competitiveness against women colleagues, so that they are not forced to conform to the same alienating demands from the male status quo that others had to face. We must acknowledge and express our nurturing, maternal feelings. This will allow us to discover the power such feelings have to enable us to stand up for values that we might not find the strength to defend if only ourselves were at stake.

MOTHERHOOD AND HETEROSEXUALITY

The issue of a feminist analysis of motherhood is analogous in many ways to that of the other defining element in woman's traditional role: her heterosexual identification with a husband. Could the radical lesbian-feminist redefinition of loving women as the only genuinely feminist expression of woman-identity provide a model for one alternative to the traditional identification of woman as mother? If one can redefine woman's sexual love outside the context of heterosexual marriage, then one might redefine the expression of women's nurturant love outside the context of motherhood. Such a view might argue, for example, that social activism that nurtures and defends the lives of other women is more authentically feminist than the nurturing care of a child fathered by a man and destined to carry on a patriarchal heritage.

But this alternative shares with Beauvoir's rejection of motherhood the problematic claim that the redefined identity is superior politically, in the case of the woman-identified-woman analogy, and ethically, in the case of Beauvoir's analysis, to motherhood itself. We once again seem to be in the presence of an impasse. How can such positions be incorporated into a feminism that also recognizes an opposing view? For example, what if one believes that one's ethnic and racial heritage must be preserved for the future and that real social transformation must begin in the family where children, exposed to nurturing care by autonomous men and women, will create a future not defined by oppressive relations?

The context-dependent character of the feminist maternal ethic provides a way out of this conceptual impasse by recognizing differences between women. Feminists espousing radically different views exist simultaneously, each addressing important problems from equally valid, if different, perspectives. But, in working separately, they often remain ignorant of one another's interests. They thus might fail to acknowledge those interests and even unwittingly work against them. A white feminist, for example, could, if unchallenged, act on unacknowledged racist fears in working for birth control among poor women and women of color. A homophobic feminist could, if unchallenged, contribute to a resurgence of heterosexist oppression and violence against lesbians while trying to build alliances with conservative women. Something like that has happened between some mothers and nonmothers.

If we are genuinely committed to combating oppression in all its forms and are willing to admit that the ever-changing diversity of women's experiences prevents any one of us from ever reaching the definitive, absolute feminist position, then what we need is a method to maintain an openness of perspective. Inviting criticism is one such method, which would seem to have application to the issue of motherhood as well as that of heterosexuality. The problem is that criticism can be seen—and be meant to be seen—as undermining the entire philosophical foundation of one's experience and identity, as radical lesbian feminism challenged women's participation in heterosexual relationships. But such criticism, especially that issued with the anger of long-silenced frustration, provides us with the all too rare opportunity to learn about ourselves and, hopefully, to grow—as heterofeminists who have answered the radical lesbian challenge have discovered.

Of course, what one discovers are the limitations, the boundaries that define one's particular identity; heterosexual marriage, for instance, does in fact require a woman to invest considerable emotional energy into a relationship with a man, energy that in a lesbian relationship would be given to a woman. Such a revelation, made possible by the radical lesbian critique, can lead a heterosexual feminist to explore the emotional roots of her heterosexuality for the first time and develop a new critical awareness and, eventually, a more profound affirmation of herself and her own values. Having one's assumptions called into question can thus be a valuable gift, especially for a philosopher. That seems to be the case here. Beauvoir radically called into question the philosophical foundations of woman's traditional role. Later feminists have responded by questioning the assumptions at the heart of Beauvoir's original critique and defending the social values embedded in woman's mothering.

This critique, and biological clocks, have, in turn, forced many women like myself to reconsider previous rejection of motherhood and face the questions about identity as women that such a reconsideration raises. "Don't I really want children?" I felt forced to ask myself. "Am I in a prolonged adolescent rebellion against my parents, denying a need that is going to appear suddenly when I'm forty-five, and it's too late?" My response to this challenge has been to formulate an alternative feminist analysis of motherhood, appreciative of the social and individual value of motherhood while reflective of the validity of my own choice not to become a mother. First, I define my position in juxtaposition to various other feminist perspectives, including Beauvoir's and the position on motherhood analogous to the radical lesbian analysis of heterosexuality, then I briefly describe the features of my experience that support my position and conclude by suggesting some of the ethical challenges present in that experience.

FEMINIST ALTERNATIVES

A third alternative, to Beauvoir's position, which advocates the adoption of men's values and the rejection of values associated with woman's traditional role, and that of a second position analogous to the radical lesbian analysis of heterosexuality, could be based upon Adrienne Rich's (1976) distinction between the valuable experience of mothering and its oppressive, institutionalized form. Such a reformist alternative would be analogous to the efforts of heterosexual women to defend the experience of heterosexual love while attacking the oppressive institution of patriarchal marriage. Both the second and this third alternative positively affirm the values implicit in women's lives and thus represent an advance over Beauvoir's position.

I would suggest that we reject any feminist position that would try to limit women's authentic alternatives by trying to find a new, fixed definition of woman's nature. Instead, we should recognize that our sense of our woman-identity results from our experiences with the various women who have been important throughout our lives, especially those who nurtured us in our childhoods. We should reclaim, with pride and with humility at our frailties, as much of our identity as we can. But we should expect and willingly acknowledge the differences between us, in our senses of who we are and what constitutes our woman-identity, without succumbing to the temptation to justify our own identity by denying our sisters'. We should celebrate the resultant spectrum of values and its vibrant oppositions as signs of our flourishing explosion out of the narrow confines of our traditional sphere, even when those values at the same time express an authentic preference for motherhood over competitive careerism; for nurturant, woman-loving, lesbian identity over heterosexual marriage; for professional involvement in social change over domesticity; and for loving men over lesbian separatism.

I would like to propose a fourth alternative that builds on the other three. It would affirm, as Beauvoir does, that some women, without false consciousness, authentically desire and value the pursuit of a career over motherhood if they are forced to choose or even if they see both as viable alternatives. This would acknowledge Beauvoir's insight and achievement in locating within her description of women's consciousness the existence of a desire for individual achievement and for the expression of productive cultural creativity that is properly understood as not being the sublimation of a supposedly more authentic desire for a child. My alternative would, however, affirm that the desire for a child can be a morally authentic desire in no way inferior to the woman's desire for individual achievement, thus rejecting Beauvoir's claim and a claim implicit in the alternative drawn by analogy from the woman-identified-woman position, that the desire for a child is by definition morally inauthentic or a sign of false consciousness.

I would also affirm, drawing on the definitions of oppression in both Rich and Beauvoir, that oppressive institutions are those that deny woman opportunities for the expression of her individual autonomy or her maternal/nurturing values. Correlatively, few women in our society experience motherhood as a real choice. For this to be a reality a woman must have other opportunities for personal development and social contribution; she must feel that she can choose to not be a mother without jeopardizing her identity as a woman or the survival of her community; and she must feel that she can have a child without jeopardizing her economic and/or physical survival —something that is not always possible today, as poverty becomes increasingly the province of women and their children. Thus moral obligations are ultimately inseparable from political change.

AN EXPERIENTIAL FOUNDATION

This feminist analysis of motherhood is based on my own experience, which reflects the increasingly prevalent reality of being raised in a family where both parents hold full-time jobs. My identity as a woman comes from the many different women in my life who have nurtured me, including my friend's grandmother who taught me to crochet, an activity I still find both comforting and womanly. Because my mother worked full-time as a grade-school teacher throughout most of my childhood, I experience my career as a teacher as an identification with her, although my career also allows me to identify with my grandfather, a retired Methodist circuit preacher who encouraged me to study philosophy by saying that we were the only two members of the family with the same profession. I feel closest to my mother in working with my students and in the intellectual probing of life's toughest questions, that's how she has expressed her mothering, and her teaching, with a courageous and sympathetic desire to help us analyze and understand our experience.

Too many analyses of women's experience, including psychoanalytic work on motherhood, fail to acknowledge the growing number of women who are daughters of working mothers, whose identities are not ideologically or emotionally shaped by the experience of having been raised by a full-time mother. Our values express that different identity. We take pride in our independence, as our mothers often did. Some of us, perhaps especially those who felt closest to our mothers during the period of their most intense, productive, joyful involvement in their careers, can feel an emotional identification with them in our own careers that is not documented in these theories. Our theories should describe the ways in which our identity as women is challenged and sustained in this experience to give ourselves support and to encourage other women to trust their feelings if they feel the desire to choose not to have children.

As long as women are mothers, motherhood will be an element in our woman-identity, but increasingly, it will not be the only, or defining, element. Nor will it be an experience women will have to give up because their job had been defined by career-obsessed men. One of the ways these changes are coming about is through the current pressure on the government to provide national health insurance, adequate day care, and equal pay for jobs of equal worth, which would enable the growing number of single mothers to provide adequate support for their children.

We have to acknowledge that for many women who are stuck in dead-end, alienating jobs, motherhood is far more meaningful and significant than work. It can also be very meaningful for women in careers they enjoy and find rewarding; the two are not mutually exclusive. What we are seeing is the expansion of roles for women and previously unimagined activities with new challenges and opportunities. What will happen in the future if babies are grown in test tubes? Will women as we know them disappear with that role? In a sense, each generation creates its nature anew, if there's any human population around to do it. Who can tell the future? Only the young.

CONCLUSION

Ethical challenges differ as situations constantly change. Trying to define an ethics is difficult, given all the shifting factors. Not just historical, political, cultural, and social, but also the biological and emotional, dimensions of mothering vary among women already and will continue to vary, in unpredictable ways in the years to come. The positive or negative feelings one has about one's membership in a community will affect one's decisions about giving birth—just as one's feelings about the future do.

Within the context of a career, the decision not to be a mother is the rejection of an opportunity that has been the source of profound meaning for many women. But it is not the only opportunity for the expression of nurturing social relationships, as is evident from the examples of great social contributions made by persons who have not been mothers. Furthermore, this experience of a moral dilemma is a new feature of moral development. It fits neither the traditional pattern of development of a young mother nor that of a professional man. Women professionals can claim maternal feelings with pride. One of my mother's most humiliating experiences came during World War II, when she was pregnant and desperate for a teaching job. She was forced to take off the enormous coat she wore to hide her pregnancy so that a male principal could decide if she "showed" too much to be allowed in a classroom. If motherhood was a sign of our shame, we should claim it with pride.

Beauvoir was wary of the return of the romantic motherhood-mystique as a return to oppressive roles. This is a political response, complicated by the French political context in which a "woman–identified" group was able to copyright the name MLF, the French equivalent of a Women's Liberation Movement. Beauvoir refused to identify "sisterhood" and maternal feelings, and she adamantly denied any motherhood feelings in her own life. But surely her relationship with her young student Olga in the 1930s, a friendship that continued throughout most of their lives, had many of the psychological colorings of her own relationship with her mother and provided her with lessons learned typically by a mother. But Beauvoir refused to consider such an interpretation of her relationships, including her close friendship in the later years of her life with a woman in her thirties. Surely this relationship also awakened emotional memories of mother and daughter in both participants, although Beauvoir denied it.

My experiences lead me to a different response. When I was in graduate school, I met my first female philosophy professor. She was a single woman in her fifties, on loan from another university as a visiting professor. She was a wonderful teacher who loved her students, a trait (with her specialization in "soft-headed" Eastern philosophy and religion) that earned her the contempt of the male faculty, who ridiculed her for "sublimating her maternal instinct." It's time we claimed our maternal feelings with pride instead of embarrassment and challenged those of our male colleagues who are locked into teaching by ridicule and training their (mostly male) students in philosophical combat to have the courage to face the very unmasculine parts of themselves buried deep within their macho exteriors. It's the least we can do for our students.

Reprinted, with changes, from *Women's Studies International Forum* 7, no. 5: 349–59, copyright 1984, with permission from Elsevier Science.

7

BEAUVOIR INTERVIEW (1985)

PARIS, 10 SEPTEMBER 1985

Margaret Simons: You know that in my critical study of the Parshley translation [of *The Second Sex*], I've uncovered numerous deletions: almost a hundred pages were cut from the original French edition. This is an important issue for the study of your philosophy—for me it's a philosophy—because the translation destroys the philosophical integrity of your work. But you've told me many times that you are not a philosopher. Well, he's done a popular [nonphilosophical] translation of your book. What do you think of this translation?

Simone de Beauvoir: Well, I think that it's very bad to suppress the philosophical aspect because while I say that I'm not a philosopher in the sense that I'm not the creator of a system, I'm still a philosopher in the sense that I've studied a lot of philosophy, I have a degree in philosophy, I've taught philosophy, I'm infused with philosophy; and when I put philosophy into my books it's because that's a way for me to view the world; and I can't allow them to eliminate that way of viewing the world, that dimension of my approach to women, as Mr. Parshley has done. I'm altogether against the principle of gaps, omissions, condensations, which have the effect, among other things, of suppressing the whole philosophical aspect of the book.

MS: You accepted this translation in 1952.

SdB: I accepted it to the extent that . . . you know, I had a lot of things to do, a creative work to write, and I was not going to read from beginning to end all the translations that were being done of my work. But when I found out that Mr. Parshley was omitting things, I asked him to indicate the omissions to me, and I wrote to tell him that I was absolutely against them, and since he insisted on the omissions on the pretext that otherwise the book would be too long, I asked him to say in a preface that I was against the omissions, the condensation. And I don't believe that he did that, which I begrudge him a great deal.

MS: Yes, it's awful. We've been studying this book for more than [thirty] years, a book which is very different from the book you wrote.

SdB: I would like very much for an unabridged translation to be done today, an honest translation, with the philosophical dimension and with all the parts that Mr. Parshley judged pointless and which I consider to have a point, very much so . . . From certain things that you've told me, I think that one will have to look at passages that weren't cut as well to see if there are not mistranslations, misrepresentations. For example, you tell me that he speaks of human nature whereas I have never believed—nor Sartre either, and on this point I am his disciple—we never believed in human nature. So it's a serious mistake to speak of "human nature" instead of "human reality," which is a Heideggerian term. I was infused with Heidegger's philosophy, and when I speak about human reality, that is, about man's presence in the world, I'm not speaking about human nature, it's completely different.

MS: Yes, exactly. These translation problems have been quite significant in feminist debate. American feminists have criticized your analysis of history and of marriage. But those discussions in *The Second Sex* contain the most extensive deletions. Parshley cut out the names of seventy-eight women from history and almost thirty-five pages from the chapter on marriage. You did a very good study of the letters of Sophie Tolstoy, and he cut almost all of it.

SdB: That's too bad, because really I liked that very much. It was Sophie Tolstoy's journal, not her letters. It's the journal, well the whole relationship was very strange, no, not very strange, on the contrary, one could say it was very banal, very typical of Tolstoy with his wife. At the same time, she is odious, but he even more odious. There. I'm enormously sorry that they cut out that passage . . . I would like very much for another translation of *The Second Sex* to be done, one that is much more faithful, more complete and more faithful.

MS: I have another question. A French philosopher friend explained to me your experience at the École Normale Supérieure [the institution responsible, under the highly centralized French university system, for training the elite professorate, as opposed to the Sorbonne, a more mass institution].

SdB: I was never at the ENS. That's false.

MS: Just a year as auditor?

SdB: No, no, never, never.

MS: You didn't . . .

SdB: I took courses at the ENS like everyone else; I took courses there when I was preparing my *agrégation* [teacher's examination]. When you are preparing an *agrégation* you have the right to take courses there, but I was never enrolled.

MS: But Sartre was [enrolled] there.

SdB: Yes, he was a student there.

MS: And Merleau-Ponty?

SdB: Yes, he as well.

MS: Were there other women who were regular students there?

SdB: There were some for a year or two. There was Simone Weil, Simone Petrement, but that was after me. I was already *agregée,* that is, I had already finished my studies, when they were at the ENS.

MS: It was a normal thing for a woman to take courses, but not to be a regular student.

SdB: No, but taking courses was normal. At the time one was preparing for the *agrégation,* one could take certain courses at the ENS. That was completely normal.

MS: Was it forbidden for women to be regular students at the ENS at that time?

SdB: No. Yes, it was forbidden and then it was allowed for a year or two, and it was just at that moment that Simone Weil, Simone Petrement, perhaps even another woman, were regular students. All that is not very pertinent between us, that is.

MS: Was it an important exclusion for you not to . . . ?

SdB: Absolutely not. I could have gone to Sèvres if I had wanted to. But I preferred to stay, not that I loved my family, but I preferred . . . Well, it wasn't even a matter of that . . . I didn't want to live on campus anywhere. That would have bothered me a lot. No, it wasn't exclusion. Well, it was completely normal. You studied at the Sorbonne and that was it. That didn't prevent me from getting my *agrégation* at a very young age; that didn't bother me at all.

MS: I once remarked to a colleague that you describe Sartre as a philosopher and yourself as a literary writer, and he replied, "Simone de Beauvoir said that she is a literary writer and Sartre is the philosopher? Ah, that's funny, *he* would prefer to be a literary writer." Is that true?

SdB: No, it's not exactly that. He thought that among his works, he was perhaps more attached to his literary works than to his philosophical ones because a literary work remains yours [*en soi*], and a philosophical work is always taken up and revised by posterity, it's changed and criticized, etc.

MS: When I started my studies with you, I was especially looking for an independent woman. It was very important to find a role model. And I looked for this role model in you. And I was angry that men said "The Great Sartreuse."

SdB: Oh, but that, that's a joke.

MS: Yes, a joke. But a lot of people told me, "Why are you working with her? Why not the man himself? She is just a follower."

SdB: My books are completely personal. Sartre never interfered. *She Came to Stay, The Mandarins,* all of that is mine. And *The Second Sex* is mine. Sartre was hardly interested at all in the education of women . . . Feminists understand very well that feminism is me and not Sartre.

MS: I heard that in 1968 or 1970, French feminists were very unhappy with *The Woman Destroyed* because they thought that it was against women.

SdB: There were critiques by certain feminists about it, but it was completely false because—well, I don't like "thesis" books, but—the story was that a woman should be independent. The heroine of *The Woman Destroyed* is completely destroyed because she lived only for her husband and children. So it's a very feminist book in a sense since it proves finally that a woman who only lives for marriage and motherhood is miserable.

MS: Now, this book is being read favorably by American feminists who see it as reflecting your own experience.

SdB: Well, of course, one puts part of oneself into any book, but it's not at all autobiographical.

MS: They refer to the rage, the fear of losing your sensuality or your tendency to sacrifice yourself, they found all those themes in that book in you.

SdB: But I never had the idea of sacrificing myself, all of that doesn't exist. They're wrong. It's hardly autobiographical at all. When one says that it's autobiographical, it's that I put in settings that I liked, that I locate the story in places, etc. But the whole story of the good wife who has sacrificed everything for her marriage and daughters, that's just the opposite. I'm completely against that, the idea of sacrificing oneself for a good husband and children. I'm completely adverse, the enemy of that idea.

MS: But you don't find that in your relation to Sartre.

SdB: No, not at all . . . I never sacrificed myself for Sartre, any more than he sacrificed himself for me.

MS: Have you read the review by Michèle Le Doeuff [1984] of your edited collection of Sartre's letters, *Les Lettres au Castor*?

SdB: There were so many articles.

MS: Le Doeuff refers to Sartre as "the only speaking subject" in the relationship.

SdB: Does that mean that I didn't give them my letters?

MS: No, it's not that. It's that Sartre really dominated the relationship.

SdB: No, that's not true. He's writing to me, so, one doesn't see my own stories, one doesn't see me, my personal life in his letters. One only sees Sartre's. That's all.

MS: So it's really Sartre who is speaking.

SdB: In his letters, yes. If I published my own, I would be the one speaking. But in my lifetime, I won't publish my letters.

MS: A friend, an American philosopher, once told me, "I am completely angry at this Simone de Beauvoir—'we, we, we'—she always says 'we' in her autobiography. Where is she? She had completely disappeared."

SdB: I'm the one speaking. Obviously, Sartre didn't write his autobiography [covering the period of our relationship]. If he had, he would have had to say "we" also.

MS: Yes, you begin a sentence and he finishes it, and afterwards you think together.

SdB: Yes, but it's the same thing. If I begin it, he finishes it; if he begins it, I finish it, afterwards, there's a moment . . . Yes, we were very, very close. But that's nothing contrary to feminism. Because I believe one can be close to a man and be a feminist. Obviously, there are feminists, especially lesbian feminists, who would not at all agree. But that's my own feminism.

MS: I am surprised that you don't say that you find the tendency to sacrifice yourself in your inner life. Because I think I saw it in your books.

SdB: Not in my memoirs. In my memoirs, there is no tendency to self-sacrifice, whereas in my novels, I described women who perhaps had a tendency to self-sacrifice. Because I'm not speaking only about myself, I'm also speaking about other women.

MS: And yet, you have told me, "Yes, when I was very young, just before leaving for Marseilles, I had a crisis of consciousness." [This question refers to Beauvoir's experience of losing a sense of direction in her life, in the early years of her intimate relationship with Sartre, after finishing her graduate study and before beginning her first position in Marseilles.]

SdB: Well, in fact, I refused to marry him after all. Thus, I remained feminist. I did not at all want to attach myself to a man by the ties of marriage. I refused marriage. I was the one who refused. Sartre proposed to me.

MS: You chose that relationship with Sartre? When one reads the memoirs, it seems that it was he who defined the relationship.

SdB: No, not at all. I also chose Sartre. I was the one who chose him. I saw a lot of other men, I even saw men who later became famous, like Merleau-Ponty, like Lévi-Strauss etc., etc. But I was never tempted to live with them, to make a life together. I was the one who chose Sartre, well, we chose each other.

MS: I have a question about choice. There is a theoretical tension in *The Second Sex* on the question of choice and oppression. In one chapter you wrote that women are not oppressed as a group. But in the next chapter, you wrote, "Yes, women are truly oppressed as a group." In another chapter, you questioned whether one can say that a girl raised to be the Other ever chooses to be the Other. But you also say that the woman is in complicity with her oppression. I find that there's a tension there. It remains even today in feminism, between choice and oppression.

SdB: I think that on the whole women are oppressed. But at the heart of their oppression—sometimes, they choose it because it's convenient for a bourgeois woman who has a little bit of money to marry a man who has even more money than she has and who will take care of everything so that she can do nothing. There is a complicity on the part of women. Very often, not always. They often find it easier to get married than to have a career, to work and be independent.

MS: And the women who are not rich, not at all rich, and I'm thinking about young girls who were [victims of] incest. Can one say that these women have the choice to be . . . ?

SdB: No, I think that they had very little choice. But all the same, there is a way of choosing at a certain moment, as soon as they get a little older, of choosing to stay in that incest situation or of refusing and even bringing their father to court.

MS: I think that many feminists understand women as victims of an absolute patriarchy. And I find certain problems with that analysis. And you understood in *The Second Sex* that women are in complicity. But also there are women who are victims of oppression but who also seek power over their children. If a woman, for example, beats her children or burns them with a cigarette. What is she doing? She is dominating.

SdB: She is getting revenge for her oppression. It's not a way of getting out of it. In the same way that making a scene in front of her husband is not a way of eliminating oppression.

MS: And the way to eliminate oppression is to . . .

SdB: To be independent. To work.

MS: Yes, especially to work. And what are you doing now in the way of work?

SdB: Well, for the moment, I am working a lot on [the journal] *Les Temps Modernes.*

MS: I have heard it said that the feminist movement in France is over.

SdB: That's not true; that's not true.

MS: No?

SdB: Not at all. It's less loud than before, it's not out in the streets because we have a lot of support from the Ministry of the Rights of Woman. So, we are more organized, we are doing more constructive work now rather than agitation; but that doesn't mean that the movement is over. Not at all. That's something that all the antifeminists say: "It's no longer in fashion, it's no longer in fashion, it's over." But it's not true at all. It's lasting. On the contrary, there are a lot of feminist researchers. There are a lot of feminists in the CNRS [the National Center for Scientific Research]. Well, that is, research, scholarships for doing research on feminism. There is a lot of work; there are a lot of foundations to help feminist or female painters, sculptors. Oh yes, yes, there are a lot of things. It's just that it's all more or less going through the ministry.

MS: Oh, that will change.

SdB: Alas, perhaps. Because Yvette Roudy, who is the minister of the Rights of Woman [during the early years of Mitterand's socialist government], is altogether a dedicated feminist. So she helps us enormously; she gives a lot of money to magazines, exhibitions, research, feminist work. For foundations also. Yes, yes. So it is not at all true that the movement is over.

This interview was transcribed and translated by Jane Marie Todd and is reprinted from "Two Interviews with Simone de Beauvoir," *Hypatia: A Journal of Feminist Philosophy* 3, no. 3 (Winter 1989): 11–27, by permission of Indiana University Press.

8

SEXISM AND THE PHILOSOPHICAL CANON: ON READING BEAUVOIR'S *THE SECOND SEX* (1990)

Feminist literary critics working with texts by women writers have exposed the sexism at work in the shaping of a literary canon. Annette Kolodny (1985), for example, in "A Map for Rereading: Gender and the Interpretation of Literary Texts," discusses the fate of Charlotte Perkins Gilman's *The Yellow Wallpaper*. Written by Gilman in the macabre style of Edgar Allan Poe, this book is the story of a middle-class wife and mother driven insane by the intellectual and social deprivation prescribed by a physician-husband unable to "read" her symptoms. Male literary critics, unable to read the connection between Gilman's story and Poe's, failed to appreciate her contribution to the literary genre. Gender bias shaped the literary canon around her, without her. An obvious question for a feminist philosopher is whether the same process has been at work in philosophy. An investigation of philosophers' readings of Simone de Beauvoir's 1949 feminist classic *The Second Sex* reveals that it has. Although *The Second Sex,* unlike *The Yellow Wallpaper,* found a wide readership among women, it, too, anticipated its own misreading within a canon shaped by men.

The Second Sex is important not only for its contribution to feminist philosophy, but for its more general contribution to existential moral and social philosophy and to our understanding of the social construction of knowledge. For Beauvoir, whose graduate degree was in philosophy, *The Second Sex* was a culmination of her existential ethics and her work on the problem of the Other, which, as a private relation of individuals, is the subject of her first published novel, *She Came to Stay* (1943).

Forced by the Nazi Occupation to confront historical and political realities, Beauvoir immersed herself in Hegel's *Phenomenology* and began what she termed the "ethical period" in her literary life, which included a play, *Useless Mouths* (1945); two novels, *The Blood of Others* (1945) and *All Men Are Mortal* (1946); and two essays on existentialist ethics, *Pyrrhus and Cineas* (1944) and *The Ethics of Ambiguity* (1947).

Beauvoir's ethics, grounded in concrete experience, contain a critique of "separation," i.e., the failure to recognize that the freedom of self and Other are interconnected. Linda Singer has described Beauvoir's philosophy as "the voice of the ethics of otherness," in which freedom emerges in a situation of relatedness and affinity (Singer 1985, 232). The importance of context, family, relationships, and the biological dimensions of human existence, along with the achievement of self, characterizes the entire body of Beauvoir's work. In *The Second Sex* Beauvoir reconceives ethical questions arising for individuals in private relationships as political questions for society as a whole, requiring an historical analysis as well as a phenomenological description. In the foreground of moral enquiry is the relationship of men and women, not the individual reasoning subject. The moral problems arising within that relationship lend themselves neither to individual solutions nor to absolute answers. They reflect a changing economic, political, legal, cultural, and technological reality that limits human freedom and shapes the experience of embodiment, the world, and other people.

Drawing on Hegel's *Phenomenology,* Beauvoir describes woman as "the Other," doomed to immanence, her freedom perpetually transcended by another. Definitions of woman's nature in myth and philosophy, science and literature, reflect men's consciousness. Beauvoir draws on Sartre's analysis of the anti-Semite to describe man's psychological motivation to become an oppressor. Men oppress women in "bad faith," attempting to flee the anxiety of their own freedom. But Beauvoir, unlike Sartre, rejects both nominalism and a Marxist reductionism. Laying the groundwork for contemporary feminism, Beauvoir argues that women's "lived experience" is the only valid theoretical basis for understanding their oppression and creating a politics of women's liberation. Tracing the politicization of women's differences from men, while refusing to reify those differences into a static essence, Beauvoir created an existential social philosophy in which individual freedom and concrete experience are privileged. Beauvoir showed that the "woman problem" that has plagued philosophy from the time of Plato and Aristotle can only be solved by women acting collectively to gain the political and economic power to define themselves.

The Second Sex broke new philosophical ground in its critical appropriation of Hegel, Nietzsche, Marx, and psychoanalysis and its transformation of feminism and existential phenomenology. In *The Second Sex*, Beauvoir succeeds where many other phenomenologists failed, in defining a social/political philosophy because of the originality of her method, which locates her critique on the margins of culture, in women's experience and the originality of her subject. Unlike most philosophers working within the phenomenological tradition, Beauvoir focused not on an individual consciousness but on a relationship. She redefined feminist discourse through her epistemological privileging of female voices, critique of male views of women as Other, and radical analysis of gender relationships. Conceived by Beauvoir as compatible with the socialist ideals of collective care and freedom from economic exploitation, *The Second Sex* provided the theoretical foundation for the emergence of radical feminism in the 1960s.

I

Despite the significance of Beauvoir's contribution to philosophy, most texts on French existential philosophy make at most a passing reference to Beauvoir, dismissing her as a follower of Sartre not worthy of autonomous study. This interpretation first appears in Jean Wahl's 1949 work *A Short History of Existentialism*: "We might mention, without discussing, Simone de Beauvoir and Merleau-Ponty, whose theories are similar to those of Sartre, though sometimes applied to different domains of experience" (Wahl 1949, 31). Walter Kaufmann's popular early anthology, *Existentialism from Dostoevsky to Sartre* (1956), does not mention her at all. Not that Beauvoir was unknown in 1956. She was well known as an existentialist writer in America, where her visit and lectures on existentialism in 1947 were well covered by the media. The Philosophical Library published an English translation of *The Ethics of Ambiguity* in 1948, and *The Second Sex* appeared in English in 1952.

Kaufmann's failure to mention Beauvoir is all the more curious given his choice of other authors for inclusion in his anthology. In addition to Kierkegaard, Nietzsche, Jaspers, Heidegger, and Sartre, Kaufmann includes selections from Rilke, Kafka, and Camus, choices that stretch the philosophical definition of existentialism much further, one would think, than would the inclusion of Beauvoir. Kaufmann acknowledges the problem in his preface: "By the time we consider adding Rilke, Kafka, and Camus, it becomes plain that one essential feature shared by all these men is their perfervid individualism" (Kaufmann 1956, 11). Including a woman might, of course, have changed another "essential feature" of the group.

In his preface Kaufmann also argues against several objections by American philosophers to Sartre's philosophy, which might also apply to Beauvoir: "Sartre is a philosopher in the French tradition which, more often than not, has produced men who stand at the borderline of philosophy and literature: Montaigne, Pascal, Voltaire, Rousseau, and even Bergson come to mind in this connection" (Kaufmann 1956, 41). For Kaufmann, Sartre is simply "one of the most interesting thinkers of our time" (Kaufmann 1956, 41, 48). Kaufmann argues as well against critics who would ignore Sartre because of his concern with sexuality, his atheism, and his leftist politics. As though to emphasize his political tolerance, Kaufmann includes a text on Marxism by Sartre in a 1975 revised edition of his anthology, although Kaufmann sees the text as in some ways indicating "the epitaph of existentialism" (Kaufmann [1956] 1975, 281). Given Kaufmann's tolerance of existentialist politics, atheism, literary style, and discussions of sexuality, that there should still be no mention in 1975 of Beauvoir's *Ethics of Ambiguity* or *The Second Sex* points to sexism as the problem.

Beauvoir is often simply identified with Sartre, their relationship misstated to exaggerate Beauvoir's dependency. Collins, writing from a conservative religious position, refers to Beauvoir, mistakenly, as Sartre's "wife" and fails to differentiate between them philosophically. "Sartre and Simone de Beauvoir have a firm grasp on the half-truth that man is not a clod and cannot become perfect after the manner of a mere thing" (Collins 1952, 77, 87). Heineman lists Beauvoir separately in the index, but the reference in the text implies that Sartre coauthored Beauvoir's *Ethics of Ambiguity*. "Sartre and his friend, Simone de Beauvoir, have seen that an ethics of absurdity does not make sense; *The Ethics of Ambiguity* which they advertise instead can hardly be accepted as a genuine ethics" (Heineman 1958, 176). The mistaken impression that Sartre coauthored *The Ethics of Ambiguity* should have been eliminated by a foot-note, which the author failed to provide. Nor is *The Ethics of Ambiguity* listed in the bibliographical notes at the end of the book; the author chose to leave Beauvoir's work uncited and its authorship unclear.

The British philosopher H. J. Blackham (1965) cannot make up his mind about Beauvoir. In his introduction he fails to credit her role in the founding of *Les Temps Modernes*; "Sartre and Merleau-Ponty were cofounders of *Les Temps Modernes* in 1945." Later, in his introduction to the selections from Merleau-Ponty, he includes Beauvoir (in the passive voice): "Maurice Merleau-Ponty is bracketed with Sartre and Simone de Beauvoir as cofounder of *Les Temps Modernes* in 1945." The only bibliographic reference to Beauvoir I could find places her in the sec-ondary role of Sartre's biographer. "Biographical material also appears in the three volumes of Simone de Beauvoir's autobiography" (Blackham 1965, 12, 350, 349).

Breisach, like Wahl, reduces not only Beauvoir but also Merleau-Ponty to a secondary figure in relation to Sartre: "Around [Sartre] have gathered such Sartre-type existentialists as Simone de Beauvoir and Merleau-Ponty" (Breisach 1962, 107). Challenging this interpretation of Merleau-Ponty can provide the basis for an analogous reinterpretation of Beauvoir, as we can see in Rabil's study of Merleau-Ponty (1967).

> But the truth of the matter seems to be that Mlle de Beauvoir did not hold Sartre's view of freedom in the early postwar period. In *The Ethics of Ambiguity*, for example, she outlines a phenomenology of freedom in which approximate realizations of freedom are described and arranged in an ascending order of validity. Here the "mixture" of man and the world is the point of departure. (Rabil 1967, 133)

Rabil's text is not unproblematic; he sees Beauvoir not as a full partici-pant in the philosophical movement he is describing but as interesting only because of her role in an argument between male philosophers— Sartre and Merleau-Ponty. His failure to include *The Second Sex* in his analysis compromises his interpretation of the influence of Kojève's reading of Hegel on French existentialism, for example, and, most im-portantly in the context of Rabil's project, his assessment of the scope of Merleau-Ponty's influence. His story of French existentialism as a movement is thus incomplete. Nevertheless, Rabil's work is worth noting because of its evidence that alternative readings of Beauvoir were possible.

For many, William Barrett's popular, and opinionated, study of existential philosophy, *Irrational Man* (1958), provided a first introduction to Continental philosophy. Beauvoir's name is not listed in the index, although an incredible assortment of other names are—from Matthew Arnold to Lao-tse. But as Kolodny points out, reading the meaning of ellipsis and absence reveals the interpretive strategies that shape a canon, and this is certainly the case with philosophers' "readings" of Beauvoir. Few of the texts I examined include a reference to Beauvoir in their index, although, as in Barrett's case, Beauvoir is sometimes mentioned in the text itself. After recognized, with Sartre and Camus, as one of a group of "brilliant and engaging writers" and "leaders" of the "Existentialist literary movement," Beauvoir gradually disappears as an individual from Barrett's text. Next referred to in tandem with Sartre ("Sartre and Simone de Beauvoir are still phenomenally productive"), she then vanishes from the discussion (Barrett 1958, 7).

I only found one other, indirect, reference to Beauvoir in Barrett's book. *The Second Sex* is listed in the index, and the reference in the text warrants a close reading. The context is a discussion of Sartre's existential psychology. Barrett is criticizing the Cartesian dualism of Sartre's "doctrine of freedom" for "not really comprehend[ing] the concrete man who is an undivided totality of body and mind." One of the counterexamples Barrett offers to this Sartrean duality contains his reference to *The Second Sex*.

> Consider the psychology of the ordinary woman. Not of the women one meets in Sartre's novels or plays; nor of that woman, his friend, who wrote a book of feminine protest, *The Second Sex,* which is in reality the protest against being feminine. (Barrett 1958, 231, 232)

The tone of this reference, as well as its content, is startling. Barrett avoids mentioning Beauvoir by name, using instead the angry phrase "that woman" and a reference to her relationship with Sartre before finally referring to her work, which he describes with a sarcastic turn of phrase. Barrett's refusal to name Beauvoir and his dismissal of *The Second Sex* warrant a careful analysis especially because many of the factors shaping Barrett's interpretation of Beauvoir might be present, in less explicit forms, in interpretations by other philosophers.

Barrett gives three objections to Sartre's dualistic psychology: man is isolated from nature, the existence of the unconscious is denied, and human relationships become "a perpetual oscillation between sadism and masochism" that "turns love and particularly sexual love into a perpetual tension and indeed warfare." It is this third objection that concerns us here. Barrett describes Sartre's analysis of relationships in frightening terms, as "a dialectical ingenuity that is almost fiendish. . . . [T]he glance of the Other, in Sartre, is always like the stare of Medusa, fearful and petrifying" (Barrett 1958, 229). The argument that follows is Barrett's attempt to explain away this dangerous human relationship. He begins by criticizing Sartre's "fundamentally masculine psychology that misunderstands or disparages the psychology of woman." He finds a strong "element of masculine protest" in

> Sartre's philosophical analysis . . . of the viscous, the thick, sticky substance that would entrap his liberty like the soft threat of the body of a woman. And the woman is a threat, for the woman is nature and Sartrean man exists in the liberty of his project, which, since it is ultimately unjustified and unjustifiable, in effect sunders him totally from nature. (Barrett 1958, 230)

Barrett could have responded to this Sartrean vision, as Beauvoir did in *The Second Sex,* by examining the roots of man's fears and myths about woman that explain male domination. Beauvoir contrasts these with women's experience of oppression and desire for liberation and argues for reciprocity. Instead, Barrett seeks to eliminate the battle between the sexes by eliminating woman/nature as a threat, thus providing a secure foundation for male domination. His solution is twofold: to reunite man with nature through the unconscious and to deny consciousness to woman.

Let Barrett himself take up the narrative at the point following his reference to *The Second Sex:*

> Take an ordinary woman, one of the great number whose being is the involvement with family and children, and some of whom are happy at it, or at least as humanly fulfilled by it as the male by his own essentially masculine projects. What sense does it make to say that such a woman's identity is constituted by her project? Her project is family and children, and these do in fact make up a total human

commitment; but it is hardly a project that has issued out of the conscious ego. Her whole life, with whatever freedom it reveals, is rather the unfolding of nature through her. (Barrett 1958, 232)

Barrett's solution to the battle of the sexes is both simple and traditional: woman is revered, and silenced, as a passive expression of nature. Since woman lacks consciousness, the oscillation between sadism and masochism stops; woman never becomes subject. Woman, whose being is involvement with the family, mediates in that role between man and nature, a relation that for man functions at the level of the unconscious, not as a subject for conscious concern.

Another problem for Barrett and others in the interpretation of Beauvoir's philosophy is that many of her texts, especially *The Second Sex,* stubbornly resist being cast in a Sartrean context. Barrett saw French existentialism as a European philosophy of despair, diametrically opposed to American optimism and belief in technology. But Beauvoir's philosophy in *The Second Sex* is optimistic, based on faith in the liberating potential of technology, which had brought violence and productivity into the physical grasp of women, as it had brought control over reproduction. Barrett could not have maintained his conceptual framework and at the same time have incorporated *The Second Sex* into his analysis.

II

One explanation for the biases in some of the earliest writings on existentialism is that they were written in the conservative 1950s before the reemergence of feminism in the 1960s. There is an exception, however, in the prefeminist era; Hazel Barnes, the translator of *Being and Nothingness*, writes that the similarity between Sartre's essay and Beauvoir's novel *She Came to Stay* (1943) "is too striking to be coincidence." Although Barnes refers to the philosophy in both texts as "Sartre's philosophy" and describes Beauvoir as wanting "to show how Sartre's abstract principles could be made to work out in 'real life,' " Barnes is careful to leave the question of influence open. "I do not at all preclude the possibility that de Beauvoir has contributed to the formation of Sartre's philosophy," Barnes writes in a footnote.

I suspect that his debt to her is considerable. All I mean in the present instance is that the novel serves as documentation for the theory, regardless of who had which idea first. (Barnes 1959, 122)

By the 1970s, with the rebirth of feminism, one would expect to find more such readings of Beauvoir. Robert Solomon's popular text *From Rationalism to existentialism* (1972), for example, promises to correct things, and on the surface it does. Solomon's text has a string of references to Beauvoir in its index. His introduction to the chapter on Sartre and French existentialism includes Beauvoir in a list of French existentialist philosophers, remarking on their "deep philosophical-personal commitment to social-political issues." Solomon even acknowledges *The Second Sex:* "Simone de Beauvoir has contributed enormously to contemporary women's liberation movements as well as to contemporary moral-social thought" (Solomon 1972, 244). But his interpretive framework retains many of the problems of an earlier, more explicitly sexist era. Beauvoir's works are treated sloppily in the footnotes and references; the references to *The Second Sex* lack information about the edition, of which there were several by the early seventies, and the wrong title is given for the original French edition of *The Ethics of Ambiguity.* Entitled in French *Pour une morale de l'ambiguité,* it is cited in Solomon's book as *L'Ethic de Ambiguité* and gives no publication information, although he gives detailed information on various editions of works by Sartre and others (Solomon 1972, 341n7).

Later in the introductory section, the differential treatment continues. Solomon describes Albert Camus as "best known for his philosophical novels, but his philosophical essays have caused his name to be one of the first mentioned in discussions of 'existentialism' (although he himself has rejected this affiliation)." The description of Beauvoir in the next sentence presents an interesting contrast. "Simone de Beauvoir is also best known as a novelist, but her two theoretical works in existentialist theory including the only explicit formulation of existentialist ethics within the movement, demonstrate her confessed allegiance to Sartre's philosophy." Where Camus does "philosophy," Beauvoir does "theory." Where Camus's "rejection of that affiliation" is no barrier to recognizing his contribution to existential philosophy, Beauvoir's "confessed allegiance" to Sartre's philosophy is. In a passage defining Sartre's relationships with Beauvoir, Merleau-Ponty, and Camus, Solomon describes Sartre as founding *Les Temps Modernes* with Merleau-Ponty, ignoring Beauvoir's role as a founding editor and focusing instead on her relationship with Sartre; "Simone de Beauvoir and Jean-Paul Sartre were and still are lovers" (Solomon 1972, 245–47).

Including a full discussion of Beauvoir's philosophy would have required Solomon to reformulate his analysis of post-1945 existentialism and its relation to Marxism and to address Beauvoir's critique of women's oppression. But no adequate account of existentialism can ignore the post-1945 texts without encountering serious difficulties, as Solomon's one reference to *The Second Sex* reveals. The reference occurs, stereotypically, within a discussion of Sartre's philosophy and his analysis of the anti-Semite as a man in bad faith who has "created the Jew from his need. . . . [T]he Jew's existence simply allows the anti-Semite to nip his anxieties in the bud by persuading himself that his place has always been cut out in the world" (Solomon 1972, 290; citing Sartre 1948, 8, 26–27). A passage from *The Second Sex* that one might expect to follow this example from Sartre would be one drawing the obvious analogy between the bad faith of the anti-Semite and that of the sexist man. Instead Solomon quotes a passage supposedly demonstrating women's bad faith in denying *themselves* freedom.

> Similarly Simone de Beauvoir points out bad faith in women . . . a woman treats herself as a sexual object (as a "woman") in order to deny her freedom. De Beauvoir declares that the common bad faith of woman is her appeal to her "feminine" nature: "Woman is a female to the extent that she feels herself as such. . . . It is not nature that defines woman, it is she who defines herself." (Solomon 1972, 290)

Actually, Beauvoir is not criticizing woman's bad faith here, although she does so elsewhere, but praising psychoanalysis for its insights into embodied consciousness. She is thus differentiating herself philosophically from Sartre rather than aligning herself with him. Solomon's interpretation, which holds the woman victim alone responsible for her oppressive situation, is an interpretation that might with some justification, and irony, be called a bad faith reading of *The Second Sex*.

Mistranslations of philosophical terminology in the current English translation of *The Second Sex* by H. M. Parshley might also be a factor in Solomon's misreading of this passage. A literal translation of the original French would read

It is not the body-object described by scholars that exists *concretely*, but the *body lived* by the subject. The woman is a female, to the extent that she *experiences* herself as such. (Beauvoir 1949, 1:77; my emphasis)

The Parshley translation reads

It is not the body-object described by biologists that *actually* exists, but the *body as lived in* by the subject. Woman is a female to the extent that she *feels* herself as such. (Beauvoir [1949] 1952, 33)

The concept of "concretely experiencing one's lived body" provides a hermeneutic link with French existential phenomenology that is lost in the phrase "actually feeling one's body as lived in."

If the lack of a full discussion of post-1945 existentialism is one source of interpretative problems, perhaps interpretations that focus directly on these later political writings might provide a more adequate reading of Beauvoir. Marjorie Grene, who puzzles over Sartre's later "interest in [childhood and] concrete individual life" (Grene 1973, 244–45), is interesting in this regard. She describes as inadequate the hypothesis that these new interests might be accounted for by Merleau-Ponty's influence, but she never thinks of the possibility that they might reflect the influence of Beauvoir, whose studies of "concrete individual life" were well known. By 1973, of course, it may have been not too early but too late, the sexist gender politics of philosophy having successfully excluded Beauvoir from the philosophical canon, so that without a feminist context for locating the effects of sexist bias, even a female philosopher was unable to trace her influence.

Finally, one must examine the representation of Beauvoir in *The Encyclopedia of Philosophy,* an ambitious multivolume project in the formalization of the American philosophical canon, published in 1967 under the editorship of Paul Edwards. The *Encyclopedia* contains no mention of Beauvoir in the index, either as a separate entry or in the four columns of listings under "French Philosophy." Had the editors alphabetized her name under "B," she would have come right after the entry on "Beauty"; instead, they jumped to Beccaria, an eighteenth-century Italian criminologist whose work on penal reform was surely no more important a philosophical contribution than Beauvoir's work on gender reform in *The Second Sex.* Nor is Beauvoir listed under "D," in which case her name would have followed the entry on "Death." That entry ended with a reference to Heidegger and Sartre but no mention of Beauvoir, although *A Very Easy Death* had been published in English translation in 1964. Beauvoir is mentioned in the entry on Sartre, where she is cited with Merleau-Ponty as one of the founders of *Les Temps Modernes*. Of the four French existentialist philosophers mentioned in this entry—Merleau-Ponty, Sartre, Beauvoir, and Camus—only Beauvoir lacks an entry under her own name in the *Encyclopedia*. The contrast with Camus is particularly interesting since many of the explanations that might account for a failure to include Beauvoir, her identity as a literary writer, for example, or the political engagement of her writings, would also apply to Camus.

Beauvoir is also mentioned in the entry on "Existentialism," although not in subsections such as "freedom and choice" or "existentialism and psychoanalytic topics," but in a subsection on Sartre. "[Sartre's psychological analyses] are employed, too, in the novels of Simone de Beauvoir, whose moral and political writings also use the Sartrean concept of choice"; a misleading reference, since Beauvoir's criticism of Sartre's concept of choice and his concept of absolute freedom define an area of philosophical difference between them. The bibliography for the entry on the history of ethics mentions Beauvoir's *Ethics of Ambiguity* with the comment "Important in its own right and in relation to Sartre." In the entry itself there is no mention of Beauvoir or her "important" work, although there is a lengthy discussion of Camus. The contrast between the treatment accorded Camus and that given Beauvoir is particularly dramatic, for the author of the entry remarks that "Camus wrote no technical philosophy" (Edwards 1967, 3–4:150, 116, 107).

III

The rebirth of feminism has not meant the end of the misreadings or even the contemptuous dismissal of Beauvoir. "Why should we read Beauvoir?" a feminist philosopher demanded of me a couple years ago. "She's out-of-date, male-identified, and just Sartrean anyway." In search of a positive approach to Beauvoir's philosophy, we might turn to a model suggested by Patrocinio Schweickart in "Reading Ourselves: Toward a Feminist Theory of Reading." She identifies a "feminist story of reading," drawn from Adrienne Rich's reading of Emily Dickinson, in which the woman reader and the woman writer are featured in the context of two settings.

> The first setting is judicial: one woman is standing witness in defense of the other. The second is dialogic: the two women are engaged in intimate conversation. (Schweickart 1986, 53)

An awareness of context is crucial in both settings. In the first, the feminist reader takes the part of the woman writer "against the patriarchal misreadings that trivialize or distort her work," a perspective that demands an understanding of the political and cultural context that both women to some extent share. In the second, a dialogic model of reading demands knowledge of the circumstances in which the author lived and worked and how her premises were shaped by her own world. It also demands an awareness of the context of reading, how a woman's reading is necessarily shaped by her own experience and interests (Schweickart 1986, 54).

Scholar/biographers can help us understand the context of Beauvoir's writing. Carol Ascher, for example, sheds new light on Beauvoir's conception of the problem of the Other through an analysis of Beauvoir's account of the death of her friend Zaza, which Beauvoir saw as the cost of her own freedom. Understanding the context of Beauvoir's writing can help us understand her preference for describing herself as a literary writer rather than a philosopher. We can also understand her idealization of men's activities, her angry attack on woman's traditional role as a threat to the development of a woman's individuality, and even her focus on relationships with men. Beauvoir was a token woman, struggling to escape woman's traditional role and survive on the fringes of the male-dominated institution of philosophy. She felt more threatened in woman's sphere than man's and considered her existence to be more of a threat to traditional women such as her mother and Zaza than to men like her father and Sartre, in spite of their sexism, which is so apparent to us now.

When writing *The Second Sex* in 1948–49, Beauvoir could not have imagined what the future, and our present, would be. She wrote before Black Power and Gay Pride, before the birth control pill and the sexual revolution, before the Battle of Algiers, the war in Vietnam, the French student rebellion of May 1968, KinderCare, and AIDS. She did not understand the depth of male violence supporting women's oppression. She could not imagine how vital female friendships would become to those who continued her assault on male-dominated institutions, nor how important and politically charged the concept of "woman-identity" would become to those leaving woman's traditional role and identity behind. But Beauvoir spoke out worldwide for women's liberation throughout the lonely years of the 1950s and 1960s, inspiring and giving personal encouragement to many of the feminist theorists who helped launch the contemporary movement. And when, in 1972, French women came to her for support, she became an active participant in a movement led by women years younger than herself. Now that she has become part of women's history, and her texts the most tangible connection with her, this relationship has become part of the "feminist story of reading" described by Schweickart.

As we have seen, the male-defined philosophical canon has erected barriers to access by, and legitimation of, women philosophers. These barriers have encouraged women in philosophy to distance themselves from their female predecessors, including Beauvoir, and to validate their identities as philosophers through reference to male-authored texts or a supposedly gender-free methodology. But with the challenge to the philosophical canon comes the possibility of reclaiming a feminist philosophical heritage and its connection with Simone de Beauvoir. Feminists may, as Schweickart suggests, "stand witness in her defense" across the differences of culture, generation, and time and join with her as "two women engaged in intimate conversation."

Reprinted, with changes, from *Journal of the History of Ideas* LI (July): 487–504, copyright 1990, with permission from Johns Hopkins University Press.

9

LESBIAN CONNECTIONS: SIMONE DE BEAUVOIR AND FEMINISM (1991)

I. BEAUVOIR AND THE HETEROSEXUAL CANON

Until recently the philosophy and life of Simone de Beauvoir have been read by most critics, both within and outside feminism, as circumscribed by her relationship with the philosopher Jean-Paul Sartre. As we have seen, most philosophical studies of existentialism have dismissed Beauvoir as merely Sartrean, a view reflected in Beauvoir's excessively modest claims that she, unlike Sartre, lacked philosophical creativity. Some feminist philosophers have criticized Beauvoir's *The Second Sex* as heterosexist, masculinist, and Sartrean. Downplaying evidence of what Elaine Marks (1986) terms a "homosexual secret" in Beauvoir's texts, biographers have similarly read Beauvoir's life in the context of her relationship with Sartre, as illustrated, for example, by the title of a 1987 biography: *Simone de Beauvoir: A Life, a Love Story* (Francis and Gontier 1987). In the opinion of most biographers, Beauvoir's relationship with Sartre is rivaled only by her affair with the American novelist Nelson Algren. Her relationships with women are consigned to a distant third place.

Deirdre Bair's popular biography of Beauvoir is no exception. For Bair, Beauvoir's relationship with Sartre is "the primary facet" of Beauvoir's identity, tragically dominating her life and work (Bair 1990b, 497). To critics, Beauvoir is Sartre's "companion" who "applies, disseminates, clarifies, supports, and administers" his "philosophical, aesthetic, ethical and political principles" (Bair 1990b, 514). Evidence of Beauvoir's sexual intimacy with women, including the remark by Beauvoir's friend Francis Jeanson that he finds Beauvoir "more sexualized in that sphere

115

[with women] than in the other" poses an interpretive challenge for Bair but is ultimately not allowed to disrupt her construction of a coherent heterosexual gender identity for Beauvoir (Bair 1990b, 511). Bair first addresses the issue in a late chapter on "The Friendships of Women," where she discusses Beauvoir's relationship with Sylvie Le Bon.

Beauvoir met Le Bon in 1960 when the eighteen-year-old philosophy student from Rennes wrote to her asking for a meeting. Beauvoir encouraged Le Bon in her studies and in her rebellion against the conservative Catholic background they both shared. In 1962, Le Bon was forcibly returned to Rennes by her family in an effort to break off the relationship with Beauvoir. After legally coming of age the following year, however, Le Bon returned to Paris and to Beauvoir. Despite the more than thirty years' difference in age between her and Le Bon, Beauvoir reports that by 1964 Le Bon was "thoroughly interwoven" in her life (Beauvoir 1972, 72). Beauvoir continued to live in her studio apartment, and Sartre spent at least one night a week there until his death. But Le Bon spent several nights a week with Beauvoir as well and saw her daily. Le Bon and Beauvoir traveled together and carried on long discussions in which Beauvoir's young companion supplanted Sartre as the sounding board for Beauvoir's ideas. And in 1980, shortly after Sartre's death, Beauvoir made Le Bon her adoptive daughter. Beauvoir's health was deteriorating, and the adoption was intended to give Le Bon the legal authority to care for her. After Beauvoir's death, Sylvie Le Bon added her adoptive mother's surname to her own, becoming Sylvie Le Bon de Beauvoir (for brevity, she will be referred to in this text simply as Le Bon).

In interviews with Bair during the 1980s, Beauvoir described her relationship with Le Bon as "an absolute relationship, because from the beginning we were both prepared to live in this way, to live entirely for each other" (Bair 1990b, 509). She called Le Bon "the ideal companion of my adult life. If I wish one thing it is only that our ages were closer, so that we could have known each other longer, earlier in our lives" (Bair 1990b, 510). Bair recalls Beauvoir's 1985 statement

> that she had elevated Sylvie to a separate plane within her life, one parallel if not equal to Sartre's. "I am fortunate" she concluded, "to enjoy a perfect relationship with both a man and a woman." (Bair 1990b, 512)

For Sylvie Le Bon, according to Bair,

> it was "love between Castor [Beauvoir's nickname, Beaver] and my-self. What made it complicated is that neither one of us was prepared, especially me, to love someone who was a woman. But that's what it was, love, that's all." (Bair 1990b, 509)

Beauvoir helped Le Bon accept the adoption and the scandal it caused by telling her, "After all, it's like marriage, because you share my name" (Bair 1990b, 509).

Despite evidence of her intimate relationship with Le Bon, Beauvoir reportedly was furious at suggestions that she proclaim a lesbian identity, "because she feared personal embarrassment and possible professional reprisal" for Le Bon, who was a philosophy teacher. Beauvoir steadfastly maintained that "it was simply a friendship and nothing more. 'We are *very very very* good friends' she insisted, her face flushing with anger at the thought that anyone might consider it in any other light." Faced with Beauvoir's intransigence, Bair declares herself at an impasse. "All this self-analysis leaves vague the question of what the friendship of Simone de Beauvoir and Sylvie Le Bon really consisted of . . . and, finally, how scholars of feminism and gender should ultimately interpret it." Bair ends by abandoning what she disparagingly terms "the recently 'trendy topic' of female friendship (Bair 1990b, 510, 508, 512, 513). Left to fill the interpretive void is a heterosexual scenario that tries unsuccessfully to explain away the troubling evidence of ambiguity in Beauvoir's gender identity.

Under this scenario, suggested by the opening sentence of Bair's chapter on "The Friendships of Women," Beauvoir turns to Le Bon in imitation of Sartre's 1965 adoption of one of his young female companions, Arlette Elkaïm.

> Sartre's adoption of Arlette served as a catalyst for many changes in Beauvoir's life that had been a long time coming. All her relationships, from Algren to her more casual friends and associates, underwent a significant shift. (Bair 1990b, 497)

But Le Bon was more than one of Beauvoir's "more casual friends" in 1965. By 1964 she was already "thoroughly interwoven" into Beauvoir's life. It was another, earlier event that transformed Beauvoir's relationship with Le Bon.

According to Bair, Sartre applied formally to adopt Elkaïm (who became Elkaïm-Sartre after her adoption, and, for brevity, will be referred to here simply as Elkaïm) on January 25, 1965. Yet Beauvoir and Le Bon had forged a deep bond some fourteen months earlier, in October 1963, following Le Bon's return to Paris from her "exile" in Rennes. The profound intimacy Beauvoir and Le Bon achieved during this period was not precipitated by anything in Beauvoir's relationship with Sartre. "It was her mother's death that brought us together," Le Bon reports (Bair 1990b, 506). In long discussions that deepened their intimacy, Beauvoir for the first time poured out her feelings to Le Bon, who encouraged her to write a moving account of her mother's death, *A Very Easy Death* (1964).

Beauvoir did not refer to her relationship with Sartre even when explicitly asked by Bair to explain her relationship with Le Bon. She referred instead to her passionate adolescent friendship with Zaza (Elisabeth Lacoin, referred to as "ZaZa" Le Coin by Bair, who claims that Beauvoir invented the nickname years later when writing her memoirs; but Beauvoir refers to "Zaza" in her handwritten journals from 1927 to 1931), who is familiar to readers of the first volume of Beauvoir's autobiography, *Memoirs of a Dutiful Daughter* (1958).

> You can explain my feeling for Sylvie by comparing it to my friendship with Zaza. I have kept my nostalgia for that my whole life. Since she died, l have often desired to have an intense, daily, and total relationship with a woman. (Bair 1990b, 76)

Le Bon also referred to Zaza in response to Bair's question:

> Ever since Zaza, she always wanted a total and intense relationship with a woman. She said she loved Zaza, that it was she who taught her the joy of loving. (Bair 1990b, 509)

Beauvoir called Zaza "the idealized love of my youth; Sylvie was the ideal companion of my adult life" (Bair 1990b, 510).

Beauvoir thus directs her reader away from the conventional heterosexual focus on Sartre for an understanding of her love of Le Bon.

What Bair describes as the "most important relationship in the last two decades of Beauvoir's life" is rooted in the most important relationships of the first two decades: those with her mother, her sister, and her friend Zaza (Portuges 1986, 107–18). As we shall see, texts published since Beauvoir's death in 1986 reveal that her passionate attachments with women spanned the middle decades of her life as well. These new texts encourage locating Beauvoir's life on what Adrienne Rich has termed the "lesbian continuum" (Rich 1980, 120) and support Marks's reading of Beauvoir's texts as transgressing the boundaries of heterosexual discourse.

II. THE LOVE OF WOMEN: NEW EVIDENCE

In spring 1990, Le Bon, Beauvoir's literary executor, completed the arduous and courageous task of editing for publication previously unavailable journals and letters from 1938 to 1945, which include accounts of Beauvoir's sexual relationships with women (Beauvoir 1990a, 1990b). At the same time, Le Bon also made available to scholars a collection of Beauvoir's manuscripts, including journals dating from 1928 to 1931, which contain similar accounts. No one who has seen the pictures of Simone de Beauvoir prostrate at Sartre's graveside or read her accounts of his death can doubt the depth of their relationship. But the new evidence from Beauvoir's journals and letters disrupts the heterosexual gender identity so carefully constructed by Beauvoir's biographers and critics and suggests a more ambiguous one.

Bair was not given access to these materials for her biography and charged Beauvoir, in an article following their publication, with evading "the hard truths of her bisexuality." But the rather clinical label "bisexual" leaves Bair's heterosexual interpretive framework intact. "Beauvoir, throughout the more than 50 years they were together, put all her needs, goals and desires second to Sartre's every impulse." For Bair, the tragedy of Beauvoir's life is that she chose the wrong man. "Why did de Beauvoir choose to remain locked in a sexless relationship with Sartre, in which she was often lied to, taken advantage of and humiliated, when she could have had a truly equal relationship with Nelson Algren?" (Bair 1990a, 34). Beauvoir's relationships with women are erased.

Overcoming this erasure requires an interpretive framework offering a more direct challenge to "compulsory heterosexuality" as a political institution. Adrienne Rich's concept of a "lesbian continuum" permits recognition of the affectional and political affinity among women that "has run like a continuous though stifled theme through heterosexual experience," providing "a history of female resistance" to the institution of compulsory heterosexuality that "has never fully understood itself because it has been so fragmented, miscalled, erased" (Rich 1980, 120, 135). Such a reading of Beauvoir's life and texts is not unproblematic, however, given Beauvoir's refusal of a lesbian identity and in light of readings of *The Second Sex* as sustaining rather than challenging compulsory heterosexuality (Card 1985, 291). But Beauvoir's refusal of a lesbian identity stems in part from a refusal to deny herself and other women the possibility of relationships with men, that is, from a rejection of the exclusionary practices of identity politics. In this case, Rich's notion of the "lesbian continuum," which is specifically designed to be inclusive, would seem to be appropriate.

Beauvoir "feared personal embarrassment and possible political reprisal for Sylvie" if she proclaimed a lesbian identity. According to Bair, Le Bon "made one cryptic remark on the subject: '[Beauvoir would only say] that we were good friends because I didn't want her to say anything more, for many reasons, many bad reasons'" (Bair 1990b, 510). This concern might have been why Beauvoir left it to Le Bon to decide—after Beauvoir's death—whether to publish the letters and journals, where we learn that it was a charge of "corrupting the morals" of a young woman student that led to Beauvoir's being fired as a teacher during the Occupation. Rich's "lesbian continuum" would thus seem appropriate here in its effort to reclaim loving connections between women that have been denied out of prejudice or fear. Furthermore, Beauvoir's refusal of the reification of gender identity can be read as challenging compulsory heterosexuality, as I will argue below.

A Woman's Heart and a Man's Brain: Unpublished Journals from 1928 to 1931

The ambiguity of Beauvoir's sexual desire would seem to mirror the ambiguity of her gender identity. Beauvoir often repeated her father's prideful description of her, his eldest daughter, as having a woman's heart and a man's brain. Diary entries from 1928 to 1931, when Beauvoir was completing her studies and beginning a life independent of her family, suggest that while her intellectual ambitions drew her into the world of men, her heart remained rooted in another world—one reminiscent of what Carroll Smith-Rosenberg, in describing the lives of nineteenth-century American bourgeois women, termed the female world of love and ritual (Smith-Rosenberg 1975, 1).

Simone de Beauvoir was born into a wealthy bourgeois family, which sought to prepare her to assume her role as wife and mother. But a series of bad investments and other financial setbacks following World War I left the family impoverished and ended its bourgeois aspirations. Beauvoir's father was a professional failure, successful philanderer, and amateur actor with aristocratic pretensions who exerted intellectual influence over his daughters but otherwise left the child rearing to his convent-bred wife, Françoise. Beauvoir's mother bitterly resented the impoverishment, domestic drudgery, and social humiliation she endured; she also suffered abuse at the hands of her husband. She had a volatile temper and took her frustration out on her daughters, trying to control every aspect of their lives and jealously prying into their affairs. But she shared a love of literature with her husband and instilled in her eldest daughter a scholastic discipline that brought Simone academic honors and eventual success as a writer. Even when money grew scarce, Françoise insisted that the pious Simone and her younger sister Hélène continue in the private Catholic girls school where they had begun their education. Without dowries, their marriage prospects were poor; unlike most of their classmates they would have to prepare for careers and learn to support themselves. Simone was a brilliant, dedicated pupil determined to be always at the head of her class; but she was unkempt, ignorant of social graces, and often ridiculed by her wealthy classmates.

The stifling presence of her mother, who had dominated Beauvoir's childhood, is in the background in her 1928 journal. At age twenty Beauvoir, who had lost her religious faith early in her teenage years, was nearing the end of her university education and preparing to become a philosophy teacher while nurturing dreams of becoming a writer. Her mother, unable to give her any guidance into the male world of the professions, could only pray for her daughter's salvation. Beauvoir's politically conservative, atheist father, who had represented the world of French literature to his intellectual daughter, vehemently opposed her progressive politics and passion for surrealism. In addition, he saw the necessity of her career as a sign of his failure and only rarely took pride in his daughter's academic triumphs.

Poupette, as Beauvoir's younger sister Hélène was called, is an important figure in the 1928–31 journals. During their early childhoods, Simone and Hélène sought solace from their mother's tyranny in each other's company, and Simone had become intensely protective of her younger sister. Relishing the opportunity to be useful and mirroring the solicitude of her mother, Simone had taken charge of Hélène's education and dominated her life. The sisters grew apart over the years as Simone, ill-dressed and covered with pimples, entered the awkward years of adolescence, and her prettier and more popular younger sister replaced her in their father's affections. But Hélène was still very important in Simone's life in 1928. Simone wrote of that time, "The person who took first place in my affections was my sister." If Jacques (a cousin she imagined being engaged to) were to die, "I would kill myself," but "if *she* [Hélène] were to vanish from the face of the earth, l shouldn't need to kill myself in order to die" (Beauvoir 1958, 296).

In spite of problems between them, Simone seems to assume the existence of a constant bond with her younger sister. During a difficult period in 1929, she wrote in her journal, "Chèri Poupette, Poupette who will always be" (Beauvoir 1929–31, 23). The sisters were to remain close throughout their lives, although Beauvoir seems impatient and critical of her sister in the 1939–41 journals when Hélène was beginning a relationship with her future husband and leaving her sister. In criticisms strikingly similar to those Simone was enduring from other women about her relationship with Sartre, Simone complained that Poupette's fiancé was too dominating, trying to transform Poupette into a "femme-esclave [a woman-slave]" (Beauvoir 1990b, 1:203).

The Idealized Love of My Youth: Zaza

But the first, most serious, threat to the sisters' relationship came in their adolescent years when Simone abandoned Poupette for her new classmate, Zaza. To the dutiful Simone, Zaza embodied rebelliousness, creativity, and freedom. She had personality and opinions of her own, including sarcastic criticisms of the hard-working Simone. She dared to talk back to the nuns and to stick out her tongue at her mother. Simone fell passionately in love with her. By 1928, in the earliest Beauvoir journal that I examined, their relationship had grown distant and then been renewed. Entries from September and October 1928 document Beauvoir's enduring love for Zaza. "I think of Zaza with an infinite tenderness, and I have as well the taste of her presence in my heart." "Coming down the stairs, l discovered a letter from Zaza, from a Zaza who loves me and to whom my tenderness has brought some sweetness" (Beauvoir 1928–29, 3, 5).

Whether or to what extent Beauvoir's love for Zaza was one-sided, as her biographers maintain, cannot be established from Beauvoir's journals. But Beauvoir's affection for Zaza is clear. Another unresolved issue is whether Beauvoir's passion for Zaza found physical expression. Beauvoir's autobiography and biographies such as Bair's describe the Beauvoir–Zaza relationship as sentimental rather than physical and emphasize Beauvoir's sexual prudery. An interesting difference between the autobiography and an unpublished journal suggests another picture. In her *Memoirs* Beauvoir recounts telling a friend, Stepha, of those times when she had felt a flush of sexual feelings sweep over her: "at a club, in the arms of certain dancers, or when at Meyrignac, sprawled in the grass of the park we were clasped in each other's arms, my sister and I" (Beauvoir 1958, 405). A nearly illegible reference to this conversation with Stepha in the 1928 journal refers not to lying entwined with her sister in the grass, but to having Zaza leaning over her bed embracing her (Beauvoir 1928–29, 6).

As interesting as the evidence of Beauvoir's erotic passion for Zaza is the indication that she censored it in her autobiography. The journals and letters show Beauvoir's awareness and concern that her feelings and behavior are lesbian. For example, in a 1939 letter to Sartre shortly after France has declared war on Germany, Beauvoir comforts GéGé, an artist friend of Poupette's, who has hurled herself on the bed sobbing about her lovers. "I threw myself down beside her; I've become such a *piège-à-loups* (wolf trap) [explained in Le Bon's editorial note: "Expression of Mme Morel, who called homosexuals of both sexes: *piège-à-loups*"], and habituated to these situations that I consoled her with the tender words 'my little girl, my *cherie,*' for a little bit I would have said 'my love'; that made me laugh" (Beauvoir 1990b, 1:91). In her journal for the same day, Beauvoir does not record that she laughed, and adds, "[GéGé] is captivating, with her charming outfit, her graceful waist and her hair in disorder, crying the tears of a girl who neglects her mascara'' (Beauvoir 1990a, 23).

By the end of the 1928–29 academic year, Zaza and Beauvoir are preparing for their different futures. Beauvoir, celebrating the completion of her graduate work in philosophy, is preparing to leave her home and enter the public literary world of men, first symbolized by her atheist father and now by her new acquaintance Jean-Paul Sartre. Beauvoir sees Zaza as involved in a hopeless struggle for independence from her wealthy family, which has discouraged their daughter's interest in a career, limited her higher education, and assigned her an endless round of domestic duties and social engagements designed to prepare her for the role of wife-and-mother. In the midst of battles with her mother over an arranged marriage, Zaza becomes gravely ill and dies, leaving Beauvoir grief stricken. Establishing a lifelong pattern, Beauvoir vowed to write as a way of dealing with her grief. "I must try to write! My only chance, my only chance!" (Beauvoir 1928–29, 28v). She made many attempts to tell the story of Zaza's tragic death, finally succeeding in her 1958 *Memoirs of a Dutiful Daughter*. In the final sentences of *Memoirs,* which concludes with an account of Zaza's death, Beauvoir seems to blame herself, reporting recurring dreams of Zaza "seeming to gaze reproachfully at me. We had fought together against the revolting fate that had lain ahead of us, and for a long time, I believed that I had paid for my own freedom with her death" (Beauvoir 1958, 360).

Beauvoir's sense of guilt and its centrality in her emotional and intellectual life becomes understandable if, as Catherine Portuges argues in her psychoanalytic study of *Memoirs,* loving Zaza was a crucial event in Beauvoir's development. Zaza, according to Portuges, enabled Beauvoir's successful differentiation from her mother and creative reconciliation of "masculine" individualism and freedom with the domestic, nurturant world of the "feminine" (Portuges 1986, 118). Portuges sees the writing of *Memoirs,* which traces the genesis of Beauvoir's intellectual creativity to the female world of her childhood, as an act of reparation to that world and to Zaza by a "feminist intellectual impelled by the desire to define herself both in relation to and separate from the mother and her 'introjects'" (Portuges 1986, 114). Ascher (1987) also provides an analysis of Beauvoir's account of Zaza's death in the *Memoirs* as relevant to her ethics, arguing that it points out the dangers of separation and autonomy for Beauvoir.

The Second Sex, published nine years before *Memoirs,* also owes its genesis to this female world—to Beauvoir's relationships with her mother, sister, and Zaza. *The Second Sex* is less a tribute to this world as the source of Beauvoir's creativity, however, than an exposé of its oppressive underside and an impassioned plea for women's liberation. A reflection on the source of her mother's bitter frustration and Zaza's hopeless struggle for freedom, *The Second Sex* analyzes the "feminine" world as a male construct designed to ensure women's enslavement as Other in a world created by men in their own interests. In this text Beauvoir no longer blames herself but instead holds male-dominated society accountable for her mother's bitter disappointments and Zaza's death.

Issues of attachment and separation and the attractions and dangers of the so-called feminine world continued to color Beauvoir's writings and intimate relationships with women throughout her life. In addition to underpinning her feminism, they also underlie the development of a central philosophical issue for Beauvoir, the "problem of the Other." Beauvoir's assumption of a fundamental attachment to the Other, which raises various ethical problems, differentiates her ethics and social philosophy from that of Sartre. The nascence of Beauvoir's intellectual odyssey in the female relationships of her childhood confirms the necessity of further philosophical study of women's traditional nurturing practices and relationships with women.

Other Women: Stepha and José

Judging from the journals, Beauvoir's lesbian connections were evident in her student days, even while her professional aspirations set her apart from many of the other women and fostered an ambiguity in her gender identity. As she wrote in *Memoirs* of her days as a student, "In many respects I set Zaza, my sister, Stepha, and even Lisa [José] above my masculine friends, for they seemed to me more sensitive, more generous, more endowed with imagination, tears, and love. I flattered myself that I combined 'a woman's heart and a man's brain' " (Beauvoir 1958, 295–96). The early journals allude to Beauvoir's intimate relationships with women besides Zaza, including Stepha, who was once a governess for Zaza's younger siblings. Upon hearing of Stepha's approaching marriage in 1929, Beauvoir writes, "I cannot recall without emotion that I had loved her so much" (Beauvoir 1928–29, 68v). In her journal entry of October 13, 1939 (although not in her letter to Sartre of the same date), Beauvoir records sitting down next to Stepha in a café, "she interrogated me to learn whether I was really homosexual [*piège*]" (Beauvoir 1990a, 88). Beauvoir does not record her reply.

José (identified as José Le Core, by Bair), a student with Beauvoir at the Sorbonne in 1929, is another woman mentioned in Beauvoir's handwritten journals. In reviewing the academic year and the end of her studies, Beauvoir remarks that it is the end of her "history" with José as well (Beauvoir 1928–29, 101). Later in the fall of 1929 she records "five passionate minutes of arms around her, and kisses" with José (Beauvoir 1929–31, 12). A year earlier, before Beauvoir's first meeting with Sartre, it was José who said to her: "What I admire about you is that you never refuse anything." Sitting with José in the bedroom, she lies down on the bed, a flower between her teeth: "I know that she suffers, but myself, I am too happy" (Beauvoir 1928–29, 61, 60).

Beauvoir's attraction to women did not end with her pursuit of heterosexual relationships. She writes in *The Second Sex*:

> It is not the organ of possession that the woman envies in the man: it is his prey. It is a curious paradox that man lives in a sensual . . . feminine world, while the woman moves in the male universe that is hard and severe; her hands keep the desire to embrace smooth skin. . . . A large part of herself remains available and wishes the possession of a treasure analogous to that which she delivers to the male. This explains the more or less latent tendency to homosexuality that survives in many women. (Beauvoir 1949, 2:169)

Entering the World of Men: Sartre

In explaining her initial attraction to Sartre, Beauvoir once remarked to Bair that she was attracted less to Sartre as a person than to the world that he represented. "I didn't want *Sartre,* I wanted to be part of his *group*" (Bair 1990b, 128). "Here," Bair writes, "her emphasis implied that she did not want Sartre the man in any physical sense" (Bair 1990b, 128). Sartre, a brilliant and rowdy student at the prestigious École Normale Supérieure (ENS), had flunked the philosophy *agrégation* the year before and was preparing for a second try. Beauvoir, although formally enrolled as a philosophy student at the Sorbonne, sat in on lectures at the ENS while preparing for the *agrégation*. Beauvoir had grown into a beautiful young woman, and she intrigued Sartre. Her reputation as an expert on Leibniz, the seventeenth-century German philosopher and mathematician, won her an invitation to cram sessions with Sartre's circle at the ENS. After she lectured the other students on Leibniz for a week, Beauvoir's place in the group was assured. After their graduation, Sartre announced that he would take Beauvoir under his wing.

Beauvoir's relationship with Sartre seems to represent both an entry into the male-dominated public world set apart from the female world of her childhood and, in some ways, an emotional continuation of Beauvoir's relationships with women—primarily her mother and Zaza. Sartre provided Beauvoir with the security once provided by God and by her mother. "I adore [Sartre's] fashion of being authoritarian, of adopting me, and of being one of so severe indulgence" (Beauvoir 1929–31, 86v). Beauvoir felt humbled by Sartre, by his self-confidence and his criticisms of her, much as she had earlier before her mother and Zaza.

> We argued for two hours about good and evil. He interests me enormously, but crushes me, I am no longer sure of what I think, if I think at all. (Beauvoir 1928–29, 87v)

She admired Sartre for his creativity, dramatic flair, and rebellious disrespect for authority as she once did Zaza and her father. As her relationship with Sartre became more passionate, she compared it with her feelings for Zaza. "Thinking of Sartre with this definitive love, this devotion that I knew for Zaza at another time, for Jacques [the cousin she had expected to marry], one time for the Lama [a male friend who first introduced her to Sartre]" (Beauvoir 1928–29, 99v). In summarizing her final year at school and her meeting with Sartre, she writes in her journal.

> June-July—the *petites camarades* [Sartre's friends] . . . Then feelings of friendship, the discovery of the world where I can live, of the thought that I love, of a choice to which I have been destined from all time. Finally! finally some people stronger than I, and near whom I am myself. . . . Intellectual blossoming out—joy, life. (Beauvoir 1928–29, 101)

Beauvoir began to enter a world of culture where she was able to find herself as an intellectual, as she had not been able to do in the "feminine" world to which women were traditionally confined. And Sartre was to be her guide.

> July-August-September. Sartre—The world has finally opened; I am learning that I have a destiny as woman and that I love it. I am learning what it is to think, what a great man is, and what the universe is. I am delirious at leaving the old prejudices, religions, morals, and false instincts. I am discovering an entire world, the freedom to think and to live her thoughts with her taste, her heart, her body, . . . the consummation of the past. . . . Discovery of the world such as I must live in it, and of my true friends. Birth of the "beaver" [Beauvoir's nickname, *castor*] who hesitated for so long between the intellectual Mlle de Beauvoir, and the passionate Mlle de Beauvoir. (Beauvoir 1928–29, 101)

But by the spring of the year following her graduation and her optimistic beginning of a new life independent of her parents, Beauvoir had fallen into a deep depression. She was grieving the loss of Zaza, who died the previous November. Without the challenge of academia, with no professional status, she seemed lost, and her relationship with Sartre was no longer able to give her what she needed.

> He talks to me as though to a very little girl. . . . I lost my pride and there I lost everything. I must try to write! My only chance, my only chance! (Beauvoir 1929–31, 28v)

The journal ends abruptly as Beauvoir nears the first anniversary of Zaza's death, the pages containing barely legible sentence fragments stained by tears.

> If you were only there, Zaza. . . . Oh . . . that everything is finished, Zaza, and that there only remains these. . . . Zaza, my friend, my dear who was close and of whom I have so much need. . . . Zaza I can't bear that you're dead—my friend, Oh! my friend, my friend. (Beauvoir 1929–31, 31, 34, 34v)

Carroll Smith-Rosenberg's analysis of the two worlds that constituted nineteenth-century bourgeois society—the public world of men and the private "world of love and ritual" of women—is useful here. Sartre could not give Beauvoir everything she needed. Her intellectual success and Sartre's support enabled Beauvoir to cross the boundary into the male intellectual world. But their relationship was always characterized by a certain distance fostered by Sartre's persistent pursuit of other women and reflected in the intellectuality of their conversations and their lifelong habit of addressing each other with the formal *vous* rather than the more familiar *tu*. Beauvoir's relationship with Sartre could not provide the emotional intimacy that characterized her closest relationships with women.

Before accepting her first teaching post, in Marseilles, Beauvoir rejected Sartre's offer to marry, which would have enabled them to request teaching posts near one another. Instead she and Sartre lived independently of one another, first in different university towns, then in separate hotels in Paris. In the 1950s, after winning the Pris Goncourt for her novel *The Mandarins,* Beauvoir purchased her own studio apartment, where she lived for the rest of her life. This arrangement allowed Beauvoir considerable independence in her relationship with Sartre, enabling her to escape the domestic servitude that her mother had so resented and to maintain her own relationships—including lesbian connections—with others.

Students: Olga, Védrine, and Natasha

After the long-anticipated but unhappy two-year vacation from academia following her success in the *agrégation* in 1929, Beauvoir took up her career in philosophy once again. She was assigned by the French sex-segregated system to teach in girls' preparatory schools, or *lycées*, first in Marseilles and then in Rouen, the northern city made famous by Jeanne d'Arc. Despite her earlier contempt for women's schools, Beauvoir reveled in the independence her profession allowed her, devoting a minimum of time to teaching and instead indulging in long country hikes and fine new clothes. Beautiful and extravagantly dressed, she was a magnetic figure to her teenage students. They fought to carry her books and to win an invitation to join their elegant teacher in a café. A few whom Beauvoir found most brilliant and interesting held a permanent and more intimate place in her life. Beauvoir's posthumously published journals and letters from 1939 to 1941 reveal that she engaged in sexual affairs with students and former students from her philosophy classes. She often led them to her hotel room to tutor them in philosophy and, eventually, take them to bed.

These relationships raise serious moral issues because of the young age of the women and because they were Beauvoir's students. Their welfare was Beauvoir's professional responsibility. Also problematic was Beauvoir's ongoing relationship with Sartre and its implications for her relationships with her young female lovers. In her critique of Beauvoir's chapter on the lesbian in *The Second Sex,* Claudia Card distinguishes between "authentic" and "inauthentic" lesbian relationships, based on Aristotle's distinction between true friendship—"where the 'object' of love is the friend"—and friendships of utility or pleasure. Card argues that a "good example of inauthenticity in lesbian behavior" is to be found in "lesbian liaisons formed by women who are still in important ways basically heterosexually oriented." In such relationships, the heterosexual woman inauthentically uses her female lovers for "consolation and regeneration" in support of her relationships with men instead of establishing authentic lesbian relationships with women, that is, loving the women for themselves (Card 1985, 296–97). Beauvoir's relationships with her young students—especially where Sartre was also involved—seem vulnerable to the charge of inauthenticity in Card's scenario and in Aristotle's broader sense as well.

Beauvoir's 1939 journal finds her involved in ongoing relationships with three young women, all émigrées from Eastern Europe: Olga Kosakiewitch and Louise Védrine (identified by Bair as Bianca Bienenfeld), both of whom were involved with Sartre as well, and Natalie Sorokine (whom Beauvoir often referred to as Natasha), whose relationship was primarily with Beauvoir. A fourth young woman, Olga's younger sister Wanda, figures prominently in the journals and letters, although her sexual relationship was exclusively with Sartre. In attempting to explain to biographer Bair her relationship with Le Bon, Beauvoir begins with Zaza, but she mentions both Olga and Natasha as well.

> I have often desired a female friendship. It did not work with Olga, it did not work with Natasha, but now I have Sylvie, and it is an absolute relationship, because from the beginning we were both prepared to live in this way, to live entirely for each other. (Bair 1990b, 509)

Although Bair does not note whether Beauvoir explained in what ways those two other relationships "did not work," a plausible reason might be that neither Olga nor Natasha remained in an exclusive relationship with Beauvoir. Both sought sexual relationships with men, which eventually disrupted their relationships with Beauvoir.

Each of these relationships recounted in the journals and letters raises the question of whether sexual relationships between professors in their thirties and teenage students can be ethical and if so, under what conditions. Olga's involvement in a relationship with both Sartre and Beauvoir began in 1933, when Olga was fifteen and Beauvoir twenty-five. In a letter from 1935, Beauvoir refers to Olga as "our [hers and Sartre's] adoptive child, lightly demonic daughter of a couple marked by the sign of Abel" (Beauvoir 1990b, 1:21). Their sexual triangle formed the subject of both Sartre's play *No Exit* and Beauvoir's novel *She Came to Stay*. The relationship was problematic for everyone involved. The problems for an adolescent in a sexual relationship with an adult multiplied when the duo became a trio. Sartre described it as "hell" in *No Exit;* Beauvoir finishes *She Came to Stay* with the adult woman murdering her younger rival. Colette Audry, a friend who was teaching at the school where Beauvoir's relationship with Olga began, called it

> an awful experience for Olga. The major complicity was between [Beauvoir and Sartre], and they required that she bend to their wishes. The poor girl was too young to know how to defend herself really. (Bair 1990b, 194)

Olga and Beauvoir first met when Olga was a student in Beauvoir's philosophy class in the *lycée* in Rouen. Since Beauvoir saw Sartre frequently although they lived in different towns, Olga must have heard a great deal about Sartre from her teacher. But Olga's relationship with Sartre came later, when Sartre suffered a period of depression and recurring hallucinations after an experimental injection with mescaline. Beauvoir, unwilling to nurse him on his frequent visits, fled to Paris at every opportunity, and Olga began caring for him. Beauvoir was later stunned to discover that Sartre was becoming obsessed with Olga. Although Sartre had had many affairs, this was apparently the first time that he had seduced one of Beauvoir's lovers. In *No Exit,* Sartre depicts hell as a relationship in which two women and one man are locked in a room together for eternity. In Sartre's characterization the older woman attempts to seduce the younger woman and is angry and jealous of the man for his success in seducing the younger woman. But Beauvoir's published depictions of the triangle with Sartre and Olga carry no suggestion of her lesbian relationship with Olga. The jealousy she recounts is heterosexual, arising from the fear that Olga was a threat to her relationship with Sartre. In her autobiography Beauvoir describes Sartre's affair with Olga as a turning point in her own life, forcing her to recognize Sartre's separateness from her and the end of the myth of their fusion in a "we." The trio did not end with the young woman's murder as did the trio in Beauvoir's novel. Bored with Sartre's obsession with her, Olga eventually dumped him and began an affair with one of his students, Bost, whom she would later marry. Although her sexual relationships with Beauvoir and Sartre apparently ended, Olga continued to occupy a central place in their lives and remained a member of their "family" of close friends until the early 1980s.

The younger women typically pushed Beauvoir toward greater independence. Beauvoir wrote in her journals from 1939 to 1941 that the younger women criticized her for devoting so much of herself to Sartre and other relationships and pitied her for what they saw as the sterility of her middle-aged life: Sartre no longer slept with her, but with them. Her response was the same as it had been to Zaza's death; she vowed to write. She wrote most of her first published novel, *She Came to Stay,* during a period early in World War II, when Sartre was gone, first in the military and then in a prison camp.

Beauvoir sought to support the efforts of the younger women to escape the domination of their families. But in the 1930s and 1940s, her behavior with these women can best be characterized as deceptive and manipulative. In 1938, for example, Sartre wrote to Beauvoir with the graphic details of an affair with a female philosophy student at the Sorbonne who "sucked his tongue like a vacuum cleaner" (Sartre 1983, 1:184). Beauvoir replied was from the mountain village where she vacationing that she had seduced his former student and closest disciple, Bost, with whom Olga was by now involved, and spent several passionate days and nights with him in various haylofts and hotels (Beauvoir 1990b, 1:62). What did not seem to concern her until much later is the reaction of Olga, for whom the relationship with Bost was a refuge. The journals and letters suggest that Beauvoir, Sartre, and Bost kept Beauvoir's continuing affair with Bost a secret from Olga for years. (Olga may not have learned of the affair until 1983 when Beauvoir published Sartre's letters; Olga broke with Beauvoir soon after.) Beauvoir suffered from acute jealousy over Olga's relationship with Bost, and her journals and letters reveal that she enjoyed the sense of superiority over Olga that the secrecy of her affair provided. Indeed, her seduction of Bost and this sense of superiority would seem to have replaced murder in her arsenal of revenge. Jealousy was almost certainly at work when Beauvoir secretly entered the room of Sartre's mistress Wanda, who wanted an exclusive relationship with him. In an effort to protect her own relationship with Sartre, Beauvoir read Wanda's diary and reported its contents to Sartre, pledging him to secrecy. It was an act oddly reminiscent of Beauvoir's mother's invasion of her daughter's privacy.

Beauvoir's descriptions of her relationships show a mixture of feelings. She remarks throughout the letters and journals how attractive, intelligent, beautiful, and "feminine" she finds both Olga and Louise Védrine. She describes herself as more sexually attracted to Védrine but jealous and angry at her in 1939 for trying to recreate the sexual trio that Olga had had with Beauvoir and Sartre. Anger transforms Beauvoir's attitude from one of authentic friendship, in which she was concerned about helping Védrine achieve her independence from her family, to one of mere pleasure.

> In bed, Védrine threw herself passionately in my arms. . . . I took more pleasure than usual in these relations but out of a sort of perversity. I had the impression of being a lout: profiting at least from her body, and a sort of amusement at feeling my sensuality empty of any tenderness. (Beauvoir 1990a, 139)

Beauvoir was less sexually drawn to Sorokine, who avidly pursued her teacher and plied her with boxes of chocolates. Beauvoir fit Sorokine into her weekly schedule, which had hours set aside for being with Olga and Védrine as well as for working and for writing letters to Sartre and Bost, both of whom were in the military in 1939. Her sexual relationship with Sorokine was just beginning. Beauvoir remarks in a letter to Sartre that she feels herself at once a male seducer "embarrassed in front of a young virgin," but lacking his clear objective to seduce and pierce the mystery, if I dare say it—while I, it is I who am at the same time the prey. It is a most incommodious situation and one exclusively reserved for homosexuals [*pièges*]. (Beauvoir 1990b, 1:173)

Beauvoir expressed great tenderness for Sorokine and was moved that Sorokine, unlike Védrine, was interested in knowing about her. "I am touched to see the extent to which . . . she makes an effort to know me, in a deep sense, and not only as an object that she loves; a concern that Védrine has not at all" (Beauvoir 1990a, 206).

Beauvoir often pitied these young women and was determined to rescue them, as she had failed to rescue Zaza, from their domineering mothers and bourgeois society. She was angry when Védrine, in demanding more of her time, said that Beauvoir only saw her other young women out of pity. But in the journals and letters Beauvoir does often describe herself as motivated by pity, and she recounts feeling pressured by Sorokine and Védrine, as well as by Olga and by her own sister Hélène, for more attention and having to defend her time and her privacy against their increasing demands. In an effort to keep her young women physically and emotionally at a safe distance, Beauvoir restricted their access to her to regularly scheduled meeting times. She continued to structure liaisons with Sorokine and Védrine around philosophy lessons. The journals contain several accounts of stormy sessions in Beauvoir's hotel room when Sorokine, impatient with the obligatory lecture on Descartes or Kant, would burst into tears, beat Beauvoir with her fists, and throw herself at Beauvoir in a mad embrace that lasted until the next appointment arrived and Beauvoir made Sorokine leave. In frustration, Sorokine once called Beauvoir a "clock in a refrigerator" (Beauvoir 1960, 574).

Beauvoir felt some guilt about her affairs with these young women—not about the appropriateness of a professor having sex with a teenage student, but about her own selfishness and her manipulation of their feelings. In a 1945 letter to Sartre, Beauvoir writes that they must see a great deal of Louise Védrine.

I'm going to try because I am full of regret. I'm shaken because of Louise Védrine. . . . She moved me and filled me with remorse because she is in a terrible and profound crisis of depression—and be-

cause it is our fault, I believe, it is the indirect but profound consequence of our affair with her. She is the only person whom we have
truly hurt, but we did it to her. (Beauvoir 1990b, 2:259, 258)

Beauvoir's regret is less about having had a relationship with Védrine
than about the way Beauvoir and Sartre tried to break it off.

The letters and journals show that Beauvoir was very upset and
angry at Védrine for trying to establish a role equal to Beauvoir's in the
trio relationship with Sartre. Beauvoir wanted to retain her privileged
relationship with Sartre, consigning the younger woman to second
place. She wrote to Sartre criticizing Védrine and urging him to break
with the young woman, although Beauvoir did not express the same
jealous possessiveness toward Sartre that she reveals in her journal (Beauvoir 1990a, 107). When Sartre, in response, did write a letter breaking
off with Védrine, Beauvoir wrote back to him criticizing him for hurting
the other woman. It was this manipulation of Védrine's relationship with
Sartre and perhaps her own exploitation of Védrine for sexual pleasure
and lack of true tenderness that is the apparent source of Beauvoir's
remorse.

Fears and concern for their safety were also a factor in Beauvoir's
relationships with these young women. Adrienne Rich (1980) argues
that legal sanctions against lesbian relationships and employment discrimination against lesbians are one way of enforcing compulsory heterosexuality. Beauvoir makes several references in her journals and letters
to her concern with keeping her sexual relationships with the young
women secret. Sorokine asked her at one point if they could be arrested
for what they are doing, and Beauvoir assured her that they were safe.
But eventually, during the Occupation, the relationship with Sorokine
caused Beauvoir's teaching contract to be terminated. Both Védrine's
and Sorokine's mothers had threatened at various times to report Beauvoir to the minister of education in an effort to put an end to Beauvoir's
relationships with their daughters. It was Sorokine's mother who finally
complained to the school; according to Beauvoir's account in her autobiography, she did so because Beauvoir encouraged Sorokine to remain
in a love relationship with a young artist of whom Sorokine's mother
disapproved and to reject a match that her mother had arranged. But
Beauvoir's letters and journals and Bair's biography support the view
that Beauvoir's own relationship with Sorokine was a significant factor
in Beauvoir's being fired. She never returned to the classroom.

Beauvoir's journals and letters from 1939 to 1941 reveal a writer on the eve of her first success, still struggling to achieve and maintain her self-esteem in the face of publishers' rejections and still learning how to carry on authentic relationships. Beauvoir's childhood fear of losing herself in her oppressive relationship with her mother may underlie her anxious concern for distance and control in her intimate relationships with women, just as it may help to explain the relationship she had with Sartre. In 1940 Beauvoir had not yet found a publisher for her first novel. She had not yet successfully established her identity in a public sense, while Sartre was already a well-known writer. Beauvoir would not open herself to a fully intimate relationship with a woman until after she had become an established writer and after the agonizing experience of her mother's final illness and death. Only then, after coming to an understanding and acceptance of her mother's life, was Beauvoir able to open her life to a commitment to another woman.

The Ideal Companion of My Adult Life: Sylvie Le Bon

The fourth volume of Beauvoir's autobiography, *All Said and Done* (1972), contains a public acknowledgment of her new companion Sylvie Le Bon, whose presence led Elaine Marks to identify the "homosexual secret" in Beauvoir's life. As noted above, their relationship began in 1960 when Le Bon, an honors student in philosophy preparing for graduate school, wrote to Beauvoir requesting a meeting. Beauvoir writes in her autobiography that "her letter was short and direct and it convinced me that she had a sincere liking for philosophy and for my books." Le Bon was shy, and Beauvoir sought to draw her out.

> I did see her again, but for two years our meetings were brief and widely spaced. I frightened her less; . . . she smiled and even laughed: she had an agreeable face and I liked her being there. . . . It was during the autumn of 1963 that I really began to grow very fond of Sylvie. . . . During my mother's last days and after her death, Sylvie was a great comfort to me, in spite of her youth. I saw more of her; our conversations became longer and longer. . . . In the year of her *agrégation* I often took her to the cinema, the theater and exhibitions of painting. In the spring and early summer we went for long drives together. (Beauvoir 1972, 66, 68, 69)

Beauvoir reports her delight in getting to know Le Bon better; once after retiring for the night in a hotel during one of their drives in the country, Le Bon awakened Beauvoir to show her a glorious moon, revealing to Beauvoir "capacities for enthusiasm and passionate feeling that her great reserve had hidden from me." Another night, Le Bon fell into a depression after Beauvoir laughingly called her "crazy." Le Bon then revealed that her parents and school had labeled her "unnatural" after discovering her passionate friendship with a fellow schoolgirl, a relationship which they violently suppressed, forcing her to repeat a grade in school to separate her from her friend. "Oppressed, lonely, shocked at finding herself turned into the black sheep, Sylvie sank into a despair that she was never to forget in later years" (Beauvoir 1972, 69, 71).

Le Bon's response was to bury herself in her studies. "She had worked with a dark fury, by way of challenge and resentment." Her parents had "meant to 'break her spirit' but she was untameable." Le Bon's defiant rebellion struck a chord in Beauvoir, reminding her, perhaps, of Zaza as well as herself.

> The better I knew Sylvie, the more akin I felt to her. She too was an intellectual and she too was passionately in love with life. And she was like me in many other ways: with thirty-three years of difference I recognized my qualities and my faults in her. She had one very rare gift: she knew how to listen. Her observations, her smiles, her silences, made one feel like talking, and even talking about oneself: I told her about my past in detail, and day by day I keep her in touch with my life. There is no one who could have appreciated more than I what I have received from her. I loved her enthusiasms and her anger, her gravity, her gaiety, her horror of the commonplace, her uncalculating generosity. (Beauvoir 1972, 72)

Beauvoir reports that she and Le Bon

> see each other every day. She is as thoroughly integrated in my life as I am in hers. I have introduced her to my friends. We read the same books, we see shows together, and we go for long drives in the car. There is such an interchange between us that I lose the sense of my age: she draws me forward into her future, and there are times when the present recovers a dimension that it had lost. (Beauvoir 1972, 72)

Surely Beauvoir's relationship with Le Bon would find a natural place in Rich's "lesbian continuum." While Beauvoir's love for Le Bon may be "narcissistic," as Marks charges, Beauvoir's account of the relationship reveals a genuine respect for Le Bon, concern for her well-being, and delight in watching her personality flower. Beauvoir's account is also free of references to her heterosexual relationships, although her relationship with Sartre continued until his death in 1980. Although Beauvoir did not identify her and Le Bon's relationship as lesbian, it was the most mature and autonomous of all of Beauvoir's relationships with women and would seem closest to what Card has defined as an authentically lesbian relationship.

Bair's biography brings some hidden details of the Beauvoir/Le Bon relationship to light, such as Le Bon's mother's discovery of her daughter's relationship with Beauvoir, which precipitated the break between Beauvoir and Le Bon in 1962. "Beauvoir described what happened as 'threatening to be a repeat of Madame Sorokine and Natasha' a reference to her dismissal from teaching for allegedly corrupting a minor." Le Bon returned to Paris in 1963, during Françoise de Beauvoir's final illness. In a later interview with Bair, Le Bon talked of the new level of emotional intimacy Beauvoir embraced after the latter's mother's death.

> We still barely knew each other when her mother died, but I remember that this day she told me virtually word for word what became the story of *A Very Easy Death*. I remember how she would stop from time to time and ask, "What do you think? Do you think I can write that? I'd like to write that." She needed catharsis, so I said, "Yes, you must do it." I suggested later that I should accompany her to the funeral, but although she was happy that I suggested it, she said no. She was right, there was no reason for me to go. At the beginning [of the renewed friendship] she was very cautious, she didn't throw herself into things. But it was her mother's death that brought us together. (Bair 1990b, 504, 506)

By 1964, Bair reports, Le Bon and Beauvoir had become inseparable.

> They spoke on the phone every day, Sylvie placing the call as soon as she arrived home from teaching. On Thursdays and Saturdays, Sylvie spent the night at Beauvoir's apartment. They were always together

on Sunday, no matter whom Beauvoir had to see or meet on that day, and Beauvoir spent every Monday night at Sylvie's apartment. On Wednesday afternoon they spent at least several hours together, and if Beauvoir did not have another engagement they frequently dined together in her apartment. (Bair 1990b, 507)

This is surely not the same woman who, as Bair claims, "put all her needs, goals and desires second to Sartre's every impulse" (Bair 1990a, 34).

Even after her death, Beauvoir's mother occupied a central place in Beauvoir's psyche and influenced more than Beauvoir's relationship with Sartre. *A Very Easy Death,* one of Beauvoir's most powerful books, has a quality of emotional catharsis that may have freed her to open herself to relationships with women that were marked by less control, greater intimacy, and freer public acknowledgment. This is apparent in her relationship with Le Bon, in contrast to her earlier relationships with women. Beauvoir writes of her mother,

I had grown very fond of this dying woman. As we talked in the half-darkness I assuaged an old unhappiness; I was renewing the dialogue that had been broken off during my adolescence and that our differences and our likenesses had never allowed us to take up again. And the early tenderness that I had thought dead forever came to life again. (Beauvoir 1964, 76)

III. CONCLUSION: LESBIAN LOVE AND FEMINIST PHILOSOPHY

Lesbian connections extend throughout Beauvoir's life, providing affective links between the female world of her childhood and the relationships of her adulthood. These connections serve as a generative source of her intellectual creativity and ethical reflections on the "problem of the Other" as well as an inspiration for and locus of feminist resistance. The discovery of lesbian connections in Beauvoir's life disrupts the boundaries of her heterosexual gender identity and suggests that biographers call into play a more fluid concept such as Rich's "lesbian continuum." But as the author of *The Second Sex,* Beauvoir was more than a private individual; she defined a theoretical framework for

the feminist movement that followed some twenty years later. The discovery of lesbian connections in Beauvoir's life raises the question of
how these connections might suggest a rereading of *The Second Sex,*
which has often been criticized as "male identified," and the history of
the contemporary feminist movement as well.

Card has criticized *The Second Sex* for failing to challenge compulsory heterosexuality as an institution. According to Card, Beauvoir attempts to recognize a "lesbian attitude" as an authentic choice without
challenging heterosexuality as an institution rooted in the biological division of the sexes. In support of her interpretation, Card quotes the
introduction to *The Second Sex:*

> The division of the sexes is a biological fact, not an event in human
> history. Male and female stand opposed within an original *Mitsein*
> [being-with]. . . . [Woman] is the Other in a totality of which the two
> components are necessary to one another. (Beauvoir 1949, 1:19)

How, Card asks, can Beauvoir claim that a woman can "choose a lesbian
orientation," implying that "any woman *can* reject a heterosexual orientation," if, as Beauvoir claims, "the [heterosexual] couple is a fundamental unity with its two halves riveted together"? And how can Beauvoir
assert that a lesbian orientation is sometimes chosen completely authentically if "woman is part of a primordial heterosexual *Mitsein* and that Man
is necessary to her? Choosing a lesbian orientation sounds like denying,
rather than assuming, her situation as a member of such a couple" (Card
1985, 292).

Card's reading assumes that biological determinism is foundational
to *The Second Sex* and radical feminism, while a challenge to institutionalized heterosexuality, is not. There are alternative readings, however.
Linda Singer reads *The Second Sex* as "a female-identified voice . . .
rewriting the discourse of freedom from the position of the oppressed
feminine" (Singer [1985] 1990, 231–32). Judith Butler provides a reading of *The Second Sex* that challenges the classification of Beauvoir as a
biological determinist and strengthens the bridge between lesbians and
feminism sought by Rich. In Butler's interpretation, Beauvoir's existentialism is the key to her philosophy of gender. Butler reads Beauvoir as
extending to gender the existentialist rejection of essentialist conceptions
of human nature and substantive views of self. This entails a rejection of

biological determinism and fixed gender identities as well. For Beauvoir, Butler reminds us,

> any effort to ascertain the "natural" body before its entrance into culture is definitionally impossible, not only because the observer who seeks this phenomenon is him/herself entrenched in a specific cultural language, but because the body is as well. The body is, in effect, never a natural phenomenon. (Butler 1986, 46)

Biology and sex differences become social constructs whose meaning is shaped through the actions of individuals.

Beauvoir's argument in *The Second Sex* that sexual activity "is not necessarily implied in the nature of the human being" would seem to support Butler's interpretation. In that argument Beauvoir claims that sexual differentiation itself need not be a feature of human reality.

> If [sexual differentiation] is assumed by existents in such a manner that in return it enters into the concrete definition of existence, so be it. It nonetheless remains that a consciousness without a body, that an immortal man is rigorously inconceivable, while one can imagine a society reproducing itself by parthenogenesis or composed of hermaphrodites. (Beauvoir 1949,1:39, 40)

Despite the strength of historical traditions of biologically based sex differences and gender roles, alternative "concrete definitions of existence" are possible.

> Beauvoir radically extends the notion of choice. To "choose" a gender in this context is not to move in upon gender from a disembodied locale, but to reinterpret the cultural history which the body wears. The body becomes a choice, a mode of enacting and reenacting received gender norms which surface as so many styles of the flesh. (Butler 1986, 48)

Gender is not a fixed identity but "a corporeal style, a way of acting the body, a way of wearing one's own flesh as a cultural sign" (Butler 1989, 256). Freedom and choice are limited, with sanctions against crossing gender boundaries severely enforced, but a woman acting "masculine" and a man dressing in "feminine" clothing claim their freedom and disrupt the social meaning of gender in the process.

Many people, Beauvoir observes in *The Second Sex*,

> fear that women in ceasing to be women, will not succeed in changing themselves into men and will become monsters. This assumes that the woman of today is a creation of nature. We must repeat once again that in the human collectivity nothing is natural. . . . Woman is defined neither by her hormones nor by some mysterious instincts but by the manner in which she reclaims her body and her relation with the world, across the consciousnesses of strangers. (Beauvoir 1949, 1:571)

Beauvoir's vision of a future with "new carnal and affectional relations of which we have no idea" (Beauvoir 1949, 2:575) seems to anticipate Butler's vision of a "carnival of gender confusion" (Butler 1989, 260).

In addition to undermining the biological basis of gender identity and sexual desire, Beauvoir's analysis in *The Second Sex* posits male dominance as integral to heterosexuality. Woman as Other is a valuable object for man in her "function of double and mediator. . . . For the man held between the silence of nature and the demanding presence of other freedoms, a being who would be at once like him and a passive thing appears as a great treasure." In heterosexual encounters, Beauvoir argues, "[man] is looking for domination, much more than fusion and reciprocity. . . . He loves the woman to feel humiliated, possessed in spite of herself; he always wants to take her a bit more than she wants to give herself." Undermining male dominance would undermine compulsory heterosexuality as well: "The child would sense around her an androgynous world and not a masculine world; were she affectively more attracted to her father—which is not even sure—her love for him would be nuanced by a will to emulation and not by a feeling of powerlessness" (Beauvoir 1949, 2:575, 162–63, 571).

Beauvoir's feminist philosophy disrupts the boundaries of heterosexual and lesbian identity just as her life did. In a 1982 interview with Alice Schwarzer, Beauvoir clearly challenged compulsory heterosexuality: "Women should not let themselves be conditioned exclusively to male desire any more" (Schwarzer 1984, 113). But in *The Second Sex* she seems just as clearly to reject a compulsory lesbian identity as a condition of women's liberation. "To emancipate woman is to refuse to enclose her in the relations that she sustains with man, but not to deny them to her" (Beauvoir 1949, 2:576). Beauvoir's life demonstrates her ability to redefine her gender identity to include the love of both women and men, to create a "family" outside the boundaries of conventional society, and to transform personal tragedy into great literature. The transformative powers of individual freedom that Butler has rediscovered at the heart of Beauvoir's existential philosophy of gender can provide an alternative to the narrow confines of essentialist identity politics. Uncovering the lesbian connections in Beauvoir's life and feminism should inspire further exploration of lesbian connections as a source of creativity in the individual lives of women and in the history of the feminist movement.

10

THE SECOND SEX AND THE ROOTS OF RADICAL FEMINISM (1995)

M any radical feminist theorists of the women's liberation movement in the 1960s have acknowledged that Simone de Beauvoir's *The Second Sex* (1949) provided a model for them. Kate Millett, for example, writes that she "owes a great debt to *The Second Sex*," claiming that she "couldn't have written *Sexual Politics* without it" and without Beauvoir's "philosophic and historical perspective."

> I think de Beauvoir realized that I probably cribbed a whole lot more in what I was doing, all my politics through literature—cultural criticism I called it. . . . Now I realize that I was probably cheating all over the place, and owed a great deal to what she had said. (Millett in Forster and Sutton 1989, 22–23)

According to Alice Echols, an historian of the women's liberation movement, Ti-Grace Atkinson, "like so many other women who helped spark the second wave of feminism," had read *The Second Sex* and been "profoundly affected by it." Echols reports that

> Roxanne Dunbar of Cell 16 cited *The Second Sex* as the book that "changed our lives." Shulamith Firestone dedicated her book *The Dialectic of Sex* to Beauvoir. And Katie Sarachild called the book "crucial to the development of the W[omen's] L[iberation] M[ovement]." (Echols 1989, 167, 337 n.155)

Despite these acknowledgments, *The Second Sex* has yet to find a secure place in the history of political philosophy. The feminist philosopher Alison Jaggar, for example, whose pioneering work defined the categories of feminist political philosophy (i.e. liberal, socialist, and radical feminism), does not include a discussion of *The Second Sex* in her definitive text *Feminist Politics and Human Nature* despite her recognition of the "historical significance" of *The Second Sex* as "a forerunner of the contemporary women's liberation movement" (Jaggar 1983, 10). Jaggar omits "religious and existentialist conceptions of women's liberation" (including Beauvoir's) because they fall "outside the mainstream of contemporary feminist theorizing" and she finds them "implausible" from her socialist feminist perspective (Jaggar 1983, 10). But I will argue in this chapter that far from being outside the mainstream of feminist philosophy, Beauvoir provides the very foundation for radical feminism in *The Second Sex*, where the historical importance of radical feminism to both socialist and radical black theorizing of racial oppression is apparent.

Demonstrating the foundational relationship of *The Second Sex* to radical feminism addresses one of Jaggar's fundamental criticisms of radical feminism, i.e., that it lacks a "comprehensive theoretical framework," in particular any psychological explanation of male behavior. Ignoring Beauvoir's work in *The Second Sex*, Jaggar traces the roots of radical feminism to a "contradictory heritage" in "the basically liberal civil rights movement and in the Marxist-inspired left" (Jaggar 1983, 10–11). Liberal feminism and socialist feminism, in contrast, have strong foundations in the philosophies of Mill and Marx, respectively. But a recovery of Beauvoir's philosophy in *The Second Sex* can both reveal a philosophical foundation for radical feminism and challenge the conception of the civil rights movement as "basically liberal," since Beauvoir drew upon the challenge to Marxist reductionism in radical black theorizing of racial oppression in formulating her theory. Her work thus challenges the definition of the feminist "mainstream" by affirming the interconnections of different forms of oppression while challenging the reductionism of identity politics.

In the discussion that follows I draw upon the definition of radical feminism provided by Echols, author of *Daring To Be Bad: Radical Feminism in America 1967–1975* (1989), the first comprehensive historical study of the radical feminist movement. Echols, unlike Jaggar, makes a helpful distinction between radical feminism and "cultural feminism," the movement that followed it in the 1970s. Jaggar charges radical feminism with falling back on biological determinism for an explanation of men's behavior, defining women's oppression under patriarchy as seamless and absolute with women as absolute victims, and focusing on the construction of a woman-culture as the sole political strategy. Echols differentiates these "cultural feminist" positions from earlier radical feminism which was "a political movement dedicated to eliminating the sex-class system." According to Echols, radical feminists were both "typically social constructionists who wanted to render gender irrelevant" and at least "implicitly" "anti-capitalists" who "believed that feminism entailed an expansion of the left analysis." Cultural feminists, in contrast, "conceived of feminism as an antidote to the left," "dismissed economic class struggle as 'male' and, therefore, irrelevant to women," and sought to establish a woman-culture where " 'male values' would be exorcized and 'female values' nurtured" (Echols 1989, 6, 7, 5).

In Echols's view, Jaggar's analysis of radical feminism reflects a misreading of the movement common to socialists:

> Most leftist and socialist-feminists mistakenly characterized radical feminism as apolitical. To them radical feminism involved changing the "cultural superstructure" and developing alternative life-styles, rather than effecting serious economic and political change. . . . So when radical feminism began to give way to cultural feminism, socialist feminists simply did not notice. (Echols 1989, 7)

Echols provides convincing evidence for the existence of a radical feminist movement that was social constructionist and leftist in its critique of racism and economic class oppression, but her focus on American movement history prevents her from identifying Beauvoir's contribution to radical feminism in writing *The Second Sex* in France some twenty years earlier. To do that, it is more useful to adopt a methodology akin to Jaggar's philosophical analysis.

Echols's history of the movement reminds us that radical feminism was born out of dissatisfaction with both liberal feminism and socialism and inspired by the transformation of the liberal civil rights struggle into the radical black power movement, a development that Jaggar does not acknowledge. In obvious parallels with radical black criticisms of the civil rights movement, radical feminists criticized liberal feminists for pursuing "formal equality within a racist, class stratified system, and for refusing to acknowledge that women's inequality in the public domain was related to their subordination in the family" (Echols 1989, 3). Much like the radical black theorists who defended the specificity of the African American experience against Marxist reductionism, radical feminists also differed from socialists "who attributed women's oppression to capitalism, whose primary loyalty was to the left, and who longed for the imprimatur of the 'invisible audience' of male leftists." For radical feminists "male supremacy was not a mere epiphenomenon" (Echols 1989, 3).

In *The Second Sex* Beauvoir rejects liberalism and its legalistic model of society as a public sphere governed by a social contract and accepts instead a Marxist model of history as shaped by material factors and class struggle. Beauvoir recognized in 1949 the importance of the hard-fought battle for legal equality but saw it as insufficient. "Abstract rights . . . have never sufficed to assure woman a concrete hold on the world." Women have yet to attain "the union of abstract rights and concrete opportunities" without which "freedom is only a mystification." Even with many legal rights won, "the institutions and the values of patriarchal civilization have largely survived." Liberal individualism is no solution. "The successes of a few privileged women can neither compensate for nor excuse the systematic degradation on the collective level" (Beauvoir 1949, 1:222–23). The analysis of the causes of women's oppression would have to go much deeper.

In an important theoretical step toward radical feminism, one paralleled by radical African American writer Richard Wright, whose work Beauvoir read and published in the 1940s, Beauvoir begins with a Marxist historical-materialist analysis of oppression and class struggle. In *The Second Sex* she argues that economic and technological developments provided the conditions for a women's liberation struggle. The industrial revolution "transformed women's lot in the nineteenth century and . . . opened a new era for her," by enabling her "to escape from the home and take a new part in production in the factory," thus "winning again an economic importance lost to her since the prehistoric era." Developments in technology made this possible by "annulling the difference in physical strength between male and female workers in a large number of cases" (Beauvoir 1949, 1:191).

New methods of birth control "permitted the dissociation of two formerly inseparable functions: the sexual function and the reproductive function.'' Reproductive technology will provide the material conditions for further gains by women.

> By artificial insemination the evolution will be achieved which will permit humanity to master the reproductive function. . . . [Woman] can reduce the number of her pregnancies, and integrate them rationally into her life instead of being a slave to them. . . . It is by the convergence of these two factors: participation in production and emancipation from the slavery of reproduction that the evolution of woman's condition is to be explained. (Beauvoir 1949, 1:199, 203)

When economic developments in advanced capitalist societies freed bourgeois women from dependence on their families, the material conditions were laid for the collective struggle by women, across economic classes, for their liberation. Beauvoir's feminism is activist; the only recourse for women is the collective struggle for their own liberation.

> Freedom remains abstract and empty in woman, and can be authentically assumed only in revolt. . . . There is no other issue for woman than to work for her liberation. This liberation can only be collective, and it demands before all else that the economic evolution of the feminine condition be achieved. (Beauvoir 1949, 2:455)

An analogy with racism was important to both 1960s radical feminists and Beauvoir, as is evident in this passage.

> Whether it's a question of a race, of a caste, of a class, of a sex reduced to an inferior condition, the processes of justification are the same: ''the eternal feminine'' is the homologue of ''the black soul'' and ''the Jewish character.'' . . . [T]here are profound analogies between the situation of women and that of Blacks: both are emancipating themselves from a same paternalism and the formerly master caste wants to keep them in ''their place,'' that is to say in the place the master caste has chosen for them. (Beauvoir 1949, 1:24)

Beauvoir's analysis of the underlying paternalism common to justifications of both sexism and racism bears striking resemblance to an essay by Alva Myrdal, ''A Parallel to the Negro Problem,'' included as an appendix in the classic text on American racism assembled by Gunnar Myrdal et al., *An American Dilemma: The Negro Problem and Modern Democracy* (1944), a book Beauvoir consulted while writing *The Second Sex*.

For Beauvoir, ethnocentrism seems historically to encompass sexism in the experience of alterity. Women were not the original, or the only, Other: "[Woman] has not represented the sole incarnation of the Other for [man], and she has not always kept the same importance in the course of history" (Beauvoir 1949, 1:234). Drawing on the structuralism of Lévi-Strauss, Beauvoir argues that

> The category of the *Other* is as original as consciousness itself. In the most primitive societies, in the most ancient mythologies, one finds the expression of a duality—that of the Same and the Other. This duality was not originally attached to the division of the sexes. . . . Jews are "others" for the anti-Semite, Blacks for the American racists, indigenous peoples for the colonialists, the proletariat for the class of owners. (Beauvoir 1949, 1:16)

According to Jaggar, the defining feature of radical feminist theory, which set it apart from liberal and Marxist theories, "was a conviction that the oppression of women was fundamental: that is to say, it was causally and conceptually irreducible to the oppression of any other group" (Jaggar 1983, 12). Echols agrees that radical feminists "expanded the left analysis" of oppression and "argued that women constituted a sex class, that relations between women and men needed to be recast in political terms, and that gender rather than class was the primary contradiction" (Echols 1989, 6, 3). Beauvoir's support for this fundamental claim is evident in the following passage from *The Second Sex*, where she acknowledges Marxist insights into the historically changing role of technology and economic factors in shaping women's lives, but criticizes Marxism for failing to recognize the irreducible nature of women's oppression.

> Engels does not recognize the singular character of this oppression. He tried to reduce the opposition of the sexes to a class conflict. . . . It is true that the division of work by sex and the oppression that results from it evokes the class division on certain points. But one must not confuse them. . . . The situation of the woman is different, singularly due to the community of life and interests that renders her in solidarity with the man, and by the complicity which he meets in

her. . . . [T]he bond that attaches [woman] to her oppressors is comparable to no other. (Beauvoir 1949, 1:101, 19)

To expand Marxism to include an analysis of gender oppression and to argue on one level for the primacy of gender contradiction, as later radical feminists would, Beauvoir returns to the philosophical roots of Marxism in Hegel's distinction between immanence and transcendence and his analysis of the master/slave relation. Turning Hegel against himself, Beauvoir argues that his description of the relationship of men, whose warfare and inventions create values that transcend the mere repetition of Life, and women, whom biology destines to immanence, the passive and dependent reproduction of Life, is more reflective of the absolute opposition of the master/slave relationship than any relationship between men.

> Certain passages of the dialectic by which Hegel defines the relation of the master to the slave would better apply to the relation of the man to the woman. . . . Between the male and she there has never been combat. Hegel's definition applies singularly to her. (Beauvoir 1949, 1:112)

Beauvoir describes the relationship between men and women as a "caste" relationship defined by struggle; "All oppression creates a state of war; this is no exception." "[W]oman has always been, if not the slave of man, at least his vassal." In the past,

> the woman confined to immanence tried to keep the man in this prison as well. . . . She denied his truth and his values. . . . Today, the combat takes on another face. Instead of wanting to enclose man in a dungeon, woman is trying to escape from it herself. She no longer attempts to drag him into the regions of immanence but to emerge into the light of transcendence. . . . It is no longer a question of a war between individuals each enclosed in their sphere. A caste with demands mounts an assault and it is held in check by the privileged caste. (Beauvoir 1949, 2:561, 1:20, 2:561–62)

For Beauvoir, an historical analysis is necessary to understand the differences between women and other oppressed groups and explain why women's liberation has been so long in coming.

> [Women] have no past, no history, no religion of their own; and they
> have no such solidarity of work and interest as that of the proletariat.
> They are not even promiscuously herded together in the way that
> creates community feeling among the American Blacks, the ghetto
> Jews, the workers of Saint-Denis, or the factory hands at Renault.
> They live dispersed among the males, attached through residence,
> housework, economic condition, and social standing to certain men—
> fathers or husbands—more firmly than they are to other women.
> (Beauvoir 1949, 1:19)

This situation elicits woman's moral complicity with her oppression, a willingness to accept dependence as a way of fleeing the responsibility of freedom facing any existent. Women are not simply victims in Beauvoir's analysis, as Jaggar charges of radical feminism. Beauvoir argues, in anticipation of the later radical feminist "pro-woman line" (Echols 1989, 91–92), that women find both material and ontological advantages in their dependence on men.

But unlike many radical feminists, Beauvoir also holds women morally responsible for complicity with their own oppression once an alternative is presented to them.

> To decline to be the Other, to refuse complicity with the man, would
> be for women to renounce all the advantages conferred upon them by
> their alliance with the superior caste. Man-the-sovereign will provide
> woman-the-liege with material protection and will undertake the jus-
> tification of her existence; thus she can evade at once both economic
> risk and the metaphysical risk of a freedom which must invent its ends
> without aid. . . . The man who makes woman an Other will then
> meet profound complicities in her. Thus, woman may fail to claim
> herself as subject because she lacks the concrete means to do it, be-
> cause she feels the necessary bond that ties her to man regardless of
> reciprocity, and because she is often well pleased with her role as
> *Other.* (Beauvoir 1949, 1:21)

The complexity of Beauvoir's analysis of gender difference and women's oppression is evident in her critiques of Marxism and psycho-analysis. Both theories attempt, unsuccessfully, to apply a model derived from men's experience to women. Beauvoir's version of existential-phenomenology provides her with the ontological and methodological grounds for reclaiming the specificity of women's experience while avoiding the essentialism of identity politics. Her criticism of the Marxist analysis of woman's situation is both existentialist and feminist. She charges Marxist economic reductionism with denying the reality of woman's lived experience.

Engels's attempt to reduce woman's situation, including her reproductive role, to economic production is "not tenable." Sexuality and maternity are dramas in the lives of individual women that defy integration into society and control by the state.

> One cannot without bad faith consider woman uniquely as a worker. Her reproductive function is as important as her productive capacity, as much in the social economy as in individual life. . . . Engels evaded the problem; he limited himself to declaring that the socialist community will abolish the family: it is an abstract solution indeed. (Beauvoir 1949, 1:102)

The practice in the Soviet Union reveals the limits of such a reductionist theory, which fails to recognize the patriarchal power of the state as oppressive to women. "Suppressing the family is not necessarily to emancipate the woman: the example of Sparta and the Nazi regime proves that by being directly bound to the State she can be no less oppressed by the males" (Beauvoir 1949, 1:102). In the interest of rebuilding its population, the Soviet Union was trying to once again

> enclose her in situations where maternity is for her the only outlet. . . . These are exactly the old patriarchal constraints that the USSR is resuscitating today. . . . This example shows well that it is impossible to consider the woman uniquely as a productive force. (Beauvoir 1949, 1:103)

For Beauvoir a true socialist revolution must affirm, not deny, individualism and thus acknowledge gender difference in individual experience and the uniqueness of women's situation.

> For a democratic socialism where class will be abolished but not individuals, the question of individual destiny will keep all of its importance: sexual differentiation will keep all its importance. The sexual relation which unites the woman to the man is not the same as that

which he sustains with her; the link which bonds her to the child is irreducible to every other. She was not created only by the bronze tool, the machine will not suffice to abolish her. Demanding for her all the rights, all the chances of the human being in general does not signify that one must blind oneself to her singular situation. And to become acquainted with it one must go beyond historical materialism that sees in man and woman only economic entities. (Beauvoir 1949, 1:103)

Marxism, by imposing a male theoretical model of economic production on women's experience, falsifies the experiences of individual women and fails to provide the grounds for challenging patriarchal oppression of women by a male-dominated socialist state. Beauvoir's rejection of the mystification of gender difference by antifeminists and cultural feminists does not entail the denial of gender differences in the lives of individual women.

Beauvoir argues that psychoanalysis as well as Marxism reduces women's experience to that of men, thus silencing women. Her argument against essentialist reductionism reflects an existentialist ontology that links her with the new left's "politics of experience" and 1960s radical feminism. It also differentiates her position from that of cultural feminism, and in its combination of cultural critique and celebration of spontaneity and the transgressing of boundaries, aligns her with postmodernism. Linda Singer argued, in a groundbreaking 1985 article, that Beauvoir's "gynocentric" feminism is an "unacknowledged source" of the postmodern discourse "of 'difference' of deconstruction." According to Singer, by "taking the insights of existentialism seriously with respect to its denial of a supervening perspective and its affirmation of the situational character of discourse, Beauvoir begins the project of writing the other side, of giving voice to the discourse of otherness" (Singer 1985, 324–25).

Beauvoir criticizes Freud's psychoanalytic theory for attempting to impose a male model onto female experience.

Freud concerned himself little with the destiny of the woman; it is clear that he modelled it on the description of the masculine destiny of which he limited himself to modifying several traits. . . . [He] admitted that woman's sexuality is as evolved as man's; but he scarcely studied it in itself. He wrote: "The libido is in a constant and regular

fashion essentially male, whether it appears in a man or a woman."
He refused to pose the feminine libido in its originality. (Beauvoir
1949, 1:78, 79)

By relying on a reductive male model of female sexuality, Beauvoir argues, Freud was unable to explain either penis envy or the Electra complex, primary features of his psychology of woman. Freud

> supposed that the woman felt herself to be a mutilated man. But the
> idea of mutilation implies a comparison and a valorization . . . it can-
> not be born from a simple anatomical confrontation. . . . Freud took
> [this valorization] for granted when it was necessary to account for it.
> (Beauvoir 1949, 1:81)

An adequate explanation of both penis envy and the Electra complex, in which Freud accounts for women's heterosexuality, would require that one leave the confines of the psychoanalytic model and examine the larger social, historical, and ontological dimensions of individual
life and woman's oppression.

> Psychoanalysis can only find its truth in the historical context. . . .
> The fact that feminine desire focused on a sovereign being [as it does
> in the Electra complex] gives it an original character; but [feminine
> libido] is not constitutive of its object, it submits to it. The sovereignty
> of the father is a fact of the social order, and Freud fails to account for
> it. (Beauvoir 1949, 1:90, 82)

Thus for Beauvoir a primary feature of the development of female
heterosexuality and the transference of a girl's attraction from her
mother to her father is the father's sovereignty, that is, the social context
of woman's oppression. Here Beauvoir extends social constructivism to
sexuality. Her alternative description of the female libido further undermines the assumption of normative female heterosexuality by postulating
an original resistance and repulsion toward men. Psychoanalysts who
have approached the female libido only from the male libido "seem to
have ignored the fundamental ambivalence of the attraction that the
male exerts on the female. . . . It is the indissoluble synthesis of attraction
and of repulsion that characterizes it." Psychoanalysis has failed to acknowledge gender difference in female sexuality. "The idea of a 'passive

libido' disconcerts because one has defined the libido on the basis of the male as drive, energy; but neither could one conceive a priori that a light could be at once yellow and blue; it's necessary to have the intuition of green" (Beauvoir 1949, 1:91). Beauvoir's social constructivist analysis of sexual difference and her challenge, albeit limited, to normative female heterosexuality anticipated the later radical feminist critiques of "compulsory heterosexuality."

In arguing for gender difference, Beauvoir avoids essentialist claims. She lays the groundwork for an appreciation of differences among women in arguing against the reductionism of Freudian psychoanalytic theory. "One must not take sexuality as an irreducible given. . . . Work, war, play, art define manners of being in the world which do not allow themselves to be reduced to any other" (Beauvoir 1949, 1:86–87). Sexuality is one manner among others of ontologically discovering the world. Thus Beauvoir, unlike the radical feminists described by Echols, rejects the a priori primacy of sexual difference. An individual woman establishes a unity among her activities as she chooses herself through her work, play, struggles, and sexuality. Beauvoir criticizes psychoanalytic theory for reducing women to passive objects in the world and for denying them the possibility of authentic choices.

> We will situate woman in a world of values and we will give to her actions a dimension of freedom. We think that she has to choose between the affirmation of her transcendence and her alienation as an object; she is not the plaything of contradictory drives; she invents solutions between which exist an ethical hierarchy. (Beauvoir 1949, 1:92)

In describing a subject's failure to effect a transference or a sublimation (and surely the most obvious example here is in the "failure" of a woman to become a heterosexual), a psychoanalyst, Beauvoir argues, "does not suppose that they perhaps refused it and that perhaps they had good reasons for doing so; one does not want to consider that their conduct could have been motivated by ends freely posed" (Beauvoir 1949, 1:92).

Freedom is a central theme of *The Second Sex*. If "one is not born a woman, but rather becomes one" (Beauvoir 1949, 2:13), then with the reality of social intervention comes the possibility of individual action, as Butler (1986) argues. Beauvoir is celebrating woman's freedom, the expansion of her choices, not confinement in a role, whether defined by Freud, or by implication here, essentialist identity politics. In her critique of psychoanalytic theory Beauvoir rejects as inauthentic the pursuit of being, of a substantive self, which was to become prominent in cultural feminism.

> In the psychoanalytic sense "to identify oneself" with the mother or the father is to *alienate oneself* in a model; it is to prefer an alien image to the spontaneous movement of her own existence, to play at being. One shows us woman solicited by two modes of alienation; it is indeed evident that playing at being a man will be a source of failure for her. But playing at being a woman is also a trap. To be a woman would be to be an object, the *Other*; and the Other remains subject in the heart of its abdication. The real problem for woman is refusing these flights in order to accomplish herself as transcendence. (Beauvoir 1949, 1:92–93)

Beauvoir's description of the contemporary struggle as one in which women claim the values of "transcendence" and refuse the limits of "immanence" differentiates her from the cultural feminist position Echols describes as seeking a womanculture where " 'male values' would be exorcized and 'female values' nurtured" (Echols 1989, 5). For Beauvoir, women's "demand is not to be exalted in their femininity; they want transcendence to prevail over immanence for themselves as for all of humanity" (Beauvoir 1949, 1:222).

> In truth women have never opposed female values to male values. It is men desirous of maintaining the masculine prerogatives who have invented this division. They have claimed to create a feminine domain—realm of life and of immanence—only in order to enclose woman there. It is beyond all sexual specification that the existent seeks her justification in the movement of her transcendence. . . . What [women] are demanding today is to be recognized as existents as men are and not to subjugate existence to life, man to his animality. (Beauvoir 1949, 1:113)

But Beauvoir's theory of gender difference is complex. She rejects both the mystification of gender difference and the abstract, gender-free nominalism of liberal modernity.

Some feminist critics, such as Iris Young (1990) have charged *The Second Sex* with typifying a nineteenth-century "humanist feminism," which, leaving gender largely unexamined, calls on women to assume men's public roles. Beauvoir does reject the mystification of gender difference typical of both nineteenth-century antifeminists, who argued that women's intellectual and physical inferiority and sensitive natures warranted their exclusion from public life and confinement to the private sphere, and their contemporaries, the "domestic feminists," who argued that women should have access to education and the vote in order to improve and extend the influence of their special moral sense. But Beauvoir does not deny there are differences.

In the introduction to *The Second Sex*, Beauvoir differentiates her position from modernism, from "the philosophy of the enlightenment, of rationalism, of nominalism.

> Women, to them, are merely the human beings arbitrarily designated by the word *woman*. . . . But nominalism is a rather inadequate doctrine. . . . Surely woman is, like man, a human being; but such a declaration is abstract. The fact is that every concrete human being is always singularly situated. To decline to accept such notions as the eternal feminine, the black soul, the Jewish character, is not to deny that Jews, Blacks, women exist today—this denial does not represent a liberation for those concerned, but rather a flight from reality. It is clear that no woman can claim without bad faith to situate herself beyond her sex. (Beauvoir 1949, 1:12–13)

Beauvoir is a social constructionist who believes women's liberation requires the dismantling of the male cultural construct of woman as Other. She certainly wants women to gain access to the public sphere, escape the confines of women's traditional roles of wife and mother, and emerge as individuals. But the public sphere will be transformed in the process; "The future can only lead to a more and more profound assimilation of the woman into the formerly masculine society" (Beauvoir 1949, 1:216). She describes how philosophy has been distorted by men who have taken their own unique perspective as absolute. Her alternative is not to argue an absolute perspective without differences, i.e., a return to the nominalism of modernity, but a critique of the male claim to objectivity and construction of a knowledge based on a phenomenological description of women's experience. Hence the title of volume two of *The Second Sex*, "Lived Experience," where Beauvoir tries to move outside the context of men's constructions of woman as Other, which are primarily useful in understanding not women but the men themselves, into women's ways of knowing their own experiences.

Beauvoir does not demand access to a gender-free objectivity of modernity but rather challenges the objective/subjective dualism itself and provides a phenomenological description of how men's perspectives shape their views of women, and reality. Laying the groundwork for women's studies in her feminist cultural critique, Beauvoir argues that men, in defining knowledge from their own point of view, have mistaken that perspective as absolute.

> [Man] seizes his body as a direct and normal connection with the world, which he believes he apprehends in its objectivity, whereas he regards the body of woman as an obstacle, a prison, weighed down by what specifies it. . . . She is defined and differentiated with reference to man and not he with reference to her; she is the inessential as opposed to the essential. He is the Subject, he is the Absolute—she is the Other. (Beauvoir 1949, 1:14, 15)

According to Beauvoir, Emmanuel Levinas exemplifies this masculinist view in his essay "Le Temps et l'Autre" where he writes that "Otherness reaches its full flowering in the feminine, a term of the same rank as consciousness but of opposite meaning." Beauvoir writes,

> I suppose that Levinas does not forget that woman is also consciousness for herself. But it is striking that he deliberately takes a man's point of view, disregarding the reciprocity of subject and object. . . . Thus his description, which is intended to be objective, is in fact an assertion of masculine privilege. (Beauvoir 1949, 1:15)

Beauvoir would have men, as well as women, claim the subjectivity of their situated consciousnesses rather than lay claim to false objectivity.

Beauvoir's psychological explanation of men's behavior is derived from her close reading of myths and male-authored texts with which she began her research for *The Second Sex*. Kate Millett, as we have seen, acknowledges that Beauvoir's analyses of the images of women in the works of Montherlant, D. H. Lawrence, Claudel, Breton, and Stendhal provided the model for Millett's cultural critique in *Sexual Politics*. Psychologically, men's oppression of women is, in Beauvoir's existential analysis, an inauthentic attempt to evade the demands of authentic human relationships and the ambiguous realities of human existence. For men who would define themselves as pure spirit, women represent an odious link to the absurd contingency of a man's own life: his birth, embodiment, and death. "In all civilizations and in our own day, [woman] inspires horror in man: it is horror of his own carnal contingence which he projects onto her" (Beauvoir 1949, 1:242). Woman as Other also seems a privileged prey of men desirous of the confirmation of self found in relationships with others and yet fearful of the dangers in relationships with their peers.

> [Woman] opposes to him neither the enemy silence of nature, nor the hard exigencies of a reciprocal recognition; by a unique privilege she is a consciousness and yet it seems possible to possess her in her flesh. Thanks to her, there is a means of escaping the implacable dialectic of master and slave which has its source in the reciprocity of freedoms. (Beauvoir 1949, 1:232–33)

Authentic human relationships, on the contrary, must be constantly created. Beauvoir's vision does not offer a comforting if static social order, but a future of ceaseless struggle in morally challenging relationships. According to Beauvoir, the master/slave dialectic can be surmounted, but only by

> the free recognition of each individual in the other, each posing at once himself and the other as object and as subject in a reciprocal movement. But friendship, generosity, which realize concretely this recognition of freedoms, are not easy virtues. They are assuredly the highest accomplishment of man, the means by which he finds himself in his truth. But this truth is that of a struggle forever opening up, forever abolished; it demands that man surmount himself at each instant. One could say also in another language that man attains an authentic moral attitude when he renounces *being* in order to assume his existence. (Beauvoir 1949, 1:232)

"One is not born, but rather becomes a woman." This familiar quotation, which opens volume two of *The Second Sex,* indicates Beauvoir's social constructionism, a position Echols sees as key in differentiating radical feminism from the biological determinism of cultural feminism. In fact, Jaggar unknowingly points toward Beauvoir as a theoretical source for the social constructivism of radical feminism in recognizing Monique Wittig as one of the few radical feminists to reject biological determinism. Wittig entitles an influential 1979 essay cited by Jaggar "One Is Not Born a Woman" in clear reference to Beauvoir.

Judith Butler has argued that Beauvoir's concept of the body as situation "suggests an alternative to the gender polarization of masculine disembodiment and feminine enslavement to the body." For Beauvoir, Butler writes,

> any effort to ascertain the "natural" body before its entrance into culture is definitionally impossible, not only because the observer who seeks this phenomenon is him/herself entrenched in a specific cultural language, but because the body is as well. The body is, in effect, never a natural phenomenon. (Butler 1986, 45, 46)

Butler draws our attention to the conclusion of the biology chapter in *The Second Sex*, where Beauvoir writes,

> it is not merely as a body, but rather as a body subject to taboos, to laws, that the subject takes consciousness of himself and accomplishes itself. . . . It is not physiology that can found values; rather, the biological givens assume those that the existent confers upon them. (Beauvoir 1949, 1:75)

If Beauvoir's view, Butler argues, is that the body exists as a locus of cultural interpretations, "then Simone de Beauvoir's theory seems implicitly to ask whether sex was not gender all along," a view radicalized in the work of Wittig and Michel Foucault, who "challenge the notion of natural sex and expose the political uses of biological discriminations in establishing a compulsory binary gender system" (Butler 1986, 47). Butler, it should be noted, claims that Foucault, a student of Merleau-Ponty, was not influenced by Beauvoir. However, an indirect influence is not unlikely given Merleau-Ponty's long association with Beauvoir.

Beauvoir "suggests," according to Butler, "that a binary gender system has no ontological necessity" (Butler 1986, 47). In fact, Beauvoir argues explicitly against the ontological necessity of sexual dimorphism earlier in the biology chapter. Beauvoir argues against Hegel that

> it is in exercising sexual activity that men define the sexes and their relations as they create the sense and the value of all the functions that they accomplish: but [sexual activity] is not necessarily implied in the nature of the human body. . . . The perpetuation of the species appears as the correlative of individual limitation. One can thus consider the phenomenon of reproduction as ontologically founded. But we must stop there. The perpetuation of the species does not entail sexual differentiation. If [sexual differentiation] is assumed by existents in such a manner that in return it enters into the concrete definition of existence, so be it. It nonetheless remains that a consciousness without a body and an immortal man are rigorously inconceivable, while one can imagine a society reproducing itself by parthenogenesis or composed of hermaphrodites. (Beauvoir 1949, 1:39, 40)

Butler's analysis provides an alternative reading of existentialist concepts of freedom and choice found in radical feminism, which Jaggar discredits as liberal and idealist (as in one "choosing a sex role" from a transsocial standpoint). For Butler,

> In making the body into an interpretive modality, Beauvoir has extended the doctrines of embodiment and prereflective choice that characterized Sartre's work. . . . Simone de Beauvoir, much earlier on and with greater consequence [than Sartre himself], sought to exorcise Sartre's doctrine of its Cartesian ghost. She gives Sartrean choice an embodied form and places it in a world thick with tradition. To "choose" a gender in this context is not to move in upon gender from a disembodied locale, but to reinterpret the cultural history which the body already wears. The body becomes a choice, a mode of enacting and reenacting received gender norms which surface as so many styles of the flesh. (Butler 1986, 48)

Beauvoir's rejection of the mystification of gender difference evident in her ontology is based, in part, on her analysis of the historical deployment of an ideology of difference in women's oppression. She concludes from her historical analysis in *The Second Sex* that

> Those epoques that regard woman as the *Other* are those that refuse most bitterly to integrate her into society as a human being. Today

she is becoming a fellow *other* only in losing her mystical aura. Anti-feminists are always playing on this equivocation. They gladly agree to exalt woman as *Other* in order to constitute her alterity as absolute, irreducible, and to refuse her access to the human *mitsein* [being-with]. (Beauvoir 1949, 1:120)

Beauvoir's intent, here as elsewhere, is not to deny gender difference as women experience it concretely, but to demystify it.

In the nineteenth century, glorification of woman's difference was common to both antifeminists such as Comte and Balzac, as well as utopian socialists such as the Saint-Simonians, who, in a foreshadowing of the Goddess worship of contemporary cultural feminism, awaited the Advent of the Female Messiah. But neither, according to Beauvoir, served well the interests of women's liberation. "The doctrines that call for the advent of the woman as flesh, life, immanence, as the Other, are masculine ideologies that in no way express feminine demands" (Beauvoir 1949, 1:217). Beauvoir's analysis of the historical relationship of socialism and Goddess worship provides an interesting context for reading the critiques of cultural feminism in the works of Jaggar and Echols. Some utopian socialists of the nineteenth century, such as Saint-Simon, Fourier, and Cabet, called for an end to all slavery and for the ideal of the "free woman." But later followers of Saint-Simon "exalted woman in the name of her femininity, which is the surest means of her disservice." Enfantin "awaited the coming of a better world from the woman messiah, and the Companions of the Woman embarqued for the Orient in search of the female savior." But for all the glorification of the feminine, with few exceptions, "women held only a secondary place in the Saint-Simonian movement." The socialist Flora Tristan, we learn later, also "believed in the redemption of the people by the woman, but she interested herself in the emancipation of the working class rather than in that of her own sex" (Beauvoir 1949, 1:189, 190). Thus socialism, which Jaggar argued could provide the only clear alternative to Goddess worship and cultural feminism, is, ironically, itself an historically problematic root of both.

Beauvoir's historical analysis reveals other limitations of socialism for feminists, problems which are still apparent in contemporary socialism. There was Charles Fourier, for example, who confused the enfranchisement of women with the rehabilitation of the flesh. . . . He considered woman not in her person but in her amorous function. (Beauvoir 1949, 1:189)

But the most serious problem for socialist feminism stems from the reductive Marxist analysis that conceives of women's liberation as contained within the proletariat revolution instead of, as Beauvoir argues, requiring women's own collective struggle as a separate development.

In arguing for the importance of recognizing gender difference in experience, Beauvoir does not maintain that the relationship between man and woman has been historically unchanging. Her analysis of women's oppression is not a simple analogy, either trivializing other forms of oppression or asserting that gender is always the primary contradiction. Class differences figure prominently in Beauvoir's analysis of how the historically different situations of bourgeois and proletariat women have undermined feminist solidarity and activism. For example, in her analysis of the bourgeois French Revolution, Beauvoir argues that neither working-class women, "who experienced, as women, the most independence," nor bourgeois women were able to make many gains.

> The women of the bourgeoisie were too integrated into the family to know any concrete solidarity among themselves; they did not constitute a separate caste able to impose their demands: economically, their existence was parasitic. Thus the women who, despite their sex, would have been able to participate in the events were prevented from doing so by their class, while those of the activist class were condemned as women to remain at a distance. (Beauvoir 1949, 1:184)

No analysis that ignores class differences can understand the history of women's oppression and the problems of feminist activism.

Beauvoir criticized the "so-called" independent French feminist movement at the turn of the twentieth century for reflecting bourgeois interests. But the "revolutionary feminism" of the same era, which "took up the Saint-Simonian and Marxist tradition," also contributed to the internal divisions that were the source of the "weakness of feminism."

> Women lacked solidarity as sex; they were first linked to their class; the interests of the bourgeois women and those of the proletariat

women did not intersect. . . . Louise Michel pronounced herself against feminism because this movement only served to divert forces which ought to be in their entirety employed in the class struggle; women's lot will find itself well ordered by the abolition of capital. . . . Since it is from the emancipation of workers in general that women await their freedom, they only attach themselves in a secondary manner to their own cause. (Beauvoir 1949, 1:205)

Beauvoir reserves her highest praise for the Woman's Social and Political Union established in Britain by the Pankhursts around 1903. Progressive without putting women's issues second, it was "allied with the laborist party" and "undertook a resolutely militant action." "It is the first time in history that one sees women try an effort as women: that is what gives a particular interest to the adventure of the 'suffragettes' in Britain and America." In a detailed account, deleted by translator H. M. Parshley from the English edition, Beauvoir pays tribute to their inventiveness. "During fifteen years they led a campaign of political pressure which recalls on certain sides the attitude of a Gandhi: refusing violence, they invented more or less ingenious substitutes" (Beauvoir 1949, 1:208).

Identifying with an earlier feminist movement, drawing on insights of radical African American theorists of racial oppression, Beauvoir laid the theoretical foundations for a radical feminist movement to come and defined a feminist political philosophy of lasting importance in *The Second Sex*.

_____

Reprinted, with changes, from "*The Second Sex*: From Marxism to Radical Feminism," in *Feminist Interpretations of Simone de Beauvoir*, ed. Margaret A. Simons (University Park: Pennsylvania State University Press, 1995), by permission of the publisher. An expanded version was published as "Beauvoir and the Roots of Radical Feminism," in *Reinterpreting the Political: Continental Philosophy and Political Theory*, ed. Stephen Watson, Lenore Langsdorf, and Karen A. Smith (Albany: State University of New York Press, 1998).

11

RICHARD WRIGHT,
SIMONE DE BEAUVOIR,
AND *THE SECOND SEX* (1997)

In the authors' preface to the 1962 edition of *Black Metropolis*, St. Clair Drake and Horace R. Cayton pay tribute to Richard Wright, who had provided the introduction to the original 1945 edition of this classic study of Chicago's African American community. They remind readers that Wright, "America's best-known Negro novelist" in 1945, had located *Native Son* in Chicago and had, years earlier, made his own "Flight to Freedom" from Mississippi to Chicago, before moving on to New York and then to Paris, France, where he lived until his death in 1960. Wright felt, as he wrote in his introduction to *Black Metropolis,* "personally identified with the material." Despite his alienation from American segregated culture, which led to his exile in France, Wright, as Drake and Cayton observe, "never became an 'escapist'. . . . The Existentialism and Pan-Africanism which he eventually adopted as a personal philosophy, and which he blended with the Marxism he had embraced in his youth, were simply additional tools for pursuing the task he had made his life work: clarifying and restating 'the race problem'" (Drake and Cayton, 1945, xvii, xliii). Wright took to Paris not only his commitment to combating racism, but also a copy of *Black Metropolis*, which he used in his effort to win international support for desegregation in America. But the impact of his efforts in Europe has been largely unrecognized. Most scholars, including Drake and Cayton, describe the European influence on Wright, leaving unaddressed the question of Wright's influence on European intellectual history.

In *The Black Atlantic* (1993), Paul Gilroy challenges scholars to broaden their interpretation of Wright to include a European context.

> On either side of the Atlantic, historians of European literature and philosophy have shown little interest in his work or in its relationship to those European writers and schools of expression with whom he interacted. . . . What would it mean to read Wright intertextually with Genet, Beauvoir, Sartre, and the other Parisians with whom he was in dialogue? (Gilroy 1993, 186)

In this chapter, I respond to Gilroy's challenge, uncovering evidence of Wright's influence on Simone de Beauvoir's philosophy, specifically in providing her with a theory of racial oppression and liberation that she utilized as a model in constructing the theoretical foundations of radical feminism in *The Second Sex* (1949). For this task, it is necessary, first of all, to understand the ways in which *The Second Sex* represents a philosophical departure for Beauvoir.

PHILOSOPHICAL INNOVATIONS IN *THE SECOND SEX*

In Beauvoir's earliest philosophical texts, her student diaries from the late 1920s, she defines an interest in the philosophical problem of "the opposition of self and other" (Beauvoir 1927, 95), which is central to *The Second Sex*. But in 1927 her primary concerns are metaphysical rather than political.

> I've understood that one can be intelligent and interested in politics; but it is far from me, because for me, what price could I attach to the search for humanity's happiness when the so much more serious problem of his reason for being haunts me? I will not make a gesture towards this terrestrial realm; the interior world alone matters. (Beauvoir 1927, 65, 66)

Beauvoir's metaphysical novels of the 1930s, with their focus on the problem of love and individual relationships, reflect her continuing interest in the "problem of the other." With the Nazi Occupation of France in 1940, Beauvoir enters what she has termed the "moral period" of her literary life, writing novels and essays on existentialist ethics with a central focus on the ethics of political resistance against oppression.

After the war, Beauvoir's interest returns, in *The Second Sex*, to love and individual relationships, but with a difference. Problems once conceived of as primarily individual or moral, are now seen as fundamentally political. In our male-dominated societies, women are the Other, an oppressed caste defined as inferior by religion and science; socialized to a psychological dependency on men; and restricted in their political and economic activities by laws and social convention. Employing a sophisticated critique of Freudian determinism and Marxist economic reductionism, Beauvoir constructs the theoretical foundations of radical feminism, arguing that women must unite in a separate political struggle to overcome their oppression.

How can we account for this radical shift in Beauvoir's frame of reference? The Allied victory in Europe brought French women the right to vote; after the war the United Nations affirmed women's equal rights. But Beauvoir had not been actively involved in any feminist organizations; nor had she been in a Marxist organization where she might have gained a firsthand understanding of its problems. One clue to Beauvoir's innovation might be her reliance in *The Second Sex* on an analogy with racism. In her introduction to *The Second Sex*, Beauvoir writes of "the profound analogies between women's situation and that of Blacks: one like the other is emancipating itself from a same paternalism and the caste of former masters wants to keep them in 'their place,' that is to say in the place that it has chosen for them" (Beauvoir 1927, 1:24). Beauvoir also relies on the analogy with racism in describing problems in psychological development when a girl is forced

> to discover inferiority in herself as a given essence; it's a strange experience for someone who poses herself for herself as the One to be revealed to herself as alterity. That is what happens to the girl when, making her apprenticeship of the world, she discovers herself [*s'y saisit*] as a woman. . . . This situation is not unique. It is also the one known by blacks in America, partially integrated into a civilization which considers them as an inferior caste. (Beauvoir 1949, 2:47)

Beauvoir was not the first feminist to use the racism analogy. Its wide use by nineteenth-century feminists reflects an earlier historic link between feminism and the African American struggle against racist oppression. But separating racism and sexism as distinct, though analogous, analytic categories can be problematic, denying the experience of African American women, for instance, for whom the effects of racism and sexism are often inseparable. In *The Second Sex* Beauvoir ignores the experience of African American women and consigns a majority of the world's women to a footnote to a discussion of Western women ("The history of the woman in the Orient, India and China was, in effect, that of a long and unchanging slavery" [Beauvoir 1949, 1:133]). But *The Second Sex* also reflects an awareness of how racism and economic class oppression can work against feminist sisterhood, an awareness that is often lacking in radical feminist theories. Scholars have not identified the sources of Beauvoir's theory of racism. Given Beauvoir's reliance on an analogy with racism, investigating the sources for her understanding of racism might shed light on the roots of her feminist theory and contribute to the larger project of challenging the legacies of racism, as Spelman (1988, 57–79) and I have argued.

AN AMERICAN DILEMMA

One source of influence on Beauvoir's theory of racism in *The Second Sex* is the massive sociological study of American race relations, *An American Dilemma* (1944), compiled under the direction of Gunnar Myrdal, which includes an appendix on women by Alva Myrdal entitled "A Parallel to the Negro Problem." Beauvoir cites *An American Dilemma* in *The Second Sex* in the conclusion to her discussion of women's history. "Just as in America, it's not a black problem but a white problem [here Beauvoir cites Gunnar Myrdal], . . . so the woman problem has always been a problem for men" (Beauvoir 1949, 1:216). The importance of Myrdal's text is also suggested by a letter that Beauvoir wrote to her American lover, Chicago writer Nelson Algren, dated December 1, 1947.

> Reading the "American Dilemma" . . . I begin again to think about the book I began about women's situation. I should like to write a book as important as this big one about Negroes; Myrdal points [to] many very interesting analogies between Negroes' and women's status; I felt it already. (Algren Papers)

In a letter written one month later, after finishing Myrdal's book, Beauvoir tells Algren that she has expanded the scope of her study of women.

"I came back to my essay about women. . . . I have a lot of reading to do: Psychoanalysis and social science, and Law, and history, and so on" (Algren Papers). The result is a book that will more closely resemble *An American Dilemma* in its encyclopedic scope.

Myrdal also seems to have contributed to Beauvoir's social constructionism, the view that race (and by analogy, gender) is socially constructed. Following Myrdal, Beauvoir substitutes the concept of caste for that of the biological category of race. Myrdal legitimates social constructionism in *An American Dilemma* as the result of a "veritable revolution in scientific thought" that "is constantly disproving inherent differences and explaining apparent ones in cultural and social terms." This trend in social science applies not only to race, according to Myrdal, but to gender as well. In tracing the theoretical roots of social constructionism on race, Myrdal places African Americans in the vanguard. "Negroes and members of other minority groups always had a tendency to find environmental explanations for differences in intelligence performance, while the 'American' scientists . . . for a long time labored under the bias of expecting to find innate differences." Referring to the essays of W. E. B. DuBois and others, Myrdal writes that "modern research has tended to confirm the Negroes' view and not the whites' " on the question of racial difference (Myrdal et al. 1944, 92, 95–96). Beauvoir's social constructionism is a central theme of *The Second Sex*; volume two opens with the claim "One is not born a woman, but becomes one."

Myrdal can thus be seen as influencing Beauvoir's theoretical framework in *The Second Sex* in four ways: by encouraging the use of an analogy with racism, providing a model for the encyclopedic scope of *The Second Sex*, introducing the concept of caste as a substitute for the biological category of race, and grounding her understanding of social constructionism in science and in the African American intellectual tradition. Despite Beauvoir's utilization of certain elements of *An American Dilemma*, Myrdal's influence on the philosophical framework of *The Second Sex* is limited by philosophical differences. *An American Dilemma* reflects Myrdal's paternalistic liberalism.

Writing as an anti-Communist and a social engineer, Myrdal largely ignores the black community and its leaders, directing his text to the white American political leadership, whose postwar ambition to be the "leader of the free world" is undermined by the continued oppression of the black people within its own borders. Myrdal appeals to both the political ambitions and the moral conscience of white America to bring practices into line with the American creed. Interested only in the negative effects of slavery and its aftermath, Myrdal finds nothing of value in African American culture and community, which he describes as "pathological," a degenerate product of oppression (*see* Southern 1987). African American women receive barely a mention and are represented in a chapter on population control (in lieu of a chapter on the family) as targets for a governmental eugenics program.

In *The Second Sex*, Beauvoir goes beyond Myrdal. She appeals to the liberal ideal of the common humanity of men and women in arguing for an end to women's oppression. She also utilizes a subjectivist, phenomenological approach and, drawing on the Marxist tradition, affirms the necessity of militant struggle to win their liberation. Defining a radical feminist position analogous to that of the black power movement in the 1960s, Beauvoir rejects both the economic reductionism of orthodox Marxism and liberal paternalism, arguing that a group in power will never willingly relinquish its privileges through moral appeals alone. Only women, united in struggle, constructing the theoretical grounds for that struggle on the basis of their own experience, can win their liberation. These differences point away from Myrdal.

Who, besides Myrdal, might have influenced Beauvoir's understanding of oppression? The author of a popular biography of Beauvoir writes that it was Beauvoir's American lover, Chicago writer Nelson Algren, "who first suggested that [Beauvoir] conduct her study of women in the light of the experience of black Americans in a prejudicial society, and who first introduced her to the contemporary literature about black Americans, starting with the Myrdal books [including *An American Dilemma*]" (Bair 1990b, 388). But this claim overlooks an earlier passage in the same December 1, 1947, letter where Beauvoir seems to be introducing Algren to Myrdal's text, rather than the other way around (Algren Papers and personal communication from Sylvie Le Bon de Beauvoir).

Could Beauvoir's lifelong companion, philosopher Jean-Paul Sartre, have guided her analysis of racism? Scholars have often assumed so, and her description of sexism in *The Second Sex* seems to have been influenced by Sartre's description of anti-Semitism (Sartre [1946] 1954). But Sartre's ahistorical analyses of bad faith and Jewish culture ([1946] 1954), and the philosophical differences in Sartre's and Beauvoir's theories of the American system of racial segregation argue against this view. Sartre, in 1945, espoused an orthodox Marxist analysis that Beauvoir rejects in *The Second Sex*. He wrote: "there is only one solution to the black problem . . . when the American proletariat—black and white— will have recognized the identity of their interests in regards to the class of bosses, the Negroes will struggle with the white workers and in equality with them, for the recognition of their rights" (Sartre 1945, 30 juillet, 2). Furthermore, in a controversial 1948 preface to a volume of *négritude* poetry, Sartre defines race not as a social construct, but as "the result of a psychobiological syncretism," in contrast to class, which he characterizes as socially constructed, "a methodical construction based on experience." In his preface, Sartre argues that "the subjective, existential ethnic idea of *négritude* 'passes' as Hegel puts it, into the objective, positive, exact idea of *proletariat*"; as "the minor term of a dialectical progression." Frantz Fanon writes of Sartre's preface, "When I read that page, I felt that I had been robbed of my last chance" (Fanon 1967, 133; citing Sartre 1948, xl). C. L. R. James describes Sartre's characterization of *négritude* as "a disaster" (James 1962, 401). Sartre's Marxist reductionism, like Myrdal's liberal paternalism, fails to appreciate culturally specific forms of struggle. Beauvoir's radical feminism, which rejects Marxist reductionism and calls for a leftist but separatist feminist struggle, thus could not have relied on Sartre's theory of racism as a model.

RICHARD WRIGHT

A more plausible source of influence is Richard Wright. The passage from *The Second Sex* cited above, where Beauvoir points to the analogy with racism in discussing the psychological problems that result from being forced to accept one's essential inferiority continues with a reference to Richard Wright's *Native Son*.

[W]hat Big[ger] Thomas experiences with so much bitterness at the dawn of his life, is this definitive inferiority, this cursed alterity which is inscribed in the color of his skin: he looks at passing airplanes and he knows that because he is black the sky is forbidden to him. Because she is [a] woman, the girl knows that the sea and the poles, that a

> thousand adventures, a thousand joys are forbidden to her. (Beauvoir 1949, 2:47)

Beauvoir refers to Wright's autobiography, *Black Boy*, in a concluding section of *The Second Sex*, where she once again draws the analogy between the situation of blacks in America and women.

> Richard Wright showed in *Black Boy* how much the ambitions of a young American Black are barred from the start and what a struggle he has to sustain to simply raise himself to the level where the problems begin to be posed for the Whites; the Blacks who have come to France from Africa also know . . . of difficulties analogous to those encountered by women. (Beauvoir 1949, 2:540–41)

As we shall see below, Wright's subjectivist approach, placing black experience at the center of his theorizing, differentiates him from Myrdal's method of objectifying blacks and marks one of several points of philosophical affinity with Beauvoir's method in *The Second Sex*. Before beginning an analysis of the similarities in their philosophical positions, it would be helpful to review the evidence of Beauvoir's contact with Wright.

My research has uncovered extensive evidence of Beauvoir's close contact with and interest in Wright, including a beautiful photograph of the two of them together during Beauvoir's visit to New York in 1947 (Webb 1968). In a 1970 interview with the French Wright scholar Michel Fabre, Beauvoir describes her long friendship with Wright, which began with the Wrights' first visit to Paris in 1946, as "especially close from 1947 to 1955." Her appreciation of Wright as a writer predates World War II. In the interview, Beauvoir recounts her first introduction to Wright's 1940 masterpiece, *Native Son*.

> Sylvia Beach [owner of a famous American expatriate bookstore, Shakespeare and Company] had told me: "You like violent books, well, here is a violent one, it will hit you hard." And I said, "Yes, I'll read it." I read it and I was very, very much impressed. So my first encounter with Wright's novels was some time in 1940, through Sylvia Beach. (Fabre 1985, 253)

Beauvoir's account seems unlikely, since *Native Son* was published in New York on March 1, 1940, and the Nazi Occupation began the following June. But her account is supported by a biography of Beach. "At the end of May . . . Sylvia placed her final order for books, including . . . Richard Wright's *Native Son*. . . . Most business (though financially negligible) was in the lending library" (Fitch 1983, 399). Beauvoir, who joined Beach's lending library in 1935, would thus have had the opportunity to borrow Wright's text.

The first public association of Wright and Beauvoir comes in 1945, when a French translation of Wright's story "Fire and Cloud" appeared in the inaugural issue of *Les Temps Modernes* [Modern Times], a journal edited by Beauvoir with Sartre and others. Wright's 1945 autobiographical story "Early Days in Chicago," later published (as "The Man Who Went to Chicago") in *Eight Men*, was published in the special 1946 issue of *Les Temps Modernes* on the U.S.A., along with excerpts from *Black Metropolis*, including one on "Crossing the Color Line." Beauvoir's first personal contact with Wright came in 1946 when Wright, an international celebrity, paid a triumphant visit to Paris as a guest of the French government (Webb 1968, 257–59). Beauvoir tells Fabre in their 1970 interview that Wright gave her several of the texts on blacks in America that were excerpted in the special 1946 issue of *Les Temps Modernes*.

> We issued a special issue on the United States with articles and extracts by black writers, and Wright was instrumental in having pieces by Horace Cayton and . . . a Chicago anthropologist, St. Clair Drake, published in that issue. He told me to read *Black Metropolis*, if I remember correctly, long before it was translated. He would always indicate and suggest new titles. (Fabre 1990, 253)

These comments by Beauvoir suggest that it might be Wright who introduced Beauvoir to Myrdal's text as well. Wright, unlike Algren, was familiar with Myrdal's text prior to 1947. He discusses *An American Dilemma* in print as early as 1944, refers to it in his 1945 preface to *Black Metropolis*, mentions it, according to Fabre, in "notes for a 1944 project, never completed, for a Negro anthology," and includes it in a "list of books, probably made in 1946, which [he] took with him on his first French trip or books he recommended to someone in Paris" (Fabre 1990, 264–65).

In the first six issues of 1947, *Les Temps Modernes* published a serial translation of Wright's autobiography, *Black Boy* (1945), alongside Beauvoir's *Ethics of Ambiguity* and Sartre's *What Is Literature?*—both of which contain references to Wright's text. In 1948, when Beauvoir was completing *The Second Sex*, *Les Temps Modernes* published Wright's essay on black American literature. According to the Algren correspondence and the Fabre interview, Beauvoir also translated Wright's speech at a 1948 political rally on "The Internationalism of the Spirit," where Camus refused to allow Beauvoir to speak in her own right. In 1948 a translation of Wright's controversial autobiographical essay "I Tried to Be a Communist," which described his break with the Communist Party, was published in *Les Temps Modernes*. The most important evidence of Wright's influence on *The Second Sex*, besides the scattered references to Wright in the text itself, is *America Day by Day* (1948), Beauvoir's account of her four-month trip to the United States in 1947. In *America Day by Day*, Beauvoir levels an attack on the American system of racial segregation and portrays Wright as her cultural and intellectual guide.

Wright's influence on Beauvoir is evidence of his contribution to what Lerone Bennett has termed "the internationalization" of the black struggle. In the section that follows I discuss Wright's influence on Beauvoir's understanding of oppression: his subjectivist approach, his critical analysis of the limitations of Marxist ideology in understanding racism and black experience, his rejection of essentialism, and his militant engagement in the black struggle. Wright, as the intellectual heir to W. E. B. DuBois, introduces Beauvoir to the concept of the "double consciousness" of blacks under racism, which serves as a model for Beauvoir's concept of woman as the Other in *The Second Sex*. Wright's phenomenological descriptions of black experience of oppression provide a methodological alternative to both Myrdal's objectifying social science methodology and the economic reductionism of Marxist orthodoxy. Finally, Wright's rejection of white-defined essentialist views of racial difference allied with an affirmation of the salience of race in the lived experience of blacks under oppression, and its strategic usefulness when defined by blacks in the interests of liberation, provide Beauvoir with a model for an anti-essentialist but militant liberation politics.

The Concept of The Oppressed Other

The first area of Wright's philosophical influence on Beauvoir's theory of oppression is in their shared concept of the oppressed Other, and their focus on the importance of social relations and recognition in the formation of the self. In *The Second Sex*, Beauvoir argues that one becomes a woman not by birth, but through the intervention of the Other. Wright described the same phenomenon years earlier in *Native Son* and *Black Boy*. In the Fabre interview Beauvoir points to Wright's description of the role of other people in shaping one's personality. In reference to *Native Son*, Beauvoir tells Fabre,

> I was impressed especially by the beginning when the adolescent says that he knows there are things he'll never be allowed to do, that he'll never fly a plane, for instance. It struck me as a new version of predestination. (Fabre 1985, 253)

In *Native Son*, Wright replaces the traditional version of predestination as given by God with a description of how one's destiny is given by man under oppression. As we have seen from the passage from *The Second Sex* cited above, Beauvoir would later draw upon Wright's "new version of predestination," which was written years before her first reading of Myrdal's *American Dilemma*, in describing how oppression distorts the psychological development of girls whose gender destines them for inferiority. This is an important step in constructing an existentialist political philosophy able to show how one's existential freedom is distorted by a situation of oppression.

Saunders Redding ([1963] 1970, 8) describes this theme of the psychological dimension of relationships of oppression as the "central stream of Wright's entire development" and attributes it to the influence of William James, whom Wright quotes in his preface to *Black Metropolis*. This central theme of the importance of the role of the Other in shaping one's personality and experience of self is also connected to the concept of "double consciousness" that can be traced not to William James, but to *The Souls of Black Folk*, W. E. B. DuBois's classic 1903 essay. DuBois writes that America

> yields [the Negro] no true self-consciousness, but only lets him see himself through the revelation of the other world. It is a peculiar sensation, this double consciousness, this sense of always looking at one's self through the eyes of others, of measuring one's soul by the tape of a world that looks on in amused contempt and pity. (DuBois 1903, 3)

DuBois's concept of double consciousness, of seeing oneself as seen by the other, has clear analogies with Beauvoir's concept in *The Second Sex* of woman as the Other, experiencing herself as defined by men.

In *America Day by Day* Beauvoir acknowledges this connection in her discussion of women's situation and character, although she is not aware that it is an intellectual legacy of DuBois: "the famous laughter of blacks . . . is often only a mask that the black dons in the presence of whites because he knows that it is demanded of him. (Richard Wright in *Black Boy*, John Dollar in *Caste and Class in a South Communauty* [*sic*], stress very much this double face of the black, one side of which is expressly destined for whites)" (Beauvoir 1948, 236). Wright, like Myrdal, also provides Beauvoir with a bridge to the larger African American intellectual tradition, specifically to W. E. B. DuBois's concept of double consciousness.

A Phenomenology of Oppression

The second area of Wright's philosophical influence on Beauvoir is a subjectivist, phenomenological approach to the study of oppression that differentiates both Wright and Beauvoir from Myrdal. In a June 3, 1945, letter, Wright proposes a book by African American writers that would do for the "inner personality, the subjective landscape of the Negro, what Gunnar Myrdal's *An American Dilemma* did for the external, social relations" (Fabre 1993, 586). His own books and essays, including *Native Son* and *Black Boy,* utilize that very methodology, describing the lived experience of American racism from the standpoint of the oppressed. Wright provides a phenomenology of racial oppression to challenge the claims by segregationists that blacks are happy and contented with their naturally inferior place in society, much as Beauvoir, in the second volume of *The Second Sex* (entitled Lived Experience), relies on a phenomenological description of women's experience to challenge the oppressive stereotypes of popular myths and Freudian psychology.

In Beauvoir's postwar efforts to expand the limits of her methodology to encompass the political, we find a source of her interest in Wright, who provided a model for linking the personal and the political. In a story of his early days in Chicago, published in the special 1946 "U.S.A." issue of *Les Temps Modernes*, Wright describes the inextricably political dimension of his personal existence. Working as a janitor at a prestigious Chicago medical research institute, Wright recalls his "adolescent dream of wanting to be a medical research worker." But the doctors ridiculed him for asking questions: " 'If you know too much, boy, your brains might explode,' a doctor said one day" (Wright 1946, 194). Describing the world of the hospital through the eyes of the janitor, whose intelligence and intellectual curiosity could have made him a researcher, reveals the injustice of racist oppression and shatters the stereotype, restoring subjectivity to the oppressed. The white doctors who thought their actions invisible to moral judgment are revealed through the eyes of the janitor they have ridiculed.

For Beauvoir, who was trying to construct an existentialist ethics in 1945, Wright's ability to trace the political dimensions of his own individual experience in *Black Boy* must have been a revelation. It is that connection of the personal and the political, of the political dimension of relationships between individual men and women once consigned to the realm of the private, that will later be a hallmark of radical feminism. In *America Day by Day*, which is dedicated to Ellen and Richard Wright, Beauvoir follows Wright's lead in using a description of ones lived, felt experience to expose the horrors of racism. Consider, for example, Beauvoir's description in *America Day by Day* of her first encounter with segregation during a bus tour across the United States.

> On the doors of the rest rooms, one reads on one side, "White Ladies," "White Gentlemen," and on the other "Colored Women," "Colored Men." There are only whites in the large hall that serves as a waiting room: blacks are packed into a little adjoining cubbyhole; beside the spacious restaurant reserved for whites the minuscule lunchroom for colored people can only accommodate four customers at a time. It's the first time we've seen with our own eyes this segregation we have heard so much about; and we've been well warned: something is falling onto our shoulders which will no longer leave us across the entire South; it is our own skin that has become heavy and stifling and whose color burns us. (Beauvoir 1948, 200)

Myrdal describes the objective signs of segregation such as those on the rest room doors. It is Wright, however, who describes how segregation feels to its victims, perhaps inspiring Beauvoir to expose her own experience, rich in details of embodiment, to an audience of readers in order to lend her support to Wright's cause. Beauvoir's graphic descriptions in *America Day by Day* of the racism of white women show how she learns firsthand that white racist allegiances and privilege can motivate white women to deny the humanity of black women.

> American kindness no longer has any place here. [I]n the line which presses at the doors of the bus, one jostles the blacks: "You're not going to let this negro woman pass in front of you," says a woman to a man, her voice trembling with fury. (Beauvoir 1948, 227)

Beauvoir leaves the South with few illusions about the possibilities of feminist sisterhood easily cutting across a racist divide.

The Critical Appropriation of Marxism

Wright also provides Beauvoir with a model of political engagement as a writer. At the beginning of their friendship in 1946, when Beauvoir had yet to integrate successfully the political realities of sexism or an analysis of Marxism into her subjectivist perspective and the personal voice that would mark her later writing, Wright was already a politically engaged writer with a broad understanding of both racism and Marxist politics. He joined the Communist Party during the 1930s because of its political commitment to achieving racial justice in America and left it in the 1940s in order to support African American demands for equality and a literary exploration of black experience free from ideological restrictions.

Wright's political development can be traced in the texts printed in *Les Temps Modernes* and elsewhere. His story "Fire and Cloud," published in the first issue of *Les Temps Modernes*, was written in 1927 when he was a postal worker in Chicago and a member of the Communist Party. The story reflects an orthodox Marxist viewpoint, in which the racist struggle is subsumed within the broader working-class struggle. But Wright's affinity for black cultural nationalism, which marked his early attraction to Garveyism and would ultimately lead to his break with Marxism, is evident in his 1938 essay "Blueprint for Negro Writing." "The Negro writer must realize within the area of his own personal experience those impulses which, when prefigured in terms of broad social movements, constitute the stuff of nationalism" (Wright

1938, 43). It was this commitment to describing the realities of black experience that would eventually lead to his break with Marxism.

Wright's 1945 preface to *Black Metropolis* marks an important philosophical turning point, as he publicly criticizes the position with which he had been so long identified. Wright criticizes Marxists for seeking "to convert the Negro problem from a complex, race, cultural, and national problem into a relatively simple one of class conflicts and interests." "The political Left," according to Wright, "often gyrates and squirms to make the Negro problem fit rigidly into a class-war frame of reference, when the roots of that problem lie in American culture as a whole." But Wright is not advocating liberalism or individual solutions. Collective struggle by blacks is a necessity so that "Negro trade unionists can make their voices heard as Negroes about their problem" (Wright 1945, xxviii, xxix). His critique of liberal individualism is as resounding as his critique of Marxism.

> The political Right, reacting traditionally, tries to smother the Negro problem as a whole and insists upon regarding Negroes as individuals and making individual deals with individual Negroes, ignoring the race consciousness which three hundred years of Jim Crow living has burned into the Negro's heart. Both the political Left and the political Right try to change the Negro problem into something that they can control, thereby denying the humanity of the Negro, excluding his unique and historic position in American life. (Wright 1945, xxix)

Wright, unlike Myrdal, argues that "race consciousness" is necessary in order to affirm the "humanity of the Negro." By joining the militancy of Marxism, freed from an economic reductionism, with a race consciousness freed of romanticism, Wright defines a radical model for black political struggle that Beauvoir adapts to the situation of women in *The Second Sex*.

A Critical Appropriation of Cultural Nationalism

In *America Day by Day* Beauvoir's narrative depicts the evolution of her own conception of race, under Wright's guidance, from a definition of racial difference designed to fulfill the needs of whites, to a self-definition of difference by blacks as the grounds for political engagement and self-realization. The narrative portrays Wright as Beauvoir's teacher, guiding her understanding of race as a social construct. Presenting Wright as her mentor, her guide not only to the sights of Harlem, but to the intellectual terrain of racism, Beauvoir's narrative legitimates Wright's analysis—perhaps the reason that an American edition of *America Day by Day* did not appear until 1953, with most of the discussion of Myrdal's text and the passages in which Wright appears to be teaching Beauvoir deleted.

Near the end of the book, Beauvoir recounts a conversation with Wright in which he criticizes an attitude reflected by Beauvoir herself earlier in the text. He tells her that he deplores whites who define blacks as "magnificently gifted for music and dance, rich in animal instincts [etc.] . . . open to religious sentiments." Whites are attracted to blacks, according to Wright, Beauvoir continues, "because they have projected onto them what they would wish to be and are not; but the most fascinated are those who feel in themselves the most profound deficiencies. . . . W[right] finds this harmful, because it tends to maintain the existence of a ditch between blacks and whites." Unfortunately, the important sentence that follows is deleted from the English edition of *America Day by Day*, as are many of Beauvoir's references to Wright and their discussions about racism, and most of Beauvoir's synopsis of sections of *American Dilemma*. "The apparent differences between the two castes come from differences of historical, economic, social, cultural situation, which could—at least theoretically—be abolished." Wright's critique of biological essentialism in this passage anticipates Beauvoir's critique of essentialist ideologies of innate gender difference in *The Second Sex*. Beauvoir's narrative recounts Wright's explanation of the changing religious practices among blacks: "whites are interested in enclosing blacks in the emotional domain in order to deny them all intellectual aptitude: blacks are refusing today to play the game . . . emotion is no longer systematically cultivated [in the churches]" (Beauvoir 1948, 266–67). When Beauvoir responds, in the conclusion of *The Second Sex*, to the charge that a world of feminine beauty will be lost with women's liberation, she accepts the prediction, without despairing of the future, that individuals will no longer be confined by the limits of stereotyped roles.

Wright rejects essentialist, biologically determined definitions of racial difference that serve the needs of whites, but he does not reject cultural difference as a ground for political struggle. Although his writings express his alienation from both the black church and the black bourgeoisie, Wright's use of black dialect and descriptions of black folk culture mark his link with a black cultural nationalism and the legacy of the Harlem Renaissance that differentiate him from Myrdal. Wright wrote within a tradition of black folk culture, a "blues" tradition, thus continuing that tradition while reflecting his alienation in the modern, individualist world (*see* Ellison 1966, Baker 1984, Werner 1990). In an unpublished 1960 preface to the second edition of *Black Metropolis* (Wright Papers), Wright warns African American leaders about the post-modern attack on humanism and turns to the blues tradition as a cultural basis for political struggle.

Beauvoir writes in *America Day by Day* of Wright's grounding his political engagement in his situation as a black writer. Most American ex-Communists lapsed into a pessimistic individualism after the war, Beauvoir writes, "except for R[ichard] Wright who by virtue of his singular situation finds himself and chooses [*se veut*] to be engaged" (Beauvoir 1948, 333). Beauvoir, who saw herself as working within a tradition of women writers, may have seen Wright as a model for her own political engagement as a woman in *The Second Sex*, although she, like Wright, is often dismissive of cultural anthropology. She also argues that women, unlike African Americans, lack a cultural identity to use as a basis for political engagement.

CONCLUSION

Responding to Gilroy's challenge in *The Black Atlantic* to read Richard Wright in a European context, I have presented evidence that Richard Wright's theory of racist oppression provided Beauvoir with a theoretical model that she utilized in *America Day by Day* to support the struggle against racism and in *The Second Sex* to construct the theoretical foundations of radical feminism. This evidence challenges the view that philosophy is the creation of only white European men and that Richard Wright, an émigré writer, was a passive recipient of French philosophical influence, exerting no influence himself on French intellectuals. My research has also identified a previously unrecognized historical moment of connection between the feminist movement and the African American liberation struggle. Wright and Beauvoir drew on Marxism and psycho-analysis to transform the theoretical frameworks of political movements rooted in the abolitionism of the 1830s, thus laying the foundations for the political radicalism of the 1960s.

But in arguing for a new interpretive model for *The Second Sex*, respectful of Beauvoir's accomplishment and appreciative of Wright's influence, I have identified an influence on feminist theory that is not unproblematic for feminists. Wright has been labeled a misogynist for his dismissive October 5, 1937, *New Masses* review of Zora Neale Hurston's *Their Eyes Were Watching God* as perpetuating the "minstrel show tradition" (Fabre 1993, 143) and for his negative fictional portrayals of female characters (*see* Walker 1988). June Jordan (1974), in an early reappraisal of Hurston, provides an interpretive context for reconciling Hurston's cultural "affirmation" and Wright's "protest." More recently, Gilroy (1993) and Barbara Johnson (1993) have argued that the complexities of Wright's portrayals of black women and masculinity warrant a more nuanced reading. This characterization of Wright as misogynist is also challenged by evidence of his role in launching the career of Gwendolyn Brooks, urging the publication of her first book of poetry, and publishing one of her poems in *Présence Africaine* (Fabre 1993, 317). Wright thus stands in an ironic relationship to feminism. Having contributed to the silencing of Zora Neale Hurston, his own influence in France has been obscured by the sexist erasure of Beauvoir's philosophical achievement. In the years to come, Wright's texts may be valued by womanist cultural criticism as an early chronicle of misogynist violence.

Reprinted, with changes, from "Richard Wright and Simone de Beauvoir: From *The Black Metropolis* to the City of Lights," *Drum Voices Revue* 8 (1998/ 99), by permission of the English Department, Southern Illinois University at Edwardsville.

12

BEAUVOIR'S EARLY PHILOSOPHY: THE 1927 DIARY (1998)

The tradition continues of reading Simone de Beauvoir's most important philosophical texts, *Ethics of Ambiguity* (1947) and *The Second Sex* (1949), as applications of Sartre's philosophy in *Being and Nothingness* (1943). Diane Raymond, in *Existentialism and the Philosophical Tradition* (1991), for example, characterizes Beauvoir's central thesis in *The Second Sex*, that under patriarchy woman is the Other, as an application of Sartre's "phenomenology of interpersonal relationships" and its "dynamic of consciousness struggling against consciousness" (Raymond 1991, 386, 389). Sonia Kruks (1995) writes that "The central claim of *The Second Sex*—'one is not born a woman but becomes one'—presupposes Sartre's argument that 'existence precedes essence': that human beings become what they are on the basis of no pre-given necessity or 'nature'" (Kruks 1995, 1). Scholars, including Le Doeuff (1989), Kruks (1990), Lundgren-Gothlin (1996a), Vintges (1996), Bergoffen (1997), and myself, have sought to differentiate the philosophies of Beauvoir and Sartre and trace their philosophical influence on one another. But the problem is a difficult one, with a tradition of sexist criticism compounded by Beauvoir herself, who discouraged recognition of her philosophy, preferring to portray herself as a defender of Sartrean existentialism.

The posthumous publication of Beauvoir's and Sartre's diaries and letters has provided scholars with a new means of challenging sexist interpretations and charting, with greater accuracy, the development of their individual philosophies. Kate and Edward Fullbrook (1994), tracing the origins of Sartre's philosophy in *Being and Nothingness* (1943) to his wartime diaries, were astonished to discover evidence that in 1939

185

Sartre modeled his philosophy on a nearly complete manuscript of Beauvoir's metaphysical novel *She Came to Stay* (1943). The Fullbrooks conclude that Beauvoir's novel, long assumed to be an illustration of Sartre's philosophy, is instead its source and that Beauvoir, long assumed to be a follower of Sartrean philosophy, is instead its originator. While the Fullbrooks' conclusion might be exaggerated, their discovery supports the theory that Beauvoir is at least *a* source, if not *the* source, of Sartrean existentialism.

Critics have attacked the Fullbrooks' claims, arguing that a novel, as literature, is not philosophy (discounting the tradition of existential literature), and Beauvoir thus cannot be said to have originated a philosophy in her novel, and that, in any case, since the original 1939 manuscript is missing, no conclusions can be drawn about what Sartre actually read in 1939. This criticism highlights the more general problem of differentiating Beauvoir's early philosophy from that of Sartre. Without a clear analysis of Beauvoir's own philosophy, especially in its earliest stages, it is difficult to address the question of influence in their relationship, which began in 1929. Beauvoir's graduate thesis on Leibniz, which could provide important clues to her early philosophy is unfortunately missing. Until recently, scholars, lacking a pre-Sartrean beginning point for Beauvoir's philosophy, have been unable to define Beauvoir's earliest philosophical position with any certainty. Fortunately, this situation has recently changed thanks to a discovery by Beauvoir's adopted daughter, Sylvie Le Bon de Beauvoir.

Following Beauvoir's death in 1986, Sylvie Le Bon de Beauvoir discovered Beauvoir's handwritten *carnets de jeunesse*, diaries dating from 1926 to 1930 when Beauvoir was a philosophy student at the Sorbonne. In 1990, Le Bon de Beauvoir donated the diaries to the Bibliothèque Nationale, where they have been made available to scholars (*see* Sylvie Le Bon de Beauvoir 1995). After reading of the Fullbrooks' discoveries, I began a study of these student diaries in the summer of 1994, looking for areas of philosophical significance, particularly in the diaries predating Beauvoir's first meeting with Sartre. If the Fullbrooks were correct in their analysis of Sartre's war diaries and Beauvoir's novel, one would expect to find in Beauvoir's 1926–29 texts an early version of "Sartrean" existentialism. Struggling to decipher Beauvoir's handwriting, I made a key discovery in the 1927 diary: Beauvoir's statement of her interest in the philosophical theme, "the opposition of self and other" (Beauvoir

1927, 95). This theme, found in both *The Second Sex*, in Beauvoir's concept of woman as the Other, and in *Being and Nothingness*, in Sartre's concept of our being-for-others, is usually read, as we have seen, as evidence of Sartre's influence on Beauvoir. Its presence in the 1927 diary means that Beauvoir, rather than Sartre, originated this theme in her own philosophy and suggests that its later presence in Sartre's philosophy might reflect Beauvoir's influence.

What other evidence could the diary provide about Beauvoir's early philosophy? Could it shed light on the influences that shaped it? Could it reveal other philosophical themes central to the existential phenomenology that Beauvoir shared with Sartre or would it point to early philosophical differences? Finally, what does Beauvoir mean by "the opposition of self and other"? Is it, as many critics charge, an indication of Beauvoir's masculinist thinking, or is it instead a reflection of what Carol Gilligan has identified as the "central moral problem for women"? The following analysis of the 1927 diary (entries dated from April 17 to October 27, 1927), which is based on a transcription prepared by Professor Barbara Klaw and myself and verified and corrected by Sylvie Le Bon de Beauvoir, attempts to answer these questions.

THE DIARY AS PHILOSOPHY

It might be objected that the diary of a nineteen-year-old girl is an inappropriate text for serious philosophical study, no matter how famous its author would later become. But diaries, despite the interpretive challenges they pose, are not unknown as philosophical texts, certainly not among the philosophers of religion Beauvoir read in 1927. Gabriel Marcel's *Journal métaphysique* (1927), for example, is an important text in the history of phenomenology in France, cited by Herbert Spiegelberg (1982, 450) for Marcel's early use of the term "phenomenology" in a diary entry dated October 20, 1920. Beauvoir may even have been encouraged to keep a philosophical diary by her mentor in philosophy at the Sorbonne, Jean Baruzi, whose colleague Charles du Bos (1948) kept a journal throughout the 1920s that chronicles, among other things, Baruzi's projects with Gabriel Marcel (Vieillard-Baron 1985). Sartre's war diaries and notebook on ethics are more recent examples of diaries as philosophical texts. Nor should the age of the author be grounds for discrediting a text. Berkeley and Leibniz authored important philosophical texts in their early twenties.

Another objection to reading Beauvoir's 1927 diary as a philosophical text might be that Beauvoir herself, in *Memoirs of a Dutiful Daughter* (1958), describes her interests at the time as literary rather than philosophical. But scholars have identified numerous omissions and misrepresentations in Beauvoir's autobiographies. Francis and Gontier (1987), for example, uncover important omissions from the *Memoirs* in their biography of Beauvoir. They reveal details of the impoverishment of Beauvoir's family following World War I and identify the figure of Pradelle, whose intransigence is portrayed (mistakenly) in the *Memoirs* as contributing to the death of Beauvoir's friend Zaza, as Maurice Merleau-Ponty. The posthumously published diaries and correspondence reveal evidence of Beauvoir's lesbian relationships omitted from the autobiographies and, most significantly in this context, evidence challenging Beauvoir's denial in the autobiographies of her influence on Sartre's philosophy (*see* Fullbrook and Fullbrook 1994). Thus, Beauvoir's autobiographies cannot be read as a definitive account but must be checked against original sources whenever possible. The discovery of Beauvoir's student diaries provides such an opportunity.

Furthermore, Beauvoir's account in the *Memoirs* of her work in philosophy at the Sorbonne contains inconsistencies that suggest the possibility of omissions and misrepresentations. Consider, for example, the account of a lengthy paper on "the personality" that Beauvoir wrote for her philosophy professor, Jean Baruzi. "I undertook for Baruzi an immense dissertation on 'the personality,' which contained the sum of my knowledge and my ignorance" (Beauvoir 1958, 364). What the knowledge contained in that essay is we are not told, despite the fact that its success apparently set Beauvoir on her course as a writer.

> Baruzi returned my essay with high praise. He greeted me at the classroom door and his faint voice breathed the hope that it was the beginning of a serious work. I was inflamed. The next day . . . I was struck by this exigency for which I had clamored for so long: I had to undertake my work. (Beauvoir 1958, 368)

Later in the *Memoirs*, Beauvoir tells of giving this essay, of which she is "excessively proud," to a fellow philosophy student to read (Beauvoir

1958, 439). Despite the apparent importance of this essay in philosophy, Beauvoir tells us nothing of its content or methodology.

The *Memoirs* contain brief but intriguing references to Beauvoir's passion for philosophy. "I studied the theory of relativity, and had a passion for it." Given the importance of the concepts of freedom and contingency in French existentialism, it is curious that Beauvoir omits from the *Memoirs* any discussion of her essay on "Liberté et contingence" for the written portion of the graduate *agrégation*. The cursory references to Beauvoir's graduate thesis (*diplôme*) in philosophy are most surprising of all. The initial reference to her *diplôme* portrays Beauvoir as passively receiving the topic from her thesis director, Léon Brunschvicg; "He advised me to write on 'the concept according to Leibniz,' and I acquiesced." But other passages reveal that Beauvoir took an active interest in her study of Leibniz. When asked by a friend, at a boring party, to explain Leibniz's system, Beauvoir reports that "during an hour I forgot my boredom" (Beauvoir 1958, 396, 460, 369, 388).

As she nears the completion of her graduate studies in philosophy, her passionate interest in Leibniz is well known. Sartre, according to the *Memoirs*, gave her a sketch of "Leibniz bathing with the monads" and later invited her to join his study group preparing for the oral philosophy exam, "counting on me to work on Leibniz." She apparently lectured the group on Leibniz for several days: "For the entire day, petrified by shyness, I commented on 'the metaphysical discourse.' . . . I returned each day, and soon began to warm up" (Beauvoir 1958, 449, 467–68). Several years later, Beauvoir's interest in Leibniz was still strong enough to lead her to make a pilgrimage, with Sartre in tow, to Leibniz's home in Hanover during a driving rainstorm (Beauvoir 1960, 209). But of the content of Beauvoir's philosophical work on Leibniz we are told nothing, and of the *diplôme*, merely the bare report that "I finished my thesis" (Beauvoir 1958, 426). If Beauvoir was as little interested in philosophy as the *Memoirs* claim, why did she pursue a graduate degree in philosophy rather than literature or some other discipline? If, on the other hand, her interest in philosophy was a passionate one, as other passages in the autobiographies imply, what philosophical subjects and methodologies and which philosophers interested her? Beauvoir's 1927 diary, where she explicitly discusses her intention of becoming a philosopher, defines a philosophical methodology, and identifies philosophical problems that will occupy her attention throughout her life, provides us for the first time with the means of answering these questions.

EARLY INFLUENCES ON BEAUVOIR'S PHILOSOPHY

Scholars interested in widening the exploration of influences on Beauvoir's philosophy beyond Sartre have focused on the influence of Husserl (Simons 1977, Bergoffen 1995), Kierkegaard and Heidegger (Lundgren-Gothlin 1996a, 1997), Hegel and Kojève's interpretation of Hegel's *Phenomenology* (Simons 1977, Lundgren-Gothlin 1996a), Marx (Simons 1977, 1995; Kruks 1990; Lundgren-Gothlin 1996a), Merleau-Ponty (Kruks 1990, Cataldi 1997), and Richard Wright (Simons ch. 11 above). Does the 1927 diary provide any evidence of early, pre-Sartrean influences on Beauvoir's later philosophy, including in *The Second Sex*? Which philosophers and writers did Beauvoir draw upon in her quest to make herself a philosopher? Is there evidence that Maurice Merleau-Ponty, whose friendship with Beauvoir is chronicled in her 1927 diary, was an important philosophical influence? Can the diary shed light on the larger historical question of the introduction of Husserl's phenomenology into France or on the origins of French existential phenomenology?

Beauvoir's study of philosophy began in 1926 at the École Normale Libre in Neuilly, under Mademoiselle Mercier, one of the first women in France to pass the graduate *agrégation* in philosophy. It was Mademoiselle Mercier who encouraged Beauvoir to pursue a degree in philosophy at the Sorbonne. Beauvoir's references to a wide range of writers in her 1927 diary reflect the influence of a rich intellectual tradition. A list of the quotations from the first few pages of the diary suggests the breadth of Beauvoir's knowledge of German philosophers and the French intellectual tradition: Alain, who may be best known as the philosophy teacher of Sartre and Simone Weil; the French poet, Paul Valéry; Schopenhauer, the German philosopher whose pessimistic philosophy focusing on the will is quoted at length in the diary; Lagneau, whose proclamation, "I have only the support of my absolute despair," Beauvoir affirms later in the diary; Henri Bergson, the leading French philosopher in the first decades of the twentieth century; Rudolph Eucken, a German philosopher of "activism"; the surrealist writer Louis Aragon; and

Nietzsche, whose *Will to Power* is quoted on the verso of the diary's second page:

> If our soul only once trembled with happiness and resonated like the strings of a lyre, all the eternities were necessary in order to provoke this sole event, and, in this sole moment of our affirmation, all eternity would be approved, delivered, justified and affirmed. (Beauvoir 1927, 2v)[1]

Although Beauvoir refers in the diary to her earlier loss of religious faith and faith in social "action" (a reference to her earlier passion for the *Équipes sociales* movement to undermine class divisions in French society, led by Robert Garric, a leftist Catholic and professor of literature at Neuilly), her continuing interest in mysticism and spirituality is evident in the sources of quotations in the first pages of her diary, dated April 17 and 18: the symbolist poet Stéphane Mallarmé; the Belgian symbolist writer Maurice Maeterlinck; the poet and writer Paul Claudel, whose mystical Catholicism Beauvoir describes as a profound early influence; the French writer Marcel Arland; the German lyric and spiritual poet Rainer Maria Rilke; the French Catholic novelist François Mauriac; the French novelist Alain-Fournier (Beauvoir 1927, 1–5). Beauvoir's diary also mentions André Gide, but not André Malraux.

In the entry for April 28, Beauvoir refers to her allegiance to "the cult of the self" of Maurice Barrès, a nationalist writer and poet, and of Charles Péguy, one of the leading modern Catholic writers in France and crusader for social justice and the ideal of spirituality in action. "It's still in this cult of the self that, at this moment, I will find the most resources because I sense my value and I'm happy to have it" (Beauvoir 1927, 21). In an entry for July 16, midway through the diary, where Beauvoir reviews her intellectual journey over the past eighteen months, she describes how her earlier allegiance to the cult of self has ended.

> I began with action, then the cult of the self for action, following Barrès and Péguy, then . . . I saw the illusion of all that and that life demanded nothing of me—how I am searching for an exigency but finding nothing of value, my despair, and the position where I am now: no longer waiting or hoping for anything, unable to either accept or refuse life. (Beauvoir 1927, 101)[2]

The despair at the loss of meaning evident in this passage marks a moment of Beauvoir's intense interest in the philosophy of Schopenhauer.

Following four pages of quotations from Schopenhauer on the meaninglessness of the past and of life that leads only to death, the fragmentation of the self, and love as only self-love and self-pity, Beauvoir defines a philosophical project on the themes of the "irrationality" of the "given [*donné*]" and "of life," "the impotence of analysis," and the "uselessness of life" (Beauvoir 1927, 54–55). Near the end of the diary, Beauvoir appeals to Péguy once again, in reaffirming her asceticism of the previous year.

> A true intellectual life, austere, implacable, which carries on, regardless. Do not allow myself to be absorbed by others. . . . Practice this asceticism which was so familiar to me last year. . . . And if I say "what good is all that?" I'll reply with Péguy. "It is not for the sake of virtue because we scarcely have any of that, it is not for the sake of duty because we have no love for that," but it is the profound law of my being, and the means of finding the peace that I long for. (Beauvoir 1927, 129–30)[3]

In an attempt to "find peace," Beauvoir returns to a notion of spiritual action that she had earlier disavowed.

The many references to writers, poets, and philosophers taken from the first entries of Beauvoir's 1927 diary demonstrate the rich intellectual context within which she began her philosophical investigations. They argue for a full analysis of the entries in Beauvoir's 1926–1930 diaries, as well as a broadening of the analysis of the influences shaping her work, not only beyond Sartre, but also beyond the confines of philosophy as a separate discipline, to include an intellectual tradition encompassing literature as well. In the present context we might, without being able to take on this extensive project, explore the influence of philosophy, in the narrow sense, asking in particular if the diary can shed light on the origins of the central philosophical themes of *The Second Sex* and on the origins of French existential phenomenology as a whole.

Of the existentialist philosophers, there is one reference to Nietzsche (cited above) and one to Pascal, to whom Beauvoir refers in defining her central philosophical concern with the search for meaning. "I know myself that there is only one problem and that it does not have a solution, because perhaps it has no sense; it is the one posed by Pascal, nearer to me Marcel Arland: I would like to believe in something—to encounter total exigency—to justify life; in brief, I would like God" (Beauvoir 1927, 62).[4] There is no mention of Kierkegaard or Jaspers, who were not well known in France at the time, or of Gabriel Marcel, whose *Metaphysical Journal* was published in 1927.

Bergson and a Descriptive Methodology

The diary provides evidence of the important, and largely unexplored, influence on Beauvoir of Henri Bergson, who in the 1920s was still the dominant figure in French philosophy. References to Bergson and his distinctive philosophical terminology are found throughout the 1927 diary. Beauvoir makes use of Bergson's concept of "presence," for example, in referring to philosophy imposing itself on one "as a living presence." Another Bergsonean concept in the diary is that of becoming and time consciousness, as in the following passage from August 4. "Oh! this perpetual and necessary flow of things and of ourselves! . . . Insane desire for the being who would be at the same time becoming" (Beauvoir 1927, 37–38, 143).[5] Bergson, in arguing against mechanistic determinism, describes free choice as springing spontaneously from one's whole personality, which is experienced as an indivisible process of becoming, united by the experience of duration and memory. Beauvoir makes prominent use of the concept of "becoming" [*devenir*] in the famous opening line of volume two of *The Second Sex*: "one is not born a woman, but becomes one [*devient*]."

There is a second element, in addition to free choice, in Beauvoir's concept of becoming a woman: it is social constructionism, i.e., the claim that gender is the result of childhood socialization. As Beauvoir explains in *The Second Sex*,

> no biological, psychic, economic destiny defines . . . the human female. . . . It is civilization as a whole that elaborates this product, halfway between the male and the eunuch, that one qualifies as feminine. Only the mediation of the other can constitute an individual as an *Other*. (Beauvoir 1949, 2:13)

Does this second element of Beauvoir's concept of becoming a woman in *The Second Sex* also find a source in Bergson's philosophy?

Although Beauvoir does not draw upon Bergson in defining the problem of the Other, which will be discussed below, his recognition of the centrality of the experience of time, duration, and memory in the creation of the self may contribute to Beauvoir's understanding of the importance of childhood experience in constructing a sense of oneself. In a diary entry dated September 5, for example, Beauvoir appeals to friendship and the surrounding memories they carry as a counter to the fragmentation of the self. "The dream, the memories, the joy of rediscovering everything at the instant that one believes that all is lost, the past which still lives and to which one offers this dreamt-of future, and which has become the present, the beauty of the evenings, of life, all this I've written to Zaza [a childhood friend]. Joy, joy! friendship as immense as my heart, that will never end." In another passage, Beauvoir reflects on the lingering effects of her Catholic upbringing in shaping her identity: "Catholicism of Mauriac, of Claudel, . . . how it's marked me and what a place there is for it in me!"(Beauvoir 1927, 159, 94).[6] Although she rejects the religious beliefs of her childhood, understanding the way that they shaped her life is part of defining her own identity, her self. As I have argued above, Beauvoir's description of the lingering effects of childhood on her consciousness marks an early difference between Beauvoirean and Sartrean existentialism. Not until after the publication of *The Second Sex* (1949), with its extended description of the social construction of gender difference in childhood, does Sartre, in *Saint Genet* (1952), begin to explore the effects of the early intervention of the Other on the becoming of consciousness.

Beauvoir employs another important Bergsonean concept, that of the "given" [*donné*] in the following diary passage where she defends her interest in a philosophy of existence. "[W]ith my intelligence alone I will try all of my life to advance as far as possible to the heart of the problem; but in accepting and living the given, without waiting to possess the absolute" (Beauvoir 1927, 72).[7] The Bergsonian concept of the given is significant for the central and unexamined place it occupies in the controversial biology chapter of *The Second Sex*, which is entitled "The Givens [*donnés*] of Biology" (a reference obscured in the English edition, where [*donné*] is translated as "data"). In the biology chapter, Beauvoir argues that a human perspective, and an ontological context, must be brought to the study of sexual difference, much as Bergson argues, in *Creative Evolution* (1911), that we must bring to the study of evolution, metaphysics, and what our intuition reveals of the creative force of life, which Bergson calls the *"élan vital"* (another Bergsonian expression found in *The Second Sex).*

A diary entry dated May 6 contains a reference to Bergson's concept of *"élan vital"* at the conclusion of a lengthy description of an experience of freedom, choice, and becoming. In this passage, which illustrates Beauvoir's use of a descriptive philosophical methodology, she describes an experience of falling in love with a fellow philosophy student, Barbier.

> This morning I experienced a strange moment the echo of which has not yet died away in me. I had just seen Barbier again, coming so spontaneously towards me. . . . He spoke to me of myself, of philosophy and literature with a genuine interest. And then . . . one instant I held in my hands an entirely new life. . . . Well! the past did not enchain me, a new passion blossomed in me, splendid, I loved him. . . . How to render that? It was not at all speculation, reasoning; nor dream, imagination; one instant it was. . . . My life is no longer a ready-made path on which already from the point where I have arrived I can discover everything and on which I need only place one foot after the other. This is a path not yet opened up, which my walk alone will create. . . . Yes, it's only by free decision, and thanks to the play of circumstances that the true self is revealed. I told Mlle Mercier, that for me a choice is never made, it is always being made; it's repeated each time that I'm conscious of it; how this is true! Well: this morning I chose Barbier. The horror of the definitive choice, is that it engages not only the self of today, but that of tomorrow which is why basically marriage is immoral. . . . One instant I was free and I lived [*vécu*] that. (Beauvoir 1927, 34–35, 35–36)[8]

This passage is interesting for several reasons: Beauvoir's methodology of describing her own lived experience, her focus on the existential themes of freedom and choice, and the interconnection of self and Other implied in the linking of freedom and choice with the experience of falling in love. The reference to Bergson, which comes at the end of the diary entry, is a reflection on the experience of self-discovery.

> It's very complicated. These possibles which are in me, it's necessary that little by little I kill off all but one; it's thus that I see life: a thou-

sand possibles in childhood, which fall little by little until on the last day there is no longer more than *one reality*, one has lived *one* life; but it is the *élan vital* of Bergson that I'm thinking of here, which divides, allowing tendency after tendency to fall away until only one is realized. (Beauvoir 1927, 37)[9]

The reference to one's choice as realizing "possibles" and her earlier reference to the "play of circumstances" suggest Beauvoir's early view of the compatibility of freedom and determinism, a position aligning her with both Leibniz and, through the concept of the "given," with Bergson.

Beauvoir's descriptive methodology of rendering an accurate account of her experience, evident in the May 6 entry, is particularly significant given its centrality in volume two of *The Second Sex*, entitled "Lived Experience" [*l'expérience vécue*], reflecting Beauvoir's methodological turn to a phenomenological description of women's concrete experience to challenge the myths of woman's nature constructed by male-defined science. Bergson's methodological focus on the "immediate givens [*donnés*] of consciousness" (as in his *Essai sur les donnés immédiates de la conscience*, 1889) has obvious affinities with phenomenology. Spiegelberg, in his history of the phenomenological movement, credits Bergson's philosophy as an important factor favoring the reception of phenomenology in France and reports that Husserl's reaction to first hearing of Bergson's philosophy of intuition in 1911 was to proclaim, "We are the true Bergsonians" (Spiegelberg 1982, 428).

Another source of influence on Beauvoir's use of a descriptive philosophical methodology might be William James. James's influence is suggested by the 1927 entry for April 20, which cites the diary of the French philosopher Maine de Biran and "the theory of emotions of William James" in reference to the claim that the "influence of the mind [*moral*] on the body is reciprocal" (Beauvoir 1927, 10).[10] Spiegelberg (1982, 63) discusses the influence of James's descriptive psychology, and his concept of the stream of consciousness, on Husserlian phenomenology. There might also be an influence of the Personalism movement; its focus, in the first decade of the twentieth century, on descriptions of consciousness makes it an important French philosophical precursor to existentialism. French Personalism brought with it a renaissance of interest in Leibniz, thanks to the work of the French Leibniz scholar and

Personalist Charles Renouvier, whose work Beauvoir would have consulted for her graduate thesis on Leibniz written in 1928–29.

In regard to Leibniz, there are intriguing references in Beauvoir's 1927 diary, suggesting that her interest in Leibniz's philosophy predates the assignment of her thesis topic. A diary entry for July 10, for example, suggests Leibniz's early relativist influence.

> I know that the laws of the mind are the same for all men. But it does not seem to me that there is only one way of judging sanely; that depends on the postulates that each has admitted either explicitly or implicitly; and the choice of these postulates is left to each one; it depends on his temperament, on his sensitivity, on this irreducible given that constitutes the individuality of each one. I ought to read Leibniz because I sense so vividly the principle of indiscernibles! I hate mechanism that, reducing quality to quantity, conjures away quality. . . . That's why I feel myself to be not phenomena but noumena, quality is the reflection of the noumena on the plane of experience. (Beauvoir 1927, 95–96)

Beauvoir thus refers to Leibniz in reflecting on the uniqueness of individuals and their varying perspectives on the world. A final, incomplete sentence in the same passage points to the existentialist reality that individuals, in the absence of the God, must create their own truth: "As soon as we truly think it's necessary to in some way create our truth" (Beauvoir 1927, 95–96).[11] These references would seem to suggest a possible Leibnizian influence on French phenomenological concern with the perspectival aspect of reality.

Jean Baruzi

There is another link with Leibniz suggested in the diary entry dated May 6: Beauvoir's mentor at the Sorbonne Jean Baruzi, for whom she wrote the essay on personality discussed in the *Memoirs*.

> I'm thinking again of Baruzi's course and of Schopenhauer: empirical character, intelligible character. Yes, it is only by a free decision, and thanks to the play of circumstances that the true self is discovered. (Beauvoir 1927, 35)[12]

Who is Baruzi? Might he have influenced Beauvoir's early use of a descriptive philosophical methodology and thus influenced her later contribution to French existential phenomenology? Jean Baruzi, who occupied the history of religion chair at the Collège de France from 1933 to 1951, taught a course at the Sorbonne in 1926–27 and 1927–28. He was a student of Bergson, a scholar of Leibniz's philosophy of religion and William James's psychology of religion, and the Catholic author of a controversial dissertation, *St. John of the Cross and the Problem of Mystical Experience* (1924). This influential text, Baruzi's existential-phenomenological description of religious anguish and the search for a truth not bounded by religious doctrine, was condemned by the French Thomists but may have inspired Etienne Gilson's existentialist reinterpretation of Aquinas as well as Bergson's work on mysticism.

Baruzi appears in Beauvoir's 1927 diary as her philosophical mentor. One of the first pages of the diary refers to Baruzi, "who attracts me this year by his scrupulous and profound faith, the intellectual ardor of his brilliant eyes, and his manner of living his thoughts to the very tips of his fingernails; he possesses an interior life." In contrast, Beauvoir characterizes Brunschvicg, the leading Sorbonne philosopher of the era and director in 1928–29 (when Baruzi was no longer teaching at the Sorbonne) of her thesis on Leibniz, as "zero": "Mr. Brunschvicg is perhaps a man of value but for me: 0." A few pages later in the diary, Beauvoir describes Baruzi's philosophy course, "where the austere and beautiful ideas give me a solemn and passionate fever." Beauvoir's reliance on Baruzi is evident in an entry midway through the diary, when, in planning her philosophical work, she declares her intention to "place [her]self in the hands of someone who criticizes and takes [her] seriously: Baruzi, G[eorgette] Lévy or Pontremoli [her fellow philosophy students]" (Beauvoir 1927, 9–10, 28, 91).[13]

Finally, in an entry near the end of the diary reflecting Beauvoir's interest in metaphysics and epistemology, Baruzi once again appears as her mentor.

> I know nothing, nothing; not only no answers but no presentable manner of posing the question. Scepticism, indifference are impossible, a religion is impossible for the moment—mysticism is tempting: but how will I know the value of a thought which leaves no place for thought? what can I lean on to reject or accept it, agree to spend two

years in reading, conversations, fragmentary meditations. I am going to work like a brute: I don't have a minute to lose. And neglect nothing: link up with Baruzi, do my homework, endeavor to know, to know. (Beauvoir 1927, 132–33)[14]

What was Baruzi's philosophical influence on Beauvoir? In drawing closer to Baruzi during his brief tenure at the Sorbonne could Beauvoir have gained access to Husserlean phenomenology?

Baruzi's interest in Leibniz and German philosophy gave him unusually broad contacts with German philosophers after World War I, which would have provided opportunities to become acquainted with Husserlean phenomenology (*see* Vieillard-Baron 1985). Spiegelberg makes no mention of Baruzi in his history of the phenomenological movement, although he remarks on the strong appeal of phenomenology in France among non-Thomist Catholics (Spiegelberg 1982, 429). Baruzi employs a descriptive methodology in *Saint Jean de la Croix*, with reference to the Bergsonean concepts of the "given" [*donné*] and "mystical becoming." There are suggestions of the influence of phenomenology in Baruzi's references to the project of determining whether the "phenomenon" of mysticism issues from an "irreducible experience," a determination Baruzi describes as inaccessible to sociological, historical, or psychological method. A reference to Husserlean phenomenology also seems apparent in Baruzi's description of his quest to discover "the lived experience" [*l'expérience vécue*] of the mystic (Baruzi 1924, xxiii, xxiv, xxvi). In his 1925 presentation to the French Philosophical Society, "Saint John of the Cross and the Problem of the Noetic Value [*la valeur noétique*] of Mystical Experience," Baruzi opens with a reference to the "phenomenology" of mystical experience. Does Baruzi provide a previously unrecognized, if minor, role in introducing Husserlean phenomenology to France, which, according to Spiegelberg, dates from the 1926 publication of the texts by Hering, Groethuysen, and Shestov (Spiegelberg appendixes, chart II)?

The answer is not clear. Baruzi's first direct reference to Husserl's phenomenology apparently does not come until his December 1926 inaugural lecture, "The Problem of Salvation in the Religious Thought of Leibniz," at the Collège de France, which may well have been influenced by the three texts on Husserlean phenomenology published earlier that year. But in this lecture Baruzi makes more than a passing reference to Husserl, apparently arguing for a phenomenological reduction. In defending the study of Leibniz, and his "critical method," by an historian of religion, Baruzi argues that Leibniz's notion of salvation, once subjected to the severe investigation of "the phenomenology of Husserl," might present us with one of Husserl's bare "essences."

> [Leibniz's] metaphysics . . . is part of . . . the very history of religion and, in the meaning given it by Husserl's phenomenology, of these essences which it will be, subsequently, after decomposition and analysis, a question of penetrating and knowing. Who says that "salvation" according to Leibniz will not present us, after some severe investigations, with one of these bare essences [*essences dépouillées*]? (Baruzi 1985, 123)

Baruzi's texts from 1924 and 1925 and especially his 1926 lecture provide evidence of his familiarity with and utilization of Husserlean phenomenology. Given Baruzi's interest in phenomenology and his role as Beauvoir's philosophical mentor in 1927, the question arises of whether Baruzi introduced Beauvoir to Husserlean phenomenology.

Beauvoir's autobiography describes her early enthusiasm for phenomenology. "I was enthused by the novelty, the richness of phenomenology: never had I seemed to approach so close to the truth." But in her autobiography she credits Sartre, who, according to her account, first learned of phenomenology from Raymond Aron, with first introducing it to her in the early 1930s (Beauvoir 1960, 231, 157, 215). Could Beauvoir have misrepresented the date of her own interest in phenomenology just as she did her own early interest in philosophy? Beauvoir's 1927 diary makes no mention of phenomenology or the concept of intentionality, or of Edmund Husserl, whose texts were not translated into French until 1931. Nor is there any mention of Hering, Groethuysen, or Shestov, whose texts, published in 1926, provided the first discussions of Husserlean phenomenology. Gurvitch's important article on phenomenology did not appear until 1928 and Levinas's book on Husserl's phenomenology not until 1930. Scheler was not translated into French until 1928, and Heidegger's influential essay "What is Metaphysics" was not published in France until 1931.

Nor does a first reading of Beauvoir's diary from 1928 to 1929, when she was completing her graduate work in philosophy at the Sorbonne, show any reference to Husserl's February 1929 Sorbonne lectures, which were later published as his *Cartesian Meditations*. There is no indication in the diaries that Beauvoir had any direct knowledge of Husserl's phenomenology, but is there evidence of Husserl's indirect influence? The influence of Husserlean phenomenology is suggested in her description of the experience of falling for Barbier and, as we shall see, in Beauvoir's bringing emotion and everyday, concrete experience into philosophy. The 1927 diary also suggests a Husserlean influence on the theme of the critique of reason evident in the 1927 diary; Beauvoir's later texts, including *When Things of the Spirit Come First* (1935–37), where the short stories are united by the phenomenological task of peeling away the layers of myths and preconceived ideas to confront the things of reality themselves; and her critique of scientific knowledge in *The Second Sex* (*see* Fallaize 1997).

Husserl, according to Spiegelberg, deemed Descartes and Kant "the two greatest pioneers" of the epistemological reduction and the critique of knowledge. One of Husserl's innovations, according to Spiegelberg, was his espousal of Kant, who had been rejected by Brentano as a speculative idealist. Husserl saw Kant, the protagonist of the critique of reason, laying the groundwork for Husserl's own, much more radical, critique. Phenomenology, as a "rigorous science," would "undertake the descriptive clarification of the immediate phenomena" that had been neglected by positivist science (Spiegelberg 1982, 107). Beauvoir's project of radically questioning everything (in the following passage from late in the diary), which might be read as simply Cartesian, could, given Baruzi's influence, also refer to this Husserlean project and the phenomenological reduction. "Write to G[eorgette] Lévy of my will to call everything into question because I believe that is a duty, to rethink every postulate, to even renounce that in which I believe" (Beauvoir 1927, 142–43). In a move also pointing to the influence of Baruzi's appropriation of Husserl for the study of mysticism, Beauvoir describes the critique of reason as opening the door to mysticism: "all explanatory philosophy confronts us with a residue, reason yields only the human, necessity of mysticism . . . it's necessary to reread and meditate on Kant, Bergson and Descartes" (Beauvoir 1927, 111–12).[15]

The combination of Kant, Descartes, and Bergson seems to point to the influence of Husserl's critique of reason, as does the following passage, where Beauvoir contrasts her position with that of her new friend and fellow philosophy student Maurice Merleau-Ponty.

> [H]e begins with an act of faith in reason—I believe with Kant that one can not attain the noumenal world. [B]eing does not equal substance—there is being in the order of the phenomenon—I said, "I believe in substance," as I said, "I believe in causality." I understood "I visualize things under the order of substance as well as that of causality" but that is not to say that there is a substance—to separate reason from the noumena with Kant and Bergson, while you assume that reason can seize the noumena. (Beauvoir 1927, 111–12)

This passage, with its interesting reference to the ontological question of the being of phenomena, continues

> Ponty rests his [philosophy] on faith in reason, I on the ineffectiveness of reason—who proves that Descartes prevails over Kant? I persist in my Sorbonne exercises—use reason, and you'll end up with residues and irrationals. (111–12)[16]

Thus it is from her studies at the Sorbonne, and almost certainly Baruzi, that Beauvoir draws her critique of reason. Since it is likely that Baruzi, in his Sorbonne lectures, discussions with Beauvoir, and critiques of her work, mentioned phenomenology and Husserl, this research also suggests that Beauvoir's autobiographical account crediting Sartre with introducing her to phenomenology might be a misrepresentation. Indeed, one wonders if Beauvoir might instead have had a hand in exposing Sartre to Husserlean phenomenology, or at least in preparing the philosophical ground for his own later discovery of Husserl. The evidence of Baruzi's influence also suggests the necessity for a reassessment of the historical development and interaction of atheistic and theistic existentialism in France. Where previously Sartrean atheistic existentialism might have been seen as unmediated by influence from theistic existentialism, the 1927 diary suggests the reverse.

Merleau-Ponty

When looking back at the academic year in July 1927, Beauvoir records "the taste for and familiarity with philosophy" (Beauvoir 1927, 87) as one of the year's conquests, which she credits to the influence of her new friend Maurice Merleau-Ponty. In one of the final diary entries, dated September 7, Beauvoir writes,

> Rereading this notebook, I understand my year; oscillation between the discouragement brought to me by love, the only great human thing where I have felt the nothingness of everything human—and the desire to search, the confused hope that there is something to do. Ponty hasn't changed me so much. He gave me the force to affirm the second tendency. (Beauvoir 1927, 159)[17]

Scholars have noted the similarities in the philosophies of Merleau-Ponty and Beauvoir, in particular their notions of embodied subjectivity and situated freedom, which differentiate them philosophically from Sartre. Does the diary provide evidence that Merleau-Ponty, during the early years of his friendship with Beauvoir, shaped the direction of her philosophical search as he encouraged her in its pursuit?

Merleau-Ponty's philosophy, as it appears in Beauvoir's 1927 diary, has little resemblance to his later position. In the diary, Merleau-Ponty attacks her for relying on emotion and tries to bring her back to Catholicism. In defending herself against Merleau-Ponty, Beauvoir defines her own philosophy.

> Well, Ponti [*sic*] is right. I do not have the right to despair. I accepted that despair was justified, but it needs to be demonstrated. . . . *But*: if trying to think without passion, I say: "I have no reason for choosing to despair," I also say, "I have no reason to move towards Catholicism rather than in any other direction." . . . And, on the contrary, it's because Catholicism appeals too much to my heart that my reason defies it: tradition, heritage, memories lead me to adhere to it. . . . raised otherwise, Merleau-Ponti [*sic*], would your reason, stripped of all passion, attract you to Catholicism? (Beauvoir 1927, 105–6)

This passage reveals Beauvoir's early critique of philosophy as pure reason, pointing instead to its social and biographical context. Beauvoir welcomes Merleau-Ponty's enthusiasm for philosophy without sharing his fondness for metaphysical absolutes. "Ponti [*sic*] says 'better to sacrifice becoming rather than being'; I say that seeing a flaw in a system, I want to sacrifice the entire system" (Beauvoir 1927, 110).[18]

Instead of being swayed by Merleau-Ponty's conservative arguments, Beauvoir rejects his appeal to faith in both Catholicism and reason.

> I realized that I had to search, but not in Catholicism. I was frightened by my inconsistencies, then in deepening them I saw all the same that my philosophy was not so up in the air as it seems—Ponti [*sic*] rests his on faith in reason, I on the powerlessness of reason. (Beauvoir 1927, 112)

Thus, in meeting Merleau-Ponty's challenge, Beauvoir claims a modernist position, affirming the process of becoming and the critique of reason. Beauvoir also affirms, against Merleau-Ponty, the value of emotion, as she tries to accommodate herself to the cold rationality of philosophy.

> Oh! tired, irritated, sure of arriving at nothing through this desperate appeal to philosophy—and yet I *want* it, I owe it to myself to do it. . . . To reason coldly. Ah! there's a lot to do to make myself a philosopher! (Beauvoir 1927, 116)[19]

The gendered context of their confrontations seems to stem from Merleau-Ponty's irritation at coming in third in the philosophy exams behind two women, Simone Weil and Beauvoir. After their first meeting following the exams at the end of June, Beauvoir describes him as "so vexed at being beaten by me, but so friendly (superficially I'm afraid and for the wrong reasons in which vanity plays a part)." Later, Beauvoir, appealing to her identity as a woman, affirms the value of feeling and sensibility: "And so, my friends, you do not like girls but consider that not only do they have a reason to satisfy but a heavy heart to restrain—and in that respect I want to remain a woman, more masculine yet in the brain, more feminine in sensibility. (Besides everyone recognizes in approaching me that I am not like other girls. Oh Ponti [*sic*], as you told me so nicely . . . !)" (Beauvoir 1927, 85, 107).[20]

Exploring the value of emotions in her experience and differentiating her position from that of Merleau-Ponty, once again as a woman, Beauvoir defends a notion of embodiment that anticipates both her own mature philosophy and that of Merleau-Ponty.

Thursday, July 28. I envy this straightforward, strong young man who lives a tranquil life with a tenderly beloved mother and who searches calmly for a truth that he hopes to find. . . . "Aristocrat" he calls me? it's true. I can't get rid of this idea that I am alone, in a world apart, being present at the other as at a spectacle. . . . Dreams are forbidden him. Ah! As for me I have riches there that I do not want to get rid of. Drama of my affections, pathos of life. . . . Certainly, I have a more complicated, more nuanced sensibility than his and a more exhausting power of love. These problems that he lives with his brain, I live them with my arms and my legs. . . . I don't want to lose all of that. (Beauvoir 1927, 126)[21]

Beauvoir's argument, in the context of a 1927 debate with Merleau-Ponty, for "living" a philosophical problem not only with one's brain, but with one's arms and legs, anticipates Merleau-Ponty's later concept of the lived body, a concept that thus may reflect Beauvoir's early influence.

As we have seen, the 1927 diary, written two years before Beauvoir's meeting with Sartre, provides evidence that her early philosophy was influenced by a wide variety of philosophers, foremost among them Schopenhauer, Kant, Descartes, Leibniz, and, perhaps most importantly, Henri Bergson and Jean Baruzi, the latter a philosophical mentor who introduced her to the descriptive phenomenological methodology that would characterize her work for the next twenty years, beginning with *When Things of the Spirit Come First* (1935–37) and *She Came to Stay* (1943), as well as *America Day by Day* (1948), and *The Second Sex* (1949). Our analysis of the 1927 diary also challenges the assumption that Merleau-Ponty originated the philosophical concepts he shares with Beauvoir, providing evidence, instead, that Beauvoir's critique of reason and her defense of emotion and embodiment might have influenced Merleau-Ponty's later concept of the lived body. But what about Sartre? Does the 1927 diary, which predates their relationship, define any of the philosophical themes later identified with Sartrean existentialism? What are the central philosophical questions, problems, and themes of the 1927 diary? Can it provide grounds for differentiating Beauvoir's philosophy from that of Sartre, or shed light on the question of influence? It is to these questions that we now turn.

NOTHINGNESS, DESPAIR, AND THE PURSUIT OF BEING

The year 1927 was one of personal crisis and transformation for Beauvoir, as she left behind the Catholic girls schools of her youth and the secure but stifling confines of family relationships, including an obsessive love for her cynical cousin Jacques that had dominated her life the previous winter, to enter the male world of secular philosophy and the Sorbonne. Beauvoir describes her search for her life's direction in an appeal to a friend, early in the diary.

> I am intellectually very alone and very lost at the entry to my life . . . looking for a direction. I sense that I have value, that there is something for me to do and to say . . . but my thought turns in the void: where should it be directed? how to break this solitude? what to achieve with my intelligence? . . . I am in a great distress at the moment to decide on my life. Can I be satisfied with what one calls happiness? or ought I walk towards this absolute that attracts me? (Beauvoir 1927, 41–42)[22]

Central themes of her 1927 diary reflect the turmoil created by a loss of faith and family ties: the search for a justification for her life and the struggle against despair, the search for self and the desire for love.

A frustrated yearning for an absolute justification for her life, for "being," leads to despair; "These miserable efforts for being!" she writes in her diary entry for May 19, "at its very base, masked by these daily diversions, the same void!" Beauvoir's concept of daily diversions as masking the "void" is significant in anticipating *Being and Nothingness*, where part one is entitled "The Problem of Nothingness." Sartre describes consciousness, the for-itself, as characterized by nothingness, frustrated in its longing for the plenitude of being. Beauvoir's references to the "void" and "nothingness" run throughout the 1927 diary, as in the entry for July 7, where her sense of the ultimate futility of human action undermines her celebration of her success on the competitive philosophy exams. "So! A fine success in life, I thought! Ah! void! nothingness, vanity" (Beauvoir 1927, 55, 87).[23] With the sense of her place in the universe in doubt, the ultimate groundlessness and contingency of her projects make the academic success, which had always been a source of pride for her, seem empty. No longer simply a sign of her progress along a path defined by God, her worldly success has become a source of despair, a reminder of her loss of direction.

The sense of nothingness that figures so prominently in Beauvoir's descriptions of her experiences in the diary extends to her sense of self.

> [April 20]: I would like to understand how I can isolate myself thus from my dearest memories and my closest desires—I often experienced that already: some mild afternoon, some moving conversation, I attribute them to an other. . . . They issue from a fiction. I can not immerse myself in them: they are not *my* memories. (Beauvoir 1927, 11)

This detachment from her memories means that the appeal to memory offered by Henri Bergson as a solution to the problem of the fragmentation of the self is inadequate or unreliable.

> [April 28]: My past is behind me like a thing gone from me; on which I can no longer act and which I regard with the eyes of a stranger, a thing in which I have no part at all. (Beauvoir 1927, 18)[24]

But while Beauvoir's description of the experience of radical detachment differentiates her from Bergson, it anticipates Sartre, for whom taking negative attitudes with respect to one's self, including the self that one has been in the past, is fundamental.

Beauvoir's early focus on the emptiness of the human pursuit of being also anticipates key philosophical themes in Sartre's *Being and Nothingness*, with its long introductory section entitled "The Pursuit of Being." Frederick Olafson writes that

> Sartre's whole philosophy can be seen as an attempt to describe a mode of being—human being—whose essence is just this aspiration [to found one's own individual being in a rational necessity of some sort], which he thinks is necessarily doomed to failure. . . . It is also the key to his moral philosophy, the fundamental imperative of which is to recognize and accept this unresolvable contradiction that defines human nature. (Olafson 1967, 288)

Olafson's reference to the "unresolvable contradiction" in Sartre's philosophy bears a striking resemblance to Beauvoir's reference, in the following 1927 diary passage, to her "paradoxical situation" and the frustrated desire to be useful.

> [April 30] Basically, I am in a paradoxical situation: I sense my intelligence, what positive power it could have; I would love to do something. . . . Only, these very qualities that demand to serve show me what an illusion it is to claim to be useful for something. (Beauvoir 1927, 24)[25]

The desire to put one's talents and energy to work in service of something in which one can wholeheartedly believe is frustrated by the recognition that no such absolute end exists. It is this frustrated desire to serve, to be useful, that Sartre captures later in his description of man as a "useless passion."

Beauvoir had lost her faith in God some time earlier; now the study of philosophy, undertaken seriously only the previous year, presented her with the radical implications of that loss.

> What has this year brought me intellectually? a serious philosophical formation that has . . . sharpened my critical spirit, alas! . . . I have everywhere noted only our powerlessness to establish anything in the realm of knowledge as in that of ethics. (Beauvoir 1927, 11–12)[26]

The absence of epistemological and moral foundations is a sign of our impotence, hence, a source of frustration. Without such foundations, how can we fulfill our desire to be of service, to put our energies to use? Where should we direct our talents and passions? How can we know that we are directing them wisely, if we have neither absolute knowledge nor definitive moral values as ends?

Beauvoir's realization of the impossibility of her desire for an absolute leaves her searching for a philosophical justification for her actions.

> There is nothing in which I believe. That is a terrible thing to have to admit. Not even in myself. I can love . . . and act on my love: that is what permits me to be alive, passionate. But I have no control of love, and as soon as it ceases, I have nothing to cling to. I hate dilettantism, and isn't it in dilettantism that I ought to end up logically? how am I so far from the skeptics that I detest? (Beauvoir 1927, 27)

Beauvoir rejects the moral relativism of "dilettantism," refusing to abandon the search for an objective standard for guiding and judging one's conduct. Ruled by her passions, since her reason has no grounds on which to rule, one has nothing "to cling to" when these unruly passions dissipate. The result is despair.

> [September 4] Again this crushing anguish: The metaphysical anguish of man alone in the unknown. How does one not go crazy? There are days when I cry from fear, when I cry from ignorance; and then I take myself in hand, I say to myself "get to work"; but alas! I know well that I will die without knowing! (Beauvoir 1927, 157)[27]

Fear joins ignorance as a source of despair, fear of being alone, cut off from the comfort of friends and family unable to share her philosophical quest, and fear of living a life ultimately bereft of meaning.

BAD FAITH

Given the depth of Beauvoir's despair, it may not come as a surprise that she struggled with the temptation to flee despair in self-deception, which Beauvoir, in her first novel, *When Things of the Spirit Come First* ([1935–37] 1982, 210), and Sartre, in *Being and Nothingness* (1943), would later term "bad faith." The following April 30 entry from Beauvoir's 1927 diary reveals an envy of those able to escape anguish and doubt.

> There are beings whom I esteem and love . . . who possess at least some convictions to which they cling: they build their lives on them; and on this solidly established plan, they have only to allow their lives to open out. I felt in awakening a short while ago how much I would like to get up hastily on these gray mornings and walk, tranquil, ardent, towards a peaceful task that I believed useful and that one had only to complete well. . . . I felt ashamed for my lack of certitudes; for not having figured out "how to live"; for being egoist. Yes, I suffered last night for being not at all as they are, and as I could perhaps be. (Beauvoir 1927, 23–24)[28]

Beauvoir envies those able to escape the doubt and anguish troubling her. She envies their belief that one's life follows a given path, that it has meaning and purpose in some absolute sense. This is the origin of bad faith, the yearning to flee the exigencies of existence, the uncertainties of contingency and nothingness, by hiding in an illusory absolute.

As the passage continues, Beauvoir's envy is counteracted by a courageous determination to face life without illusions. She moves beyond her shameful recognition of her inadequacies in the eyes of her friends, laying the grounds for an ethic of authenticity.

> Basically, it's ridiculous to still allow myself to be bothered by the certainty of others. I can not stop myself from envying them because it seems that there is something more complete in faith and happiness than there is in doubt, disquietude. But I *know* well, however, that their God is not. . . . No, truly; that which I love above all, is not ardent faith . . . it's the broken élans, the searches, the desires, it is the ideas above all, the intelligence and criticism, the weariness, the flaws, those beings who can not allow themselves to be duped and who struggle to live despite their lucidity. (Beauvoir 1927, 26)[29]

Beauvoir's contrast of the fullness of faith with the negativity ("broken élans," "weariness," and "flaws") of critical consciousness anticipates Sartre's characterization of consciousness and bad faith in the important second half of part one of *Being and Nothingness*. Despite the attractions of being, Beauvoir's admiration is for those who "cannot allow themselves to be duped," those who struggle against despair to maintain their lucidity.

Debra Bergoffen, in an analysis of *Ethics of Ambiguity*, identifies two important philosophical differences between Beauvoir and Sartre centering on their different understandings of bad faith. Sartre, in *Being and Nothingness*, sees bad faith as grounded ontologically in the intentionality of consciousness. Our consciousness, which is always (of) the world, reveals the world to us, at the same time as it reveals the gulf, our freedom, that separates us from being. For Sartre, our frustrated desire to be being, leads us inevitably to the attempt to flee the anxiety and separation and to deny our freedom in bad faith. Beauvoir also defines consciousness as intentionality, but she then "pauses," as Bergoffen points out, "to distinguish between two moments of intentionality, the moment of disclosure and the moment of the object disclosed" (Bergoffen 1997, 181). The first moment of intentionality, the moment of the disclosure of being, unlike the second, does not result in frustration.

Desiring the disclosure of the object, consciousness is rewarded for its curiosity with the joys of discovery.

> In this expression of its desire, consciousness forgoes the bad faith project of forgetting that it reveals the objects it desires. It recalls its delight in disclosing the object of its desire. In order to live the complexity of its desire, it desires the tensions bad faith would escape. (Bergoffen 1997, 182)

So Sartre, focusing on the second intentional moment of desiring to be being, sees bad faith as ontologically grounded, while Beauvoir, focusing on the first moment of desiring to disclose being, presents an alternative to bad faith in the joys of disclosure. Both Bergoffen (1997, 76–93) and Lundgren-Gothlin (1996a, 161) characterize Beauvoir's description of the "conversion" of the failed desire of being into a desire for the joys of disclosure of the phenomenal world and of the self, through an existential bracketing of the "will to be" analogous to Husserlean reduction, as a mark of Beauvoir's philosophical difference from Sartre. Lundgren-Gothlin (1997) traces Beauvoir's concept of disclosure to Heidegger, identifying further evidence that her appropriation of the phenomenological tradition was not mediated by Sartre.

But if bad faith is not ontologically necessary, what is the ground of its appeal? Bergoffen argues that

> unlike Sartre who links anxiety and freedom ontologically, Beauvoir links them historically. Bad faith is one of the ways we express our nostalgia for the securities of childhood. (Bergoffen 1997, 182)

The 1927 diary confirms Bergoffen's observation that Beauvoir locates the source of bad faith in a nostalgia for childhood, as the following diary entry dated July 10 indicates.

> Mademoiselle Mercier is trying to convert me; she speaks to me of Father Beaussard who would like to see me and I'm thinking of the remark of G[eorgette] Lévy [Beauvoir's friend and fellow philosophy student]. "You will be tempted that way"; it's true. This morning . . . I passionately desired to be the girl who takes communion at morning mass and walks in a serene certainty. Catholicism of Mauriac, of Claudel . . . how it's marked me and what place there is in me for it!

and yet I know that I will know it no longer; I do not desire to believe: an act of faith is the most despairing act there is and I want my despair to at least keep its lucidity, I do not want to lie to myself. (Beauvoir 1927, 94)[30]

Beauvoir's linking of faith with the temptation "to lie to myself" provides key elements in the concept of bad faith that is central to Beauvoir's later philosophy and to Sartre's as well. But the passage also reflects a philosophical difference in their understandings of childhood, which marks an area of Beauvoir's later philosophical influence on Sartre. An April 28, 1927, diary entry contains another reference to a nostalgia for childhood, a desire to still be "the awestruck child that I was a year ago" able to bring to her work "the infinity of a love and a devotion" (Beauvoir 1927, 17).[31] But, as we have seen from the July 10 entry, Beauvoir vows to resist these nostalgic desires at the root of bad faith, thus affirming the power of choice.

Beauvoir's discussion of bad faith in her 1927 diary also provides us with insight into certain problematic features of this concept as it appears in her later texts. Terry Keefe (1983) has identified what he terms a puzzling ambiguity in Beauvoir's concept of bad faith, where it tends to be confused with the problem of coherence and noncontradiction. This confusing association becomes clearer if Beauvoir's concept of bad faith is traced not to Sartre's discussion in *Being and Nothingness*, but to her own much earlier formulation of the problem of bad faith in the 1927 diary, where an alternative to bad faith lies in the construction of a unified, authentic self. For example, in the diary entry cited above, on being bothered by the certainty of others, Beauvoir writes, "But me, what am I? my unity comes from no principle, not even from any emotion to which I could subordinate everything: it is made only within my self" (Beauvoir 1927, 26).[32] Where for Sartre, any appeal to identity is a bad faith attempt to evade the negativity of the for-itself, for Beauvoir, the disclosure of self, as a joyous disclosure of being, can be an authentic alternative to the nostalgic appeal of bad faith. But it raises the question of how to unify a set of disparate feelings and interests. Not being duped means being true to one's experience rather than seeking refuge in a false ideal. Beauvoir's turn to philosophy in search of an answer raises other problems, as we shall see, as she struggles to reconcile her "woman's heart" with the cold rationality of philosophy.

PHILOSOPHY AND THE SEARCH FOR SELF

Beauvoir's turn to philosophy and the disclosure of being is part of her search for a self and her effort to reconstruct a system of beliefs undermined by critical consciousness: "Mademoiselle Mercier yesterday spoke in a very profound fashion . . . of the horror of ruined syntheses for those who lack the force to rebuild them. It's necessary that I rebuild." "Too many diverse syntheses equally understood, oblige me to construct my own." This entails moving beyond cynicism and criticism. Once one has "destroyed the idols" of faith, one must discover "in oneself a profound call." She is determined to take charge of her own life, which means creating a meaning uniting disparate elements. "I want to live. I must therefore be able to live. In order to do that it's necessary that I make *my* unity." What she asks of life is to "realize" herself, to discover "the law of [her] being." Establishing the "profound unity of my thought," she writes, is the only way to avoid being the "plaything of my capricious desires" (Beauvoir 1927, 48, 62, 50, 48, 49, 51–52).[33]

In this search for self, one must "be sincere" and not "limited by a rigid ideal." Reminded of the full range of her emotions, her silliness as well as her intellectual ardor, Beauvoir rejects as inaccurate a "solemn image of myself," despite the attractions of asceticism. She vows to avoid an "artificial unity," confident that she can discover "a strong unity of [herself] underlying this apparent dispersion" and "establish a hierarchy" where she might "recognize herself" and find a home base from which "to stray." She vows to use "this diary to recount [her] experiences" however "varied and even absurd" and to pair it with a work of thought marked by a "strong, detached, and disdainful judgment." Her diary thus becomes a tool for self-discovery and understanding through the description of her experience, the "states [of consciousness she's] lived through," inspiring her to believe in her ability to undertake a serious work (Beauvoir 1927, 52–53).[34]

In this search for self, Beauvoir discovers once again the joys of disclosing being, which, as Bergoffen has noted, counteract the anguished temptation to bad faith. Reconstructing the philosophical basis of her self allows Beauvoir to transform her "absolute despair" into grounds for joy.

> Lagneau's saying is beautiful "I have only the support of my absolute
> despair"; I would want no other motto. On this despair I will raise

my joy; I will surmount the inexplicable. Courageously each day, to reconstruct everything. . . . as long as I don't abdicate. (Beauvoir 1927, 64)

In response to cynics, she defends her turn to the positive as an inner law.

My self is sufficient for imposing laws on myself. I sense that I *must* walk in this direction. I will do so. (Beauvoir 1927, 64)[35]

Beauvoir's constructive alternative to despair and bad faith lies in a turn toward a description of her own experience as the foundation of life's meaning.

I know myself that there is only one problem and that it does not have a solution, because perhaps it has no sense. . . . I would like to believe in something—to encounter total exigency—to justify life; in brief, I would like God. Once this is said, I will not forget it. But knowing that this unattainable noumenal world exists where alone could be explained to me why I live, in the phenomenal world which is not for all that so negligible, I will construct my life. I will take myself as an end. (Beauvoir 1927, 62)

Noting her method of deducing a philosophical system from the premises revealed by her friends, she asks "but what are *my* premises?" (Beauvoir 1927, 62).[36] The effort to unify herself has become an effort to define the premises of her own philosophical position.

Beauvoir's attraction to philosophy is evident early in the diary, where she describes her attraction to a fellow philosophy student, Barbier, because a relationship with him represents the possibility, ridiculed by her cynical cousin Jacques, of developing her own philosophy.

There is the serious possibility, austerity, philosophy, Barbier: oh! his strong attraction, my need to realize what I sense in myself; to do something, to believe in something. My intellectual passions, my philosophical seriousness! Things Jacques can reverse with a smile: naturally one can show the vanity of everything, in terms of intelligence; but what if it imposes itself upon one as a living presence? Jacques would say, and I as well, I've said it on numerous occasions when I resemble him—: what good is it to dedicate one's life to philosophy, knowing that one will find nothing? But if I love this vain research? No! I refuse! I have only *one* life and many things to say. [Jacques] will not deprive me of my life. (Beauvoir 1927, 37–38)[37]

This passage is particularly interesting for Beauvoir's description of philosophy as an intellectual passion that reflects a need within herself, a love whose loss would be as though she had been deprived of her life.

As we've seen in the discussion of Merleau-Ponty, Beauvoir records "the taste for and familiarity of philosophy" as one of the year's conquests. Late in the diary, describing her intellectual development to Pontrémoli, a friend whom she has described as sharing an "understanding of literature and philosophy," Beauvoir recounts her turn to philosophy. "I wrote to [Pontrémoli] . . . telling him my history, my initial ecstasy of life, then my despair before a life without meaning, my desire to die, the harshness of my friendships, and finally my effort to find [meaning], my act of faith in philosophy" (Beauvoir 1927, 90, 142).[38] Belying the claims in the *Memoirs* of Beauvoir's primary interest in literature, the 1927 diary suggests that literature takes second place to philosophy at this time in her life. But her interest in literature is far from insignificant, as is evidenced by her interest in shaping a methodology that combines philosophy and literature, later exemplified in her novel *She Came to Stay* (the subject of Merleau-Ponty's 1945 article "Metaphysics and the Novel") and defended in her 1946 essay "Literature and Metaphysics."

Making herself a philosopher, Beauvoir must make philosophy her own, incorporating her passions as well as her reason. She describes her project of combining literature with philosophy, as she tries to integrate passion and reason in philosophy itself, using a fictional narrative to link together philosophical meditations.

> I must work on a work in which I believe. . . . To write "essays on life" which would not be a novel, but philosophy, linking them together vaguely with a fiction. But the thought would be the essential thing and I would be searching to find the truth, not to express it, to describe the search for truth. (Beauvoir 1927, 54–55)

As the diary nears its conclusion, Beauvoir's dedication to philosophy has become unmistakable:

[July 28] Oh! I see my life clearly now . . . a passionate, frantic search. . . . I didn't know that one could dream of death by metaphysical despair; sacrifice everything to the desire to know; live only to be saved. I didn't know that every system is an ardent, tormented thing, an effort of life, of being, a drama in the full sense of the word and that it does not engage only the abstract intelligence. But I know it now, and that I can no longer do anything else. (Beauvoir 1927, 133–34)[39]

The search for self and the philosophical quest for meaning are united by Beauvoir's descriptive philosophical methodology, which draws on Bergsonean and phenomenological traditions to incorporate the passion of lived experience into philosophy. In the 1927 diary Beauvoir records her growing philosophical interest in the problems of her own life, an interest that leads her to define philosophy as her life's work and the problems arising from her own life as her focus. Those problems, and the central theme of her work for the next two decades, concern relations with others. In a 1927 diary entry dated May 28 comparing the love of others with the love of God, Beauvoir makes clear her intention that love, and the problem of setting limits to love, should be the subject of her graduate thesis in philosophy; "even for the most beloved there is a measure [of love] since it is not God. In fact, perhaps not . . . I'll deepen this for my *diplôme*" (Beauvoir 1927, 68). On July 7, Beauvoir writes,

It's necessary to study very profoundly the questions that interest me. There is this subject of "love" which is so fascinating and of which I've traced the broad lines; it would be necessary to start from there . . . and then as an easier but related problem friendship—its dangers, the nature of the education that it brings, in brief how souls can act one upon the other—It would be necessary to have the courage to write not in order to display ideas but to discover them, not in order to clothe them artistically but to make them live. The courage to believe in them. (Beauvoir 1927, 92)[40]

Philosophy is clearly not a game or a matter of simply critiquing or applying the ideas of others.

Rereading her diary, Beauvoir defines her central philosophical theme, one that will recur throughout her later work as the problem of the Other:

> [July 10] I must rework my philosophical ideas . . . go deeper into the problems that have appealed to me. . . . The theme is almost always this opposition of self and other that I have felt since beginning to live. Now is the time to work out a synthesis of it. Foreign influences are set aside, as are all concerns with writing style. I will write my work in my own style seeking only to express well what I sense. (Beauvoir 1927, 95)[41]

In identifying in 1927 the philosophical theme of the opposition of self and Other, two years before her first meeting with Sartre, Beauvoir originates a theme central not only to her first published novel, *She Came to Stay* (1943), and to *The Second Sex* with its description of woman as Other, but to Sartre's *Being and Nothingness* (1943) as well. But, as we shall see below, this theme, arising for Beauvoir not from within a solipsistic context as it does for Sartre but from within a context of intimate personal relationships, defines another area of Beauvoir's philosophical difference from Sartre.

INTERSUBJECTIVITY AND THE OPPOSITION OF SELF AND OTHER

In *Being and Nothingness*, Sartre describes human relations as fundamentally an opposition of self and Other. For Sartre, the Other intrudes into the solipsistic world of consciousness, the for-itself, which is faced with the shameful, fearful, anguished recognition of its own being-for-others and the proof of the existence of an alien consciousness. The hostile gaze of the sniper epitomizes the Look of the Other. The for-itself reasserts itself as subject by objectifying the Other in turn, thus launching an endless cycle of sadism and masochism. As Everley (1996) notes, *Being and Nothingness* presents no nurturing relationships or evidence of one's genuine need to help or be helped by the Other. Sartre asserts the primacy of "ontological separation," denying that the "we" can be an ontological fact or that the experience of the "we-subject" can be primary. He claims that the *Mitsein* (Heidegger's concept of "being-with") is merely psychological rather than ontological, represents the oscillation between masochism and sadism as inescapable, and denies the possibility of reciprocal "recognition" between consciousnesses, calling "respect for other's freedom" an "empty word" (Sartre 1943, 328, 536, 549–51, 474, 529, 531).

This conception of the origins of the opposition of self and Other makes a striking contrast with that of Beauvoir. For Beauvoir, the self-Other conflict arises not within a solipsistic context from hostile encounters with strangers, but within an intersubjective context where the identity of the self is both sustained and threatened by friendship and love for the Other. To understand this conception, it is necessary first to understand the intersubjective context, the ways in which the self is sustained by identification with the Other. There seem to be three basic ways that relationships with the Other nurture the self. The Other brings comfort and consolation, a sense of utility through service, and expansion of the self into the world of the Other.

One of the earliest entries in the diary describes the comfort and consolation to be found in friendship. The diary begins, much as Sartre begins his discussion of relations with the Other in *Being and Nothingness*, with a description of the experience of being seen in the eyes of the Other. But unlike Sartre's account where one experiences one's objectification by the Other's hostile Look, in Beauvoir's account, our being-for-others can be a comfort and encouragement to the self. "[April 18] I'm lonely to the point of anguish today. . . . To console myself I must glance at this 'me' of multiple faces that is reflected in the eyes of my friends." Although Beauvoir, anticipating Sartre, begins by describing the experience of being seen by the Other, the meaning of that experience, and thus the meaning of the problem of the Other, is radically different. In thinking of the image of herself in the admiring eyes of her younger sister, Beauvoir is reminded of "the joy of being able to find refuge in this real tenderness when all else fails me." The image of herself in the eyes of her childhood friend Zaza, her "confidante, [her] other self," also "comforts [her]." In one of the last diary entries, Beauvoir credits her long friendship with Zaza as providing a sense of identity with her own past: "[September 5] the past which lives on and to which one offers this future of which one dreamt, and which has become the present" (Beauvoir 1927, 5, 6, 159).[42] Friendship can provide the comfort of an identity, a connection and continuity with one's past, which one's own consciousness annihilates.

Beauvoir also describes the consolation she finds in her love for Jacques: "[June 3] we cling to one another so tightly that we can support the great vertiginous void; we will not fall into the abyss" (Beauvoir 1927, 74).[43] In this passage, Beauvoir's use of the phrase "the vertiginous void" anticipates a phrase that Sartre will later incorporate into *Being and Nothingness*. But for Beauvoir, the encounter with the Other is not always a bad faith attempt at evasion, as it is for Sartre. Friendship gives one the strength to face the harsh realities one could not bear alone, even when that reality is a recognition of one's individual accomplishments. This is evident in key passages from the diary recording Beauvoir's ambivalent response to her success on the competitive philosophy exams in June 1927.

On the one hand, Beauvoir enjoys her individual success in this conflict of self and Other, which brings her new acquaintances and encourages her to pursue a career in philosophy. "Excitation a bit feverish, project of study and of camaraderies; it appeared to me at one moment desirable to prepare for the *agrégation* and I felt in myself the soul of a *normalien* [a reference to the prestigous, and traditionally male, École Normale Supérieure which Sartre attended and which Merleau-Ponty and Simone Weil were preparing to enter]!" On the other hand, she is disconcerted by her sudden fame and by the image of herself in the eyes of envious strangers. "I feel stunned, a little diminished by my success which my camarades have felt too keenly; diminished by the sympathetic curiosity that they feel towards a 'young woman of merit.' Basically what have I accomplished this year? nothing" (Beauvoir 1927, 83, 84).[44]

Disgusted by the evidence of her preoccupation with worldly success, which seems a betrayal of her ascetic ideals, Beauvoir vows to reclaim her autonomy and return to her work. "I will not allow myself to be absorbed by the Sorbonne. Not to be 'Mademoiselle Bertrand de Beauvoir'; to be myself" (Beauvoir 1927, 86). But Beauvoir's reaction to this experience of public recognition for her individual achievement, which affirms her, goes beyond a simple determination to maintain an inner focus. Her immediate reaction is one of acute anguish.

[July 7] To think that last Thursday I spent all morning and afternoon at Mlle Mercier's [Beauvoir's mentor at the Institute Catholique in Neuilly, who had first encouraged her to study philosophy] sobbing from nerves. What a fine success in life, I thought! oh! emptiness! nothingness, vanity. Once again, I am stronger from the love that others have for me. Charming afternoon at G[eorgette] Lévy's reading poetry together and touching beautiful books—long conversations with Miquel who becomes very dear to me. (Beauvoir 1927, 87)[45]

In response to the anxiety surrounding competitive success and confirmation of self, Beauvoir retreats for comfort and consolation to a circle of intimate friends.

But even the comfort of friends is not immune from the annihilating powers of consciousness, nor free from conflict. In the important passage dated July 10, cited above, Mademoiselle Mercier responds to Beauvoir's anguish over the exam by "trying to convert" her. Beauvoir, though "tempted" by a nostalgia for the Catholicism of her childhood, characterizes faith as "the most desperate act there is" and vows to keep the "lucidity" of her despair and not "lie to myself." The passage concludes with Beauvoir's affirmation of her determination to do philosophy and her identification of the theme of the "opposition of self and other" (Beauvoir 1927, 94–95). The temptation to conform to the direction of one's cherished mentor, whose guidance is necessary to help one find one's way in life, is challenged by the necessity of being true to oneself and defining one's own philosophical position. This experience of the differentiation of self within a nurturant relationship provides the immediate context of Beauvoir's definition of the theme of the opposition of self and Other, in contrast to Sartre's examples of encounters with hostile strangers that frame his discussion of relations with the Other in *Being and Nothingness.*

Any experience of difference from friends can lead to an anguished confrontation with nothingness for Beauvoir. "I had a moment of vertigo, with nothing for me to cling to," she writes after conversations with various friends in which their differences were made apparent. Her response is a defiant avowal of her autonomy: "Once again, this necessity to be strong! to be always alone if I do not abdicate." Beauvoir is aware of her tendency to subsume the Other within her self in certain relationships, especially those with her younger sister and Zaza. This tendency to dominate the Other, which Sartre refers to as sadism, characterizes Françoise's initial attitude toward Xavière in *She Came to Stay.* The diary presents ample evidence of Beauvoir's early interest in this attitude. "When I am feeling malicious, as I am this evening," Beauvoir writes in the entry for April 18, "it seems to me that as in Poupette [her younger sister], yet less, I especially love in [Zaza] a reflection of myself" (Beauvoir 1927, 138, 6).[46] Dominating the Other provides security and comfort, but it can lead to conflict when the Other's assertions of independence bring an anguished perception of one's difference and isolation.

Beauvoir describes herself as "plunged into the abyss of reflection" by the shameful recognition that her own critical consciousness can appear to her pious sister as egoism and a lack of certitude. "I feel ashamed for my lack of certitude, for not having resolved the question of 'how to live'; for being an egoist." In this passage Beauvoir anticipates Sartre's description of the experience of shame as evidence of the subjectivity of the Other. Beauvoir's response is to reaffirm her critical rejection of religion, refusing to allow herself to be "troubled by the certitude of others" (*see* n. 29). But she does not simply try to objectify the Other in turn, as Sartre would argue that one must. In order to maintain these important relationships, Beauvoir takes a relativist position, trying to acknowledge differences. "I can only love them and rejoice in their differences from me, but without desiring to be such as they are" (Beauvoir 1927, 26).[47] She reserves her respect for those who refuse to be "duped" and "who struggle to live despite their lucidity" (*see* n. 29), thus anticipating the concepts of bad faith and authenticity. While more disturbing than comforting, the conversation with Poupette, like the conversation with Mlle Mercier discussed above, does enable Beauvoir to see herself more clearly. But her description of her shameful apprehension of herself as an object in the gaze of another whose admiration she had taken for granted reveals how conflict and the anguished experience of nothingness ["the abyss"] can arise from within even the most comforting relationships.

This passage also provides an interesting contrast to Sartre's discussion of sadism in *Being and Nothingness*. Despite the many common elements in their phenomenological descriptions of the shameful experience of the Other's gaze, and the instability of a relationship in which the Other is subsumed by the self, they present different alternatives following upon the collapse of sadism. For Sartre, sadism alternates with masochism. But Beauvoir, in her relativist stance, tries to define a third alternative, in which differences are acknowledged and a relation with the Other is maintained. The experience of the objectivity of the Other's judgment is thus not simply an obstacle to the realization of one's own subjectivity, as it is for Sartre, requiring that one attempt to reestablish one's domination of the Other. Beauvoir's relativist ethics is grounded in her determination to respect the differences between self and Other while maintaining a relationship.

SERVING OTHERS

A second aspect of the connection of self and Other that Beauvoir describes in her 1927 diary is serving the Other, a service that allows one to discover a sense of life's utility despite the ultimate "uselessness of everything" (Beauvoir 1927, 12), a theme that anticipates Sartre's definition of man as a "useless passion." In 1927 Beauvoir was still involved in the social activism of *Les Équipes sociales*, an idealistic movement to end class divisions, although she had realized its limitations and the limitations of the philosophy of its leader, Garric. Her interest in philosophy also reflects the importance of service.

> Basically, I'm in a paradoxical situation: I sense my intelligence and . . . I would love to do something . . . I would love to become impassioned for a philosophical work. . . . Only, these very qualities that want to serve show me what an illusion it is to claim to serve something. (Beauvoir 1927, 23)

Serving others relieves this despair by providing a sense of utility on a human scale, without appeal to an illusory absolute. One of Beauvoir's pleasures in her relationship with her younger sister is the sense of being needed: "the pleasure that she has need of me" and "I do a lot for her and almost all of the passion of her life comes to her from me." Beauvoir's love for her cousin, Jacques, also stems in part from her perception that "[August 1] J[acques] needs me." This desire to be of service to someone is part of the attraction of Jacques over Maurice Merleau-Ponty; "[September 6] I can do something for Jacques; for the other it would be only from pleasure" (Beauvoir 1927, 5, 139, 159).[48]

Just as the need for comfort can lead to conflicts of self and Other, the need to serve the Other can also lead to conflicts when one abdicates the self attempting to serve the Other. Beauvoir anticipates Sartre's later description of the instability of masochism and love in her description of the course of her love for her cousin Jacques. Her description shows how, in serving the Other, one can become aware of the Other's weaknesses and one's own strength. The more one abases the self and takes on responsibility for the Other in serving the Other, the more the Other comes to seem incapable of acting for himself. Midway through the diary, when Beauvoir describes a letter from Jacques in which he writes of his despair and sense of uselessness, her response is no longer to idolize her hero, but to want to take him in hand.

> I will gladly force you to love yourself if you will love me, because the image of yourself that you will see in my eyes will be beautiful and true. Each one will be strong from the weakness of the other. (Beauvoir 1927, 74)[49]

Serving him has revealed his weaknesses and her own strengths. With Beauvoir's growing determination to overcome despair and construct a philosophy out of her own experiences, Jacques's despair, which had once seemed to his younger cousin an indication of his profundity, now seems a sign of his weakness, an inability to find a positive alternative.

Beauvoir, distressed by Jacques's failure to answer her letters and fearing that their love is finished, tries to excuse him by taking responsibility herself.

> But it is so much as though everything were finished! . . . and it is my fault, it is when I love less that I sense myself less loved. I can not imagine what you are today. Perhaps you are thinking about me, perhaps you are painfully meditating. O my friend, forgive me! (Beauvoir 1927, 103)

Refusing to accept Jacques's lack of response to her letters as evidence of his lack of interest, she prefers to imagine him suffering over her absence, an evasion of a bitter reality that Beauvoir will face two years later when she is surprised to learn of Jacques's affair with another woman during this same period and of his marriage, in 1929, to someone else. Beauvoir assumes responsibility for Jacques's actions and comes to think of him as weaker and weaker, more and more pitiable and dependent on her. On the diary's final page, she declares, "I no longer love

Jacques." But her desire to serve, to be useful, seems unabated. In one of the final entries of the diary, Beauvoir writes, "I dream of immense sacrifices; but I have nothing large enough for . . . a gift" (Beauvoir 1927, 168v, 165).[50]

Beauvoir's fundamental commitment to give of herself in service to others may be a foundation for what Karen Vintges (1996) has identified as Beauvoir's most important contribution to moral philosophy. While Sartre and Foucault share with Beauvoir a rejection of moral absolutes, Vintges argues that only Beauvoir refuses to abandon a moral obligation to provide guidance to others. According to Vintges, Beauvoir provides young women with practical guidelines on the art of living through her autobiographical stylization of herself into an intellectual woman. In her autobiographies, Beauvoir tries to help young women with the problem of reconciling their need for individual freedom with their need for love. Reading Beauvoir's ethics within the context of *Being and Nothingness*, Vintges tries unsuccessfully to trace the development of this ethic from an initial philosophical solipsism. We can succeed in grounding it, however, if we begin instead with the intersubjective philosophy of Beauvoir's 1927 diary, where serving others is seen as supportive of the self. In serving others one is able to achieve a sense of the usefulness of one's life on a human scale, if not in an absolute sense, thus relieving the despair of meaninglessness that follows the loss of faith. Serving others can thus assist one in opting for lucidity rather than evasion and avoiding the temptations of bad faith.

LEARNING

A third aspect of the intersubjective context of Beauvoir's 1927 philosophy is that the self can learn from the Other, who can open up a world aspired to by the self. The Other also provides us with objectivity, not in a hostile sense, but in the sense of correcting the limitations of our own perspective. Friendship, according to Beauvoir, "even simple camaraderies," can open up new worlds for us, take us out of ourselves; "There alone can I tear myself away from my own manner of thinking." Beauvoir's younger sister provides "[April 18] an ear for listening to that which would take on too much importance if I didn't say it." In planning her philosophical work for the next year, Beauvoir vows to "confide in someone who critiques and takes me seriously: Baruzi [her philosophy professor, Jean Baruzi], G[eorgette] Lévy or Pontrémoli [another philosophy student]" (Beauvoir 1927, 59, 61, 5, 90).[51] Criticism by the other is indispensable to the development of the self.

Beauvoir sees others as representing different philosophical systems. "I think a great deal at this moment of those beings whom I know, or rather of the ideas that are for me these beings . . . in deducing them logically from their point of departure." In identifying with an admired Other, one can move beyond the limits of a personal philosophy one has come to see as inadequate. Beauvoir defines the stages of her own philosophical development in terms of relationships: the stage of her activist involvement in the *Équipes sociales* movement with her love for Garric, its leader, and the stage of her despair and disillusionment with her love for Jacques. The desire to move beyond that despair attracts her to Barbier, a fellow philosophy student who, as we have seen above in our discussion of Bergson, represents the "serious" alternative of "austerity, philosophy" (Beauvoir 1927, 25, 37).[52]

When Beauvoir falls in love with Barbier, it is an experience of freedom and a revelation of her true self.

> one instant I held in my hands an entirely new life. . . . Well! the past did not enchain me, a new passion blossomed in me. . . . I loved him. . . . Yes, it's only by free decision, and thanks to the play of circumstances that the true self is revealed. . . . One instant I was free and I lived [*vécu*] that. (*see* n. 8)

It is through a relationship with the Other that Beauvoir discovers her freedom and her true self. But identification with the Other can lead to conflict for a self defined by becoming. "For me a choice is never made, but is always being made. . . . The horror of the definitive choice, is that one engages not only the self of today, but that of tomorrow, and it is why, basically, marriage is immoral" (*see* n. 8).

The identification with the Other in love can be especially problematic when it entails complete self-abdication as it does in 1927 for Beauvoir, who defines love as "feeling oneself dominated." Beauvoir has come to see her love for Jacques as a betrayal of herself, as "the supreme defeat." An effort at the fusion of their selves that had obsessed her the previous winter is no longer appealing. "My self does not want to let itself be devoured by his." But in breaking free from Jacques, she does not abandon the ideal of domination, describing Barbier as "the unknown who knew how to conquer me." Indeed, what Beauvoir finds attractive about Barbier is "his manner of dominating, of being strong and such that one could simply walk in the light reflected in his eyes" (Beauvoir 1927, 136, 38, 39).[53] In domination, the Other becomes an absolute, the source of absolute consolation and fulfillment with the abandonment of one's annihilating consciousness. In this passage, which anticipates Beauvoir's later critique of marriage in *The Second Sex*, we begin to see Beauvoir's early formulation of the ethical problem of reconciling freedom and love that, as Vintges argues, represents Beauvoir's legacy to generations of women.

LOVE AND SELF-DECEPTION

Beauvoir recognizes the impossible desire for complete fusion with the Other as an inauthentic desire to abdicate responsibility for herself. But the yearning for love seems to overcome her critical consciousness, as in the April 18 entry, addressed to Jacques:

> I have a total confidence in you and your love. . . . But, in order to be supported by this confidence, I would have to ignore too many parts of you. . . . I refuse to take them into account under the pretext that the essential is stable. I see you in your entirety and it's in your entirety that I love you. (Beauvoir 1927, 7)[54]

Abandoning herself in her love for the Other is only possible by the conscious pretext of ignoring or refusing to take account of reality. Self-deception is an effort to avoid the anguished experience of her solitude, the reality of her separate existence as an individual.

Late in the diary, in the August 26 entry, Beauvoir describes the desire for love as a form of idolatry that demands self-deception; "love is a fact to which one must submit; the only sin is that of idolatry. Don't think too much about that!" This temptation of self-deception is grounded, once again, in nostalgia for girlhood, as is illustrated in the entry for May 28. "Ah! How large and how small is love! if it were only small! or if it were only large as it is for a little awestruck girl!" The May

11 entry acknowledges the force of this nostalgic desire and the necessity of denying it: "Oh! to love again as simply as I once knew how to do. Only realize that: despite what I want, my love must keep its limits." Even recognizing the impossibility of her desire and the risk to herself in accepting domination by another, Beauvoir is unable to suppress it, as is evident in the entry for July 7. Referring to Jacques, she writes, "I will sacrifice my exams for him; but not my work if I can create one, nor myself. . . . Refuse to submit to any slavery. And yet, deep down, I don't know . . . maybe I will sacrifice everything for him, everything and it will not be a sacrifice" (Beauvoir 1927, 154, 70, 47, 90).[55]

Such is the fantasy and the temptation in the search for love, analogous to the temptation of self-deception and evasion in religious faith. In Beauvoir's 1927 diary, there is a vicious dynamic driven by the anguish of separation and the desire for fusion with the Other, which no mere friendship could fulfill. Egoism leaves her isolated and awakens a nostalgic yearning for the Other;

> my life is so empty! . . . Whether Zaza, Garric, Jacques; the Sorbonne or the *équipes* . . . the passions of my childhood and youth were passions: boiling, crushing, and me oppressed by their weight, tiny, *absorbed* by them; now it is my self that absorbs them all . . . the affections that I experience are not at all the center of my life: I could so do without them! they leave me so alone! quite alone! (Beauvoir 1927, 18)[56]

This sense of loneliness awakens a yearning for fusion with the Other and the desire to be dominated.

With the failure of fusion, one seems condemned to a solitary life bereft of love.

> [May 13] I speak mystically of love, I know the price. . . . I am too intelligent, too demanding, and too rich for anyone to be able to take charge of me entirely. No one knows me or loves me completely. I have only myself. (Beauvoir 1927, 51)

Even surrounded by friends she feels lonely, for lack of the one person who can be everything to her. "I must live, knowing that no one will help me to live. . . . Alone I will live, strong in what I know how to be." The attempt at fusion can fail when either the self rebels against the "mutilation," or when the Other resists the attempt at fusion. The diary's final entry refers to the loneliness of love when the Other refuses fusion and of friendship, which precludes fusion. "[E]veryone is alone; and that's a beautiful thing. Jacques taught me that, painfully because I loved him. Ponty taught me that in joy; beautiful friendship, without harshness, without abandon, spontaneous, new, happy and tender which asks nothing more than is good to give" (Beauvoir 1927, 51, 64, 168v).[57]

When the attempt at fusion fails, Beauvoir's response is to defend an egoism that verges on solipsism until despair reminds her once again of her need for the Other and the cycle repeats itself. Mere friends, separated from her by their differences, ultimately cannot protect her from this experience of nothingness; only a relationship in which the self is wholly absorbed into the Other can provide complete comfort. Rejecting relationships offering lesser fulfillment, one is thrown back to egoism. When the anguish of isolation becomes too acute, the desire for love returns, and the self renews its attempt to merge with the Other, seeking to be dominated. While Beauvoir's early formulation of a relativist ethics reflects an attempt to appreciate difference and maintain friendship, the unrelenting anguish of isolation and separation drives this attempt at fusion, despite its inevitable failure, setting the stage for Beauvoir's work on the problem of the Other in the 1930s and 1940s.

EGOISM AND INDIVIDUAL FREEDOM

But what of the espousal of individual freedom, for which Beauvoir is so well known? Beauvoir's philosophy, including her feminism in *The Second Sex,* has been criticized by many feminists as masculinist, and Sartrean, precisely because of its valuation of individual action (*see,* for example, Keller 1985, 258–59). In *Memoirs of a Dutiful Daughter,* Beauvoir avows her early individualism.

> [A fellow student] announced abruptly that he was an individualist. "Me, too," I said. "But I thought you were Catholic, Thomist and social?" I protested, and he congratulated me on our agreement. (Beauvoir 1958, 435)

How is this individualism reconciled with the dependence on the other in Beauvoir's 1927 diary?

The diary's final entries, dated October 17 and 27, constitute a proclamation of autonomy. "No, I will love no longer. . . . I have my force in me. I love and keep my self; I give of myself without losing anything. I have need of no one!" This is a sharp contrast with a passage from the opening pages of the diary where Beauvoir describes Jacques as "everything—my sole reason for living" and herself as awaiting "with so much impatience the day when you will no longer be 'the other' or 'me,' but when there will be only and definitively 'we.' " But the diary does not show a clear development from fused relationships to a solipsistic individualism. First of all, egoism is not represented in the diary as implying a complete detachment from the Other. "I feel ashamed . . . for being an egoist, for a radical egoism which can be qualified only in that I direct it towards those I love or directly on myself" (Beauvoir 1927, 168v, 6–7, 24).[58] Egoism encompassing others implies the interconnection of self and Other. Whether finding comfort in old friendships, serving others, or learning from another whose philosophical position she admires, relationships with the Other, for Beauvoir, can serve the interests of the self.

Furthermore, not all of the early diary entries espouse the ideal of fusion, and the later entries egoism. In some entries, the opposite is the case. An early diary entry critiques the dream of fusion and self-abdication.

> The other can no longer be for me anything definitive and complete: the great renunciation of which I have dreamed is impossible! They are only themselves as I am only myself, and above all I have no need of them. (Beauvoir 1927, 18–19)

That the desire to abdicate the self remains alive at the diary's conclusion is evident from a marginal notation, dated "1929," on the following entry late in the diary: "one moment in the Luxembourg [garden], I felt faint from sadness, thinking that after 18 months of such passionate loves, I found myself with an empty heart and knowing that the one who could fulfill everything does not exist." This last phrase is underlined in a different color ink, and in the margin is written "Sartre—1929" (Beauvoir 1927, 137).[59] Beauvoir's fantasy of self-abdication and fusion with the other thus remained alive well after the conclusion of the 1927 diary.

Indeed, other passages in the 1927 diary suggest that Beauvoir is holding the desire for fusion in abeyance until the completion of her education in two years, when she will have to make a choice about marriage. Beauvoir's philosophical project of resolving the opposition between self and Other, which she defines in the 1927 diary, thus remains unresolved at the diary's end. We can see its reappearance, twelve years later, in *She Came to Stay*, where Françoise, the central character, struggles with the problem of selflessness. It is not resolved until *The Second Sex*, where Beauvoir provides a historical, political analysis of woman's desire for self-abdication and fusion with the Other, which, in 1927, was seen as natural.

In the 1927 diary, Beauvoir recognizes that the dilemma created by the desire for fusion with the Other and the desire for self is related to being a woman, a sign of her woman's "heart." In the following passage, Beauvoir imagines her future of solitary isolation, cut off from the intimate relationships implicit in a woman's traditional role of wife and mother. "Yesterday how I envied M. de Wendel so pretty and unaffected! without pride as without envy, I cried in thinking of the lot which was reserved for me, and of all the force, and the tension required so that I could find it preferable to any other." Beauvoir experiences her future career, necessitated by her family's financial situation, as her given lot, requiring an exhausting effort to assume as her own future. There is a sense of reconciling herself to a future that has been imposed on her. When she actively plans her writing projects, she can experience a joyous discovery of her individual power in a future defined by her own action. "Friday I established with force a life's program; in such moments my solitude is an intoxication: I am, I dominate, I love myself and despise the rest" (Beauvoir 1927, 107, 57).[60]

But there remains an underlying ambiguity to the experience, the loneliness that accompanies egoism, that leaves Beauvoir yearning, in despair, for woman's traditional feminine role. "But I would so like to have the right me as well of being simple and very weak, of being a woman; in what a 'desert world' I walk, so arid, with the only oasis my intermittent esteem for myself." In this passage, which anticipates the analysis in *The Second Sex* of woman's complicity with her oppression, we can see Beauvoir's own experience of that temptation. The depth of her anguish is evident in the concluding lines of this entry: "I count on myself; I know that I can count on myself. But I would prefer to have no need to count on myself." Accompanying this passage is a marginal notation, dated May 18, 1929: "Could I again bear to suffer as I suffered in writing these lines?" (Beauvoir 1927, 57).[61]

Planning for a career can be both an intoxicating experience of individual empowerment and an experience of loss and denial of self. Denied a woman's traditional dependency, Beauvoir experiences a sense of isolation. Prideful of her self-reliance, she still yearns to escape the need for it. In this passage we find the source of Beauvoir's description in *The Second Sex* of woman's traditional role as a temptation to flee the loneliness and dread of one's freedom. If Vintges is correct and Beauvoir's most important contribution to ethics lies in the practical guidelines for young women in the art of living, then the painful lessons in reconciling love and freedom that Beauvoir endured, and recorded in her 1927 diary, are surely the foundation of this ethics. But what can we conclude from the diary about Beauvoir's philosophical understanding of the problem of love and the theme of the opposition of self and Other at the heart of this ethics?

Reading Beauvoir's philosophy within a Sartrean context, Vintges, as well as Kate and Edward Fullbrook, traces the origins of Beauvoir's concept of the opposition of self and Other to an initial concern with the philosophical problem of solipsism. The Fullbrooks, in their analysis of *She Came to Stay*, credit Beauvoir with originating the proof of the existence of other minds in her description of the experience of being seen in the eyes of the Other. Vintges, in her analysis of *Ethics of Ambiguity*, credits Beauvoir with solving the problem of ethical solipsism through her concept of emotion as providing an embodied connection of self and Other. But if we begin instead with Beauvoir's 1927 diary, rather than these later works, and try to define Beauvoir's initial concept of the opposition of self and Other, the problem of solipsism seems secondary. Her own initial philosophical concern would seem to be with an opposite problem, which we might term, not solipsism (only-self), but solaltrism (only-other).

In solipsism, ethical egoism is the problem; for Beauvoir, selflessness, or the temptation to self-abdication, is the problem. In Sartre's philosophy, "hell is other people"; for Beauvoir, hell is isolation or the absence of other people. It is not the presence of a hostile Other, but the absence of the beloved Other that is a source of anguish for Beauvoir.

The existence of the Other is in doubt for Sartre; Beauvoir doubts the existence of the self. While relations with the Other seem to be inevitably in bad faith for Sartre, the comfort and opportunity for service they provide the self, in Beauvoir's philosophy, would seem to encourage lucidity and the avoidance of bad faith. Hence, Beauvoir's philosophy defines a different epistemological and moral problem. If solaltrism is foreign to the philosophical tradition, which has been largely shaped by men writing of their own experiences, it is not foreign to the experience of women. The feminist psychologist Carol Gilligan, in her analysis of a woman's moral voice, has argued that much as a "latent egocentrism" is the "potential error in justice reasoning" that characterizes moral development in men, so "a tendency to see oneself as selfless" by defining oneself in others' terms is a "potential error in care reasoning" characteristic of women (Gilligan 1987, 31). Gilligan also sees the desire for abdication of the self in fusion with the Other as setting the stage for a "conflict of self and other" that she terms "the central moral problem for women, posing a dilemma whose resolution requires a reconciliation between femininity and adulthood" (Gilligan 1982, 71). Thus, Beauvoir's concept of the opposition of self and Other, which has been traditionally attributed to the influence of male philosophers including Hegel and Sartre, has origins instead in her own experience, and defines a problem faced by many women, for which Beauvoir provides one of the first philosophical analyses.

Beauvoir's 1927 diary suggests a new reading of the problem of the Other in Beauvoir's texts, including *She Came to Stay*, *Ethics of Ambiguity*, and *The Second Sex*, which have been traditionally read within a Sartrean context framed by the problem of solipsism. Beauvoir's work on the philosophical problem of the Other, by providing a different kind of "different voice," also challenges an essentialist reading of gender difference. While many feminist philosophers interested in using Gilligan's work to define an ethics of care have looked to the experience of motherhood, and the relationship of mother and child, as a model for a maternal ethics of care, Beauvoir's work reflects a very different experience and a very different model. In *She Came to Stay*, the central conflicts arise within extramarital heterosexual and lesbian relationships modeled on Beauvoir's own life. Her mature moral voice offers, instead of a maternal ethics, a radical feminist critique of men's oppression of women, a call for women's collective struggle to win their own liberation, and, as

Vintges argues, practical guidelines for young women in reconciling freedom and love. If philosophy is to serve the interests of young women, as it has historically served the interests of young men, then Beauvoir's contribution to defining the problem of the Other, or what we might term "solaltrism," must receive a prominent place in the philosophy curriculum.

Earlier versions of this chapter were published as "The Search for Beauvoir's Early Philosophy," *Simone de Beauvoir Studies* 14, (1997): 13–28 and "Philosophical Beginnings: Beauvoir's 1927 Diary," in *The Existential Phenomenology of Simone de Beauvoir*, ed. Dorothy Leland and Lester Embree (Dordrecht: Kluwer Academic Publishers, forthcoming). Quotations from Beauvoir's 1927 diary by permission of Sylvie Le Bon de Beauvoir and the Bibliothèque Nationale.

NOTES

All page references are to Beauvoir 1927 unless otherwise indicated.

1. "Si notre âme si frémi de bonheur et résonné comme les cordes d'une lyre, ne fût ce qu'une seule fois, toutes les éternités étaient nécessaires pour provoquer ce seul évènement, et, dans ce seul moment de notre affirmation, toute éternité était approuvrée, délivrée, justifiée et affirmée. Nietzsche. (Volonté de Puissance)" (p. 2v).

2. "Je n'ai de soutien que mon désespoir absolu." (p. 1). "C'est encore dans le culte du moi qu'en ce moment je trouverai le plus de ressources parce que je sens ma valeur et je suis heureuse d'en avoir" (April 28, p. 21). July 16: "comment j'ai commencé par l'action, puis le culte du moi pour l'action suivant Barrès et Péguy, puis comment j'ai vu l'illusion de cela et que la vie n'exigeait rien de moi—comment je cherche une exigence et que je trouve que rien ne vaut, mes désespoirs, et la position où je suis maintenant: n'attendant, n'espérant plus rien, ne pouvant ni accepter, ni refuser la vie" (p. 101).

3. "Une vraie vie intellectuelle, austère, implacable, qui passe outre. Ne pas me laisser absorber par les autres; . . . Pratiquer cet ascétisme qui m'était si familier l'an dernier. . . . Et si je dis 'a quoi bon tout cela'? [J]e réponds avec Péguy. 'Ce n'est pas par vertu car nous n'en avons guère, Ce n'est pas par devoir car nous ne l'aimons pas,' mais c'est la loi profonde de mon être, et le moyen de trouver la paix que je veux" (p. 129–30).

4. "Je sais moi qu'il y a qu'un probleme et qui n'a pas de solution, parce qu'il n'a peut être pas de sens; c'est celui qu'a posé Pascal, plus près de moi Marcel Arland: je voudrais croire à quelque chose—rencontrer l'exigence totale—justifier la vie; bref, je voudrais Dieu" (p. 62).

5. "4 Août—oh! ce perpétuel et nécessaire écoulement des choses et de nous mêmes! . . . Désir fou de l'être qui serait en même temps du devenir" (p. 143).

6. [September 5] "Et dire aussi le rêve, les souvenirs, la joie de tout retrouver au moment qu'on croit tout perdu, le passé qui vit encore et auquel on offre cet avenir qu'il rêva, qui est devenu du présent, la beauté des soirs, de la vie, tout ce que je viens d'écrire à Zaza. Joie, joie! amitié immense comme mon coeur, qui ne finira pas" (p. 159). "Catholicisme de Mauriac, de Claudel, . . . comme il m'a marquée et quelle place il y a en moi pour lui!" (p. 94).

7. "[A]vec mon intelligence seule j'essaierai toute ma vie de m'avancer aussi loin que possible au coeur du problème; mais en acceptant le donné et en vivant le donné, sans attendre de posséder l'absolu" (p. 72).

8. "Ce matin j'ai connu une minute étrange dont l'écho n'est pas encore mort en moi. Je venais de revoir Barbier, si spontanément venu vers moi. . . . Il m'a parlé de moi, philosophie, de littérature avec un intérêt non dissimulé. Et alors . . . un instant j'ai tenu dans mes mains une vie toute neuve. . . . Eh bien! le passé ne m'enchaînait pas, une passion nouvelle s'épanouissait en moi, splendide, je l'aimais. . . . Comment rendre cela? Ce n'était point spéculation, raisonnement; non plus rêve, imagination; un instant cela a été . . . ma vie n'est plus un chemin tracé que déjà du point où je suis arrivée je puis découvrir toute et dans laquelle il n'y aura qu'à poser un pas après l'autre. C'est une route non frayée que ma marche seule créera" (p. 34–35). "Oui, c'est par la décision libre seulement, et grâce au jeu des circonstances que le moi vrai se découvre. Je disais à Mlle Mercier, que chez moi un choix n'était jamais fait, mais toujours se faisait; il se répète chaque fois que j'en prends conscience; combien c'est vrai! Eh bien: ce matin j'ai choisi Barbier. L'horreur du choix définitif, c'est qu'on engage non seulement le moi d'aujourd'hui, mais celui du demain et c'est pourquoi au fond le mariage est immoral. . . . Un instant j'ai été libre et j'ai vécu cela" (p. 35–36).

9. "C'est très compliqué. Ces possibles qui sont en moi, il faudra que peu à peu je les tue tous sauf un; c'est ainsi que je vois la vie: mille possibles dans l'enfance, qui tombent peu à peu et si bien qu'au dernier jour il n'y a plus qu'*une réalité*, on a vécu *une* vie; mais c'est l'élan vital de Bergson que je retrouve ici, qui se divise, laissant tomber tendances après tendances pour qu'une seule se réalise" (p. 37).

10. "L'influence du moral sur la physique est réciproquement: journal de Maine de Biran et théorie des émotions de James" (p. 10).

11. "Je sais que les lois de l'esprit sont les mêmes chez tous les hommes. Mais il ne me semble pas qu'il n'y ait qu'une manière de juger sainement; cela dépend des postulats que chacun a admis explicitement ou implicitement; et le choix de ses postulats est laissé à chacun; il dépend de son tempérament, de sa sensibilité, de ce donné irréductible qui constitue l'individualité de chacun. Je devrais lire Leibniz car je sens si vivement le principe des indiscernables! Je hais le méca-

nisme qui réduisant la qualité à la quantité escamote la qualité. . . . C'est pourquoi je me sense non phénomène mais noumène, la qualité est un reflet du
noumène sur le plan de l'expérience." "[D]ès que nous pensons vraiment il faut
en quelque sorte créer notre vérité" (p. 95–96).

12. "Je repense au cours de Baruzi et à Schopenhauer: caractère empirique,
caractère intelligible. Oui, c'est par la décision libre seulement, et grâce au jeu
des circonstances que le moi vrai se découvre" (p. 35).

13. "Baruzi cette année qui m'attire par sa foi scrupuleuse et profonde, l'ar-
deur intellectuelle de ses yeux brillants, et sa manière de vivre ses pensées jusqu'au bout de ses ongles; il possède une vie intérieure. Mr. Brunschvicg est peut
être un homme de valeur mais pour moi: 0" (p. 9–10). "cours de Baruzi où les
idées austères et belles me donnent une fièvre grave et passionnée" (p. 28). "me
confier à quelqu'un qui critique et me prenne au serieux: Baruzi, G. Lévy ou
Pontremoli" (p. 91).

14. "Je ne sais rien, rien; non seulement pas une réponse mais aucune manière
sortable de poser la question. Le scepticisme, l'indifférence sont impossibles, une
religion est impossible pour l'instant—le mysticisme est tentant: mais comment
connaîtrai-je la valeur d'une pensée qui ne laisse pas place à la pensée? sur quoi
m'appuyer pour la rejeter ou l'accepter. accepter de passer deux ans en lectures,
conversations, méditations fragmentaires. Je vais travailler comme une brute: je
n'ai pas une minute à perdre. Et ne rien négliger: me lier avec Baruzi, faire des
devoirs, tâcher de savoir, de savoir" (p. 132–33).

15. "A G. Lévy écrit ma volonté de tout remettre en question parce que je
crois cela un devoir, de repenser tout postulat, de renoncer même à ce que je
crois" (p. 142–43). "toute philosophie explicative nous met devant un résidu, la
raison ne donne que de l'humain, nécessité d'une mystique. . . . il faut relire et
méditer Kant, Bergson et Descartes" (p. 111–12).

16. "[I]l part d'un acte de foi en la raison—je crois avec Kant qu'on ne peut
atteindre le monde des noumènes. [L]'être n'égale pas le substance—il y a de
l'être dans l'ordre du phénomène—j'ai dit, 'je crois à la substance,' comme j'ai
dit 'je crois à la causalité,' j'entendais 'je me représente les choses sous l'ordre de
la substance comme sous l'ordre de la causalité' mais cela ne veut pas dire qu'il y
ait une substance—séparer la raison du noumène avec Kant et Bergson, tandis
que vous admettez que la raison peut saisir le noumène. . . . Ponti appuie la
sienne sur la foi en la raison, moi sur l'impuissance de la raison—qui prouve que
Descartes l'emporte sur Kant? [J]e maintiens mon devoir de Sorbonne—servez-
vous de la raison, vous aboutissez à des résidus et à des irrationnels" (p. 111–12).

17. "Jeudi 7 juillet . . . J'ai conquis deux choses cette année: le goût et l'habi-
tude de la philosophie—la connaissance des êtres" (p. 87). "Mercredi 7 Septembre—Relisant ce cahier, je comprends mon année; oscillation entre le décourage-
ment que m'apportait l'amour, seule grande chose humaine où je sentais le néant

de tout l'humain—et le désir de chercher, le confus espoir qu'il y avait quelque chose à faire. Ponty ne m'a pas tant changée. Il m'a donné la force d'affirmer la seconde tendance" (p. 159).

18. "Eh bien! Ponti [*sic*] a raison. Je n'ai pas le droit de désespérer. J'ai admis que le désespoir se justifiait: mais il exige d'être démontré. . . . *Mais*: si essayant de penser sans passion je dis: 'Je n'ai pas de raison pour choisir le désespoir', je dis aussi, 'je n'ai pas de raison pour m'acheminer vers le catholicisme plutôt que dans aucune autre voie.' . . . Et au contraire, c'est parce que le catholicisme parle trop à mon coeur que ma raison s'en défie: traditions, hérédité, souvenirs me porteraient à donner mon adhésion à cela. . . . élevé autrement, Merleau-Ponti [*sic*], est-ce que votre raison dépouillée de toute passion vous attirerait vers le catholicisme?" (p. 105–6). "Ponti [*sic*] dit 'mieux vaut sacrifier le devenir que l'être'; moi dis que je vois un vice dans un système, je veux sacrifier le système entier" (p. 110).

19. "[J]'ai reconnu que je devais chercher, mais pas dans le catholicisme. Je me suis effrayée de mes inconséquences, puis en les approfondissant, j'ai vu tout de même que ma philosophie n'était pas si en l'air qu'elle semble— Ponti [*sic*] appuie la sienne sur la foi en la raison, moi sur l'impuissance de la raison" (p. 112). "Oh! fatiguée, énervée, sûre de n'aboutir à rien par ce désespéré recours en la philosophie—et pourtant je *veux*, je me dois de le faire. . . . Raisonner froidement. Ah! il y a à faire pour faire de moi une philosophe!" (p. 116).

20. "Sûrement Merloponti [*sic*] si vexé d'être battu par moi mais si sympathique (extérieurement je crains et pour de mauvaises raisons où la vanité se mêle)" (p. 85). "Et puis, mes chers amis, vous n'aimez pas les jeunes filles mais songez que non seulement elles ont une raison à satisfaire mais un coeur lourd à comprimer—et en cela je veux rester femme, plus masculine encore par le cerveau, plus féminine par la sensibilité. (D'ailleurs tous reconnaissent en m'approchant que je ne suis pas comme les autres jeune filles. ô Ponti [*sic*], comme vous m'avez dit ça gentiment!)" (p. 107).

21. "Jeudi 28 Juillet. Je l'envie ce garçon simple et fort qui vit une vie tranquille auprès d'une mère tendrement chérie et cherche calmement une vérité qu'il espère trouver. 'Aristocrate' m'a-t-il dit? c'est vrai. Je ne peux me défaire de cette idée que je suis seule, dans un monde à part, assistant à celui ci comme à un spectacle. . . . Il s'interdit le rêve. Ah! moi j'ai là des richesses dont je ne veux pas me défaire. Drame de mes affections, pathétique de la vie. . . . Certes, j'ai une sensibilité plus compliquée, plus nuancée que la sienne et une plus épuisante puissance d'amour. Ces problèmes qu'il vit avec son cerveau, je les vis avec mes bras et mes jambes. . . . Je ne veux pas perdre tout cela" (p. 126).

22. "Je suis intellectuellement très seule et très perdue à l'entrée de ma vie . . . cherchant une direction. Je sens que j'ai de la valeur, que j'ai à faire et à dire quelque chose . . . mais ma pensée tourne à vide: vers quoi la diriger? comment

rompre cette solitude? que réaliser avec mon intelligence?" (p. 41) "Je suis dans une grande détresse au moment de décider de ma vie. Puis je me satisfaire avec ce qu'on appelle le bonheur? où dois-je marcher vers cet absolu qui m'attire?" (p. 42).

23. "Ces misérables efforts pour être!" "tout au fond masqué par ces divertissements d'un jour, le même vide!" (p. 55). "Ça! une belle réussite de la vie, pensais-je! ah! vide! néant, vanité" (p. 87).

24. "Je voudrais comprendre comment je puis m'isoler ainsi de mes souvenirs les plus chers et de mes plus proches désirs—J'ai souvent éprouvé déjà cela: telle après midi si douce, tel entretien si ému, je les attribue à une autre. . . . [I]ls sortents d'une fiction. Je ne puis m'y baigner: ils ne sont pas *mes* souvenirs" (April 20, p. 11)."Mon passé est derrière moi comme une chose sortie de moi; sur laquelle je ne puis plus rien et que je regarde avec des yeux étrangers, une chose à laquelle je n'ai point de part" (April 28, p. 18).

25. "Au fond, je suis dans une situation paradoxale: je sens mon intelligence, et quelle puissance positive elle pourrait avoir; j'aimerais faire quelque chose. . . . Seulement, ces qualités mêmes qui demandent à servir me montrent quelle illusion c'est de prétendre servir à quelque chose" (April 30, p. 24).

26. "Que m'a apporté intellectuellement cette année? une serieuse formation philosophique qui a . . . aiguisé mon esprit critique hélas! . . . Je n'ai partout constaté que notre impuissance à rien fonder dans l'ordre de la connaissance comme dans celui de la morale" (p. 11–12).

27. "Il n'y a rien à quoi je croie. Cela, c'est la chose terrible qu'il faut bien m'avouer. Même pas à moi. Je peux aimer . . . et agir selon mon amour: c'est ce qui me permet d'être vivante, passionnée. Mais de l'amour, je ne suis point maîtresse, et dès qu'il cesse, je n'ai rien à quoi m'accrocher. Je hais le dilettantisme; et n'est ce pas au dilettantisme que je devrais aboutir logiquement? en quoi suis-je si loin des sceptiques que je déteste?" (p. 27). "Encore cette angoisse écrasante: L'angoisse métaphysique de l'homme seul dans l'inconnu. Comment ne devient-on pas fou? Il y a des jours où je crie de peur, où je pleure d'ignorance; et puis je me reprends, je me dis 'travaillons sagement'; mais hélas! je sais bien que je mourrai sans connaître!" (p. 157).

28. "Il y a des êtres que j'estime et aime . . . qui possèdent du moins quelques convictions auxquelles ils s'accrochent: ils bâtissent leur vie là dessous; et sur ce plan solidement établi, ils n'ont qu'à laisser épanouir leur vie. J'ai senti en me réveillant tout à l'heure combien je voudrais dans ces matins gris me lever hâtivement et marcher, tranquille, ardente, vers une tâche paisible que je croirais utile et qu'il s'agirait seulement de bien remplir. . . . je me sentais honteuse de manquer moi de certitudes; de n'avoir pas résolu le 'comment vivre'; d'être égoïste. Oui, j'ai souffert hier soir de ne point être telle qu'ils sont, et que j'aurais pu être peut être" (April 30, p. 23–24).

29. "Au fond, c'est ridicule de m'être encore laissée troublée par la certitude des autres. Je ne peux m'empêcher de les envier parce qu'il semble que dans la foi et le bonheur il y a quelque chose de plus complet que dans le doute, l'inquiétude. Mais je *sais* bien pourtant que leur Dieu n'est pas. . . . Non vraiment; ce que j'aime par dessus tout, ce n'est pas la foi ardente . . . c'est l'intelligence et la critique, les lassitudes, les défauts, ce sont les êtres que ne peuvent pas se laisser duper et que se débattent pour vivre malgré leur lucidité" (p. 26).

30. "Mademoiselle Mercier essaie de me convertir; elle me parle de l'abbé Beaussard qui voudrait me voir et je pense du mot de G[eorgette] Lévy. 'Vous serez tentée de ce côté là;' c'est vrai. Ce matin . . . j'ai passionnément désiré d'être la jeune fille qui communie aux messes matinales et qui marche dans une certitude sereine. Catholicisme de Mauriac, de Claudel . . . comme il m'a marquée et quelle place il y a en moi pour lui! et pourtant je sais je ne le connaîtrai plus; je ne désire pas croire: un acte de foi est l'acte le plus désespéré qui soit et je veux que mon désespoir garde du moins sa lucidité, je ne veux pas me mentir à moi même" (p. 94).

31. "encore l'enfant émerveillée que je fus il y a un an." "l'infini d'un amour et d'un dévouement" (p. 17).

32. "Mais moi, que suis je? mon unité ne vient d'aucun principe, ni même d'aucun sentiment auquel je subordonne tout: elle ne se fait qu'en moi même" (p. 26).

33. "Mademoiselle Mercier parlait hier de façon très profonde . . . de l'horreur des syntheses écroulées pour qui n'a la force d'en réédifier aucune. Il faut que je réédifie" (p. 48). "trop de synthèses diverses également comprises m'obligent à construire la mienne propre" (p. 62). "on commence par 'détruire les idoles.' Mais une fois cela fait, il se peut qu'on retrouve en soi un appel profond" (p. 50). "Je veux vivre. Je dois donc pouvoir vivre. Pour cela il faut que je fasse *mon* unité" (p. 48). "je sais ce que je demande à la vie: me réaliser. . . . C'est la loi de mon être" (p. 49). "le jouet des caprices de mes désirs . . . Et l'essentiel sera d'obtenir la profonde unité de ma pensée" (p. 51–52).

34. "Or, aujourd'hui déjà je n'ai plus pour l'image grave de moi la ferveur de mercredi. Donc cette image n'est pas tout à fait juste. Si j'ai envie de faire des sottises et de causer avec des imbéciles, il faut le faire. Prendre garde seulement à ce que je puisse toujours ne pas le faire. Pas d'unité artificielle. Je sais si bien que sous cette dispersion apparente il y a cette forte unité de mon moi! si je me juge du dehors seulement je suis effrayée de me voir ardente avec équipes, intellectuelle ici, pleurante et abattue à la maison, jouisseuse et sotte ailleurs. Tout cela est moi. Mes fois comme mes désarrois. Il faut seulement établir une hiérarchie pour que je m'y reconnaisse, avoir un port d'attache fixe d'où je pourrai ensuite m'écarter" (p. 52). "sur ce cahier je conterai mes expériences que j'accepte variées et même absurdes; ce sera sur le plan de ma faiblesse. Puis

je m'attacherai à une oeuvre de pensée où tout aboutira dans un jugement fort, détaché et dédaigneux" (p. 52–53). "Relisant les premières pages de ce cahier, je m'émerveille de tout de lucidité, de précision dans l'analyse et de don pour décrire les états que je traversais. . . . Je pourrais donc moi aussi faire quelque chose? il faut que je travaille à un travail auquel je croirai et pour lequel je ne désirerai aucune louange" (p. 53).

35. "Le mot de Lagneau est beau 'je n'ai de soutien que mon désespoir absolu'; je ne voudrais pas d'autre devise. Sur ce désespoir j'élèverai ma joie; je surmonterai l'inexplicable. Courageusement chaque jour, tout reconstruire . . . Il suffit de ne pas abdiquer. Moi même suffit pour imposer à moi même des lois. Je sens qu'il me *faut* marcher dans ce sens. J'y marcherai" (p. 64).

36. "Je sais moi qu'il y a qu'un probleme et qui n'a pas de solution, parce qu'il n'a peut être pas de sens; c'est celui qu'a posé Pascal. . . . je voudrais croire à quelque chose—rencontrer l'exigence totale—justifier la vie; bref, je voudrais Dieu. Ceci pose, je ne l'oublierai point. Mais sachant qu'existe ce monde noumenal que je ne puis atteindre oú seulement pouvrait m'être expliqué apourquoi je vis, dans le monde phenomenal qui n'est pas pour autant negligeable, j'édifierai ma vie. Je me prendrai comme une fin" (p. 62). "(Curieux de voir comment je construis: je pars de ce qu'un être m'a livré de sa position et j'essaie de ces prémisses de déduire tout un système; continuons; mais où sont *mes* prémisses?)" (p. 62).

37. "Il y a le possible sérieux, austérité, philosophie, Barbier: oh! son attrait si fort, mon besoin de réaliser ce que je sens en moi; de faire quelque chose, de croire à quelque chose. Mes passions intellectuelles, mon sérieux philosophique! Des choses que Jacques renverse d'un sourire: naturellement on peut montrer la vanité du tout, en termes d'intelligence; mais si cela s'impose comme une présence vivante? Jacques dirait, et moi aussi, je le dis aux jours nombreux où je lui ressemble—: à quoi bon consacrer sa vie à la philosophie, sachant qu'on ne trouvera rien? Mais si j'aime cette recherche vaine? Je ne peux me résoudre à ne rien faire, à vivre agréablement. Non! je ne veux pas! Je n'ai qu'*une* vie et beaucoup de choses à dire. Il ne m'enlèvera pas ma vie à moi." (p. 37–38).

38. "J'aimerais infiniment l'amitié de Pontrémoli . . . qui comprend comme moi la littérature et la philosophie et dont la sympathie pour moi est si évidente" (p. 90). "Relu les lettres de Pontrémoli: Je lui ai écrit . . . en lui racontant mon histoire, mon ivresse première de vivre, puis mon désespoir devant la vie qui n'a pas de sens, mon désir de mourir, la dureté de mes amitiés, et enfin mon effort pour trouver, mon acte de foi dans la philosophie" (p. 142).

39. "Il faut que je travaille à un travail auquel je croirai. . . . Ecrire des 'essais sur la vie' qui ne soient pas du roman, mais de la philosophie, en les reliant vaguement d'une fiction. Mais que la pensée soit l'essentiel et que je cherche à trouver la verité, non à exprimer, à décrire la recherche de la verité" (p. 54–55).

"Oh! je vois bien ma vie maintenant . . . une recherche passionnée, éperdue. . . . J'ignorais qu'on pût rêver la mort par désespoir métaphysique; tout sacrifier au désir de savoir; ne vivre que pour se sauver. Je ne savais pas que chaque système est chose ardente, tourmentée, effort de vie, d'être, drame au plein sens du mot et n'engage pas que l'intelligence abstraite. Mais je sais cela à présent, et que je ne peux plus faire autre chose" (July 28, p. 133–34).

40. "même pour le plus aimé il y a une mesure puisqu'il n'est pas Dieu. Au fait, peut être non . . . J'approfondirai ceci pour mon diplôme" (p. 68). "Il faut étudier très profondément les questions qui m'intéressent. Il y a ce sujet de 'l'amour' qui est si passionnant et dont j'ai tracé les grandes lignes; il faudrait partir de là . . . et puis comme sujet plus facile et s'y rattachant pourtant l'amitié— ses dangers, la nature de l'éducation qu'elle donne, bref comment les âmes peuvent interagir les unes sur les autres— . . . . Il faudrait avoir le courage d'écrire non pour exposer des idées mais pour les découvrir, non pour les habiller artistement mais pour les animer. Le courage d'y croire" (p. 92).

41. "Il faut que je mettre au net mes idées philosophiques . . . approfondir les problèmes qui m'ont sollicitée. . . . Le thème est presque toujours cette opposition de moi et l'autre que j'ai senti au commençant de vivre. Maintenant est venu le temps d'en faire une synthèse. Les influences étrangères sont écartées, et aussi le désir de toute recherche d'écriture. J'écrirai mon oeuvre dans mon propre style en cherchant seulement à bien exprimer ce que je sens" (July 10, p. 95).

42. "Je suis seule jusqu'a l'angoisse aujourd'hui. . . . Il faut pour me consoler que je jette un coup d'oeil sur ce moi aux multiples visages que refletent les yeux de mes amis" (April 18, p. 5). "la joie de pouvoir me refugier quand tout le reste me fait defaut dans cette tendresse reelle" (April 18, p. 5). "confidente, l'autre moi–meme," "cette image . . . me reconforte" (p. 6). "le passé qui vit encore et auquel on offre cet avenir qu'il rêva, qui est devenu du présent" (September 5, p. 159).

43. "[M]ais nous nous appuierons l'un sur l'autre si fort que nous saurons supporter le grand vide vertigineux; nous ne tomberons pas dans le gouffre" (June 3, p. 74).

44. "Excitation un peu fiévreuse, projet d'étude et de camaraderies; il m'a paru un moment désirable de faire l'agrégation et je me suis sentie une âme de normalien! . . . Je me sens abrutie, un peu diminuée par mes succès que mes camarades on trop sentis; diminuée par la curiosité sympathique qu'ils éprouvent à l'égard d'une 'jeune fille qui a de la valeur'. Au fond qu'ai je fait de cette année? rien" (June 29, p. 83, 84).

45. "Je ne me laisserai pas absorber par la Sorbonne. Ne pas être 'Mlle Bertrand de Beauvoir'; être moi" (p. 86). "Dire que jeudi dernier toute la matinée et l'après midi chez Mlle Mercier j'ai sanglotté d'énervement. Ça! une belle

réussite de la vie, pensais-je! ah! vide! néant, vanité. De nouveau, me voilà plus forte de l'amour que d'autres ont pour moi. Après midi charmante chez G.Lévy à lire des vers ensemble et toucher de beaux livres—longues conversations avec Miquel qui me devient très cher" (July 7, p. 87).

46. "J'ai eu un moment de vertige, sans rien pour me raccrocher. . . . De nouveau, cette necessité d'être forte! d'être seule toujours si je ne m'abdique pas" (p. 138). "Lorsque je suis méchante, comme ce soir, il me semble que comme en Poupette, moins pourtant, j'aime surtout en elle un reflet de moi" (p. 6).

47. "Il n'y a qu'à les aimer et à me rejouir de ce qu'ils ont de différent de moi, mais non désirer être telle qu'ils sont" (p. 26).

48. "inutilité de tout" (p. 12). "Au fond, je suis dans une situation paradoxale: je sens mon intelligence, et . . . j'aimerais faire quelque chose . . . j'aimerais . . . me passionner pour une oeuvre philosophique. . . . Seulement, ces qualités mêmes qui demandent à servir me montrent quelle illusion c'est de prétendre servir à quelque chose" (p. 23). "le plaisir qu'elle ait besoin de moi." "je fais beaucoup pour elle et presque toute la passion de sa vie lui vient par moi" (April 18, p. 5). "je crois que J[acques] a besoin de moi" (August 1, p. 139). "Je peux quelque chose pour Jacques; pour l'autre ce serait de la joie seulement" (September 6, p. 159).

49. "Je te forcerai bien à t'aimer si tu m'aimes, parce que l'image de toi que tu verras dans mes yeux sera belle et vraie. Chacun sera fort de la faiblesse de l'autre" (p. 74).

50. "Mais c'est tellement comme si tout était fini! . . . et c'est ma faute, c'est quand j'aime moins que je me sens moins aimée. Je ne peux pas me représenter ce que tu es aujourd'hui: peut être penses tu à moi. peut être médites tu douloureusement. O mon ami, pardon!" (p. 103). "Je n'aime plus Jacques" (p. 168v). "Je rêve à d'immenses sacrifices; mais je n'ai rien d'assez grand pour en faire un don inutile" (p. 165).

51. "meme les simples camaraderies" (April 18, p. 59). "Là seulement je peux m'arracher à ma propre manière de penser" (April 18, p. 61). "une oreille pour écouter ce qui prendrait trop d'importance si je ne le disais pas" (April 18, p. 5). "me confier à quelqu'un qui critique et me prenne au serieux: Baruzi, G. Lévy ou Pontremoli" (p. 90).

52. "Je pense beaucoup en ce moment aux êtres que je connais, ou plutot aux idées que sont pour moi ces êtres . . . en la deduisant logiquement de leur point de départ" (p. 25). "le possible serieux: austerité, philosophie" (p. 37).

53. "mais qu'est ce enfin qu'aimer? se sentir dominée" (p. 136). "mon *moi* ne veut pas se laisser dévorer par le sien. C'est affreux! Je n'ai rien fait cette année (comme pensée personnelle) tant l'image de la vie calme auprès de lui me disait l'inutilité d'un effort dans un autre sens; quand j'aurai cette vie, quand je

serai arrivée, installée, je ferai bien moins encore. Mais c'est la défaite suprême!'' (p. 38). "Je me dis que ce qui m'attire, c'est sa manière de dominer, d'être fort et tel qu'on puisse marcher dans la lumière simplement que reflètent ses yeux'' (p. 39).

54. "J'ai une confiance totale en toi et en ton amour; je suis sûre de ce que tu es et de ce que tu es pour moi. Mais pour pouvoir reposer sur cette confiance, il faudrait méconnaitre trop de parties de toi . . . je refuse de n'en pas tenir compte sous prétexte que l'essentiel est stable. Je te vois tout entier et c'est tout entier que je t'aime'' (p. 7).

55. "l'amour est un fait auquel il faut se soumettre; le seul péché est d'idolâtrie. Ne pas trop penser à cela!'' (p. 154). "Ah! c'est si grand et si petit l'amour! si ce n'était que petit! ou si ce n'était que grand comme pour la petite jeune fille émerveillée!'' (p. 70). "Oh! de nouveau l'aimer si simplement comme j'ai parfois su le faire. Seulement savoir cela: c'est qu'en dépit de ce que je voulais, mon amour doit garder des limites'' (p. 47). "Je lui sacrifierai mes examens; mais non mon oeuvre si j'en peux faire une, ni moi même. . . . Refus de subir aucun esclavage. Et au fond je ne sais pas . . . peut être que je lui sacrifierai tout, tout et que ce ne sera pas un sacrifice'' (p. 90).

56. "si vide est ma vie! . . . Que ce soit Zaza, Garric, Jacques; la Sorbonne ou les équipes . . . mes passions d'enfance et de jeunesse étaient des passions: bouillantes, écrasées, et moi oppressée de leur poids, toute petite, *absorbée* par elles; maintenant c'est mon moi qui les absorbe toutes . . . les affections que j'éprouve ne sont point le centre de ma vie: je pourrais tellement m'en passer! elles me laissent tellement seule! tout à fait seule!'' (p. 18).

57. "Je parle mystiquement de l'amour, j'en sais le prix. Mais je sais aussi qu'il ne rompt pas ma solitude, d'ailleurs il n'est pas fait pour ça. Je suis trop intelligente, trop exigeante et trop riche pour que personne puisse se charger de moi entiérement. Personne ne me connait ni ne m'aime tout entiére. Je n'ai que moi'' (p. 51). "Il faut que je vive, sachant que personne ne m'aidera à vivre. . . . Seule je vivrai, forte de ce que je sais être'' (p. 51). "naturellement on cherche la compénétration, la création d'un "nous" qui ne soit ni moi ni toi. . . . Le mutilerai je, mutilant aussi celui de l'autre par de mutuelles concessions? Quel mot hideux!'' (p. 64). "[C]hacun est seul; et c'est cela qui est beau. Jacques m'a enseigné cela, douloureusement car je l'aimais. Ponty me l'enseigne dans la joie; la belle amitié, sans dureté, sans abandon, spontanée, neuve, heureuse et tendre qui ne demande rien de plus que ce qu'il est bon de donner'' (p. 168v).

58. "Non, je n'aimerai plus jamais. . . . J'ai ma force en moi. J'aime et me garde; je me donne sans rien perdre. Je n'ai besoin de personne!'' (October 17 and 27, p. 168v). "ce qu'il est pour moi: tout—ma seule raison de vivre. . . . J'attends avec tant d'impatience le jour où tu ne sera plus 'l'autre' ni 'moi', mais il y aura seulement et définitivement 'nous.' '' (p. 6–7). "je me sentais honteuse

. . . d'être égoïste, d'un égoïsme radical qui peut se nuancer seulement en ce que je le ferai porter sur ceux que j'aime ou directement sur moi même" (p. 24).

59. "Autrui ne peut plus rien être pour moi de définitif et complet: le grand renoncement auquel j'avais rêvé est impossible! Ils ne sont qu'eux comme je ne suis que moi, et surtout je n'ai pas besoin d'eux" (p. 18–19). "un instant au Luxembourg, j'ai defailli de tristesse, songeant qu'apres 18 mois de si passionns amours, je me trouvais le coeur vide et sachant que n'existe pas celui qui remplirait tout" "Sartre—1929" (p. 137).

60. "Et puis, mes chers amis, vous n'aimez pas les jeunes filles mais songez que non seulement elles ont une raison à satisfaire mais un coeur lourd à comprimer—et en cela je veux rester femme, plus masculine encore par le cerveau, plus féminine par la sensibilité" (p. 107). "[C]omme hier j'ai envié M. de Wendel si jolie et simple! sans orgueil comme sans envie, j'ai pleuré en songeant au sort qui moi m'est réservé, à toute la force, et la tension exigée pour que je le puisse trouver préférable à tout autre" (p. 57). "Vendredi j'établissais dans la force un programme de vie; en de tels instants ma solitude est une ivresse: je suis, je domine, je m'aime et méprise le reste" (p. 57).

61. "Mais je voudrais tant avoir le droit moi aussi d'être très simple et très faible, d'être une femme; dans quel 'monde désert' je marche, si aride, avec les seules oases de mon estime intermittente pour moi même. . . . Je compte sur moi; je sais que je peux compter sur moi. Mais j'aimerais bien ne pas avoir besoin de compter sur moi" (p. 57). "Pourrais je encore supporter de souffrir comme je souffrais en écrivant ces lignes?" (p. 57).

REFERENCES

Algren, Nelson. Papers. Rare Books and Manuscripts. Ohio State University Library.

Apuzzo, Ginny, and Betty Powell. 1977. Confrontation: Black and White; An Interview with Ginny Apuzzo and Betty Powell. *Quest* 3, no. 4 (Spring), n.p.

Ascher, Carol. 1987. The Anguish of Existence: Remembering Simone de Beauvoir. Paper presented at Eastern Division, American Philosophical Association, December 30.

Aury, Dominique. 1945. Qu'est-ce que l'existentialisme? Bilan d'une offensive [Interview article with Jean-Paul Sartre]. *Les Lettres Françaises*, 24 novembre.

Bair, Deirdre. 1989. Introduction to the Vintage Edition. In *The Second Sex*, by Simone de Beauvoir. Trans. H. M. Parshley, xiii–xxiii. New York: Vintage Books.

———. 1990a. Do as She Said, Not as She Did. *New York Times Magazine*, 18 November, 32, 34.

———. 1990b. *Simone de Beauvoir: A Biography*. New York: Summit.

Baker, Houston A., Jr. 1984. *Blues, Ideology, and Afro-American Literature: A Vernacular Theory*. Chicago: University of Chicago Press.

Barnes, Hazel. 1959. *Humanistic Existentialism: The Literature of Possibility*. Lincoln: University of Nebraska Press.

Barrett, William. 1958. *Irrational Man*. New York: Doubleday.

Baruzi, Jean. [1924] 1931. *Saint Jean de la Croix et le problème de l'expérience mystique*. 2nd ed. Paris: Alcan.

———. 1985. *L'intelligence mystique*. Ed. Jean-Louis Vieillard-Baron. Paris: Berg International.

Beal, Frances M. 1970. Double Jeopardy: To Be Black and Female. In *Sisterhood Is Powerful: An Anthology of Writings from the Women's Liberation Movement,* ed. Robin Morgan. New York: Random House.

Beauvoir, Simone de. [1927]. 4e cahier. Holograph manuscript. Paris: Bibliothèque Nationale. Transcription by Barbara Klaw, Sylvie Le Bon de Beauvoir, and myself; my translation.

———. [1928–29]. Carnet 6. Holograph manuscript. Paris: Bibliothèque Nationale; my transcription and translation.

———. [1929–31]. Carnet 7. Holograph manuscript. Paris: Bibliothèque Nationale; my transcription and translation.

———. [1935–37] 1982. *When Things of the Spirit Come First*. Trans. Patrick O'Brian. New York: Pantheon.

———. [1943] 1949. *She Came to Stay* [*L'Invitée*]. Trans. L. Drummond. London. Reprint, trans. Yvonne Moyse and Roger Senhouse, New York: World, 1954. Reprint, New York: Norton, 1990.

———. 1944. *Pyrrhus et Cinéas*. Paris: Gallimard.

———. 1945. *Les Bouches inutiles* [Useless mouths]. Paris: Gallimard. Trans. Claude Francis and Fernande Gontier as *Who Shall Die?* Florissant, Mo.: River Press, 1983.

———. 1945. *Le Sang des autres* [The blood of others]. Paris: Gallimard. Trans. Roger Senhouse and Yvonne Moyse, New York: Knopf, 1948.

———. 1946. *Tous les hommes sont mortels* [All men are mortal]. Paris: Gallimard. Trans. Leonard M. Friedman, New York: World, 1955.

———. 1946. Littérature et métaphysique. *Les Temps Modernes* 1(7) avril.

———. 1947. *Pour une morale de l'ambiguïté* [Ethics of ambiguity]. Paris: Gallimard. Trans. Bernard Frechtman, Secaucus, N.J.: Citadel Press, 1948.

———. 1948. *L'Amérique au jour le jour* [America day by day]. Paris: Morihien; my translation unless otherwise indicated. Reprint, trans. Patrick Dudley. New York: Grove Press, 1953.

———. 1949. *Le Deuxième Sexe* [The second sex]. 2 vols. Paris: Gallimard; my translation unless otherwise indicated. Trans. H. M. Parshley, New York: Knopf, 1952; Reprint, New York: Bantam, 1961 and 1970; Reprint, New York: Random House, 1974.

———. [1954] 1956. *The Mandarins*. Trans. Leonard M. Friedman, New York: Popular Library.

———. 1958. *Mémoires d'une jeune fille rangée* [Memoirs of a dutiful daughter]. Coll. Folio. Paris: Gallimard; my translation unless otherwise indicated. Trans. James Kirkup, New York: Harper & Row, 1959.

———. 1960. *La Force d'age* [Prime of life]. Coll. Folio. Paris: Gallimard; my translation unless otherwise indicated. Trans. Peter Green, New York: Lancer Books, 1962.

———. [1964] 1975. *A Very Easy Death*. Trans. Patrick O'Brian, New York: Pantheon.

———. [1968] 1969. *The Woman Destroyed*. Trans. Patrick O'Brian, New York: Putnam.

———. [1972] 1975. *All Said and Done.* Trans. Patrick O'Brian, New York: Warner Books.

———. 1975. Simone de Beauvoir interroge Jean-Paul Sartre. *L'Arc* 61: 3–12; my translation.

———. 1977. Preface to *Histoires du M. L. F.,* by Anne Tristan and Annie de Pisan. Paris: Calmann-Lévy; my translation.

———. 1979. De l'urgence d'une loi antisexiste. *Le Monde,* 19 mars, 1; my translation.

———. [1981] 1984. *Adieux: A Farewell to Sartre.* Trans. Patrick O'Brian. New York: Pantheon.

———. 1990a. *Journal de guerre: Septembre 1939-Janvier 1941.* Ed. Sylvie Le Bon de Beauvoir. Paris: Gallimard; my translation.

———. 1990b. *Lettres à Sartre.* 2 vols. Ed. Sylvie Le Bon de Beauvoir. Paris: Gallimard; my translation.

———. 1992. *Letters to Sartre.* Ed. Sylvie Le Bon de Beauvoir. Trans. and ed. Quintin Hoare. New York: Arcade.

Beauvoir, Sylvie Le Bon de. 1995. Simone de Beauvoir au seuil d'une nouvelle vie [and] Sylvie Le Bon de Beauvoir et les archives de la Bibliothèque Nationale de France. *Simone de Beauvoir Studies* 12: 5–9.

———, ed. 1997. *Lettres à Nelson Algren: Un Amour transatlantique; 1947–1964,* by Simone de Beauvoir. Paris: Gallimard.

Bennett, Lerone, Jr. 1982. *Before the Mayflower: A History of Black America.* 5th ed. New York: Penguin Books.

Bergoffen, Debra B. 1995. Out from Under: Beauvoir's Philosophy of the Erotic. In Simons (1995).

———. 1997. *The Philosophy of Simone de Beauvoir: Gendered Phenomenologies, Erotic Generosities.* Albany: State University of New York.

Blackham, H. J. 1965. *Reality, Man and Existence: Essential Works of Existentialism.* New York: Bantam.

Boston Women's Health Collective. 1973. *Our Bodies, Ourselves.* Boston: New England Free Press.

Breisach, Ernest. 1962. *Introduction to Modern Existentialism.* New York: Grove.

Butler, Judith. 1986. Sex and Gender in Simone de Beauvoir's *Second Sex.* In *Simone de Beauvoir: Witness to a Century,* ed. Helene Vivienne Wenzel, special issue of *Yale French Studies* 72:35–49.

———. 1989. Gendering the Body: Beauvoir's Philosophical Contribution. In *Women, Knowledge, and Reality: Explorations in Feminist Philosophy,* ed. Ann Garry and Marilyn Pearsall. Boston: Unwin Hyman.

———. 1990. *Gender Trouble: Feminism and the Subversion of Identity.* New York: Routledge.

Card, Claudia. [1985] 1990. Lesbian Attitudes and *The Second Sex.* In Simons and Al-Hibri (1990).

Cataldi, Sue L. 1997. The Body as a Basis for Being: Simone de Beauvoir and Maurice Merleau-Ponty. Paper presented at FAU/CARP Research Symposium on Beauvoir, Delray Beach, Florida, May.

Collins, James. 1952. *The Existentialists: A Critical Study*. Chicago: H. Regnery.

Conger, Carol. 1983. Child Abuse: A Lesbian Anarchist Perspective. *The Lesbian Inciter* 11 (July), 1:20–21.

Contat, Michel, and Michel Rybalka. 1970. *Les Ecrits de Sartre*. Paris: Gallimard.

Cotera, Martha P. 1976. *Diosa y Hembra: The History and Heritage of Chicanas in the U.S.* Austin, Tex.: Information Systems Development.

———. 1977. *The Chicana Feminist*. Austin, Tex.: Information Systems Development.

Daly, Mary. 1973. *Beyond God the Father: Towards a Philosophy of Women's Liberation*. Boston: Beacon Press.

Daniels-Eichelberger, Brenda. 1977. Voices on Black Feminism. *Quest* 3, no. 4 (Spring):16–28.

———. 1977/78. Anglogynophobia. *Women's News . . . For a Change* 1, nos. 7, 8, 10; vol. 2, no. 1 (November, December 1977 and February, April 1978).

David, Catherine. 1979. Beauvoir elle-même. *Le Nouvel Observateur*, 22 janvier; my translation.

Davis, Angela. 1981. *Women, Race, and Class*. New York: Random House.

Dayan, Josée, and Malka Ribowska. 1979. *Simone de Beauvoir*. Paris: Gallimard; my translation.

Delaplaine, Jo. 1978. Mujeres y la Comunidad Latina/Women and the Latin Community. *Quest* 4, no. 4 (Fall):6–14.

Dinnerstein, Dorothy. 1976. *The Mermaid and the Minotaur: Sexual Arrangements and Human Malaise*. New York: Harper and Row.

Drake, St. Clair, and Horace R. Cayton. [1945] 1993. *Black Metropolis: A Study of Negro Life in a Northern City*. Chicago: University of Chicago.

DuBois, W. E. B. [1903] 1989. *The Souls of Black Folk*. Introduction by Henry Louis Gates, Jr. New York: Bantam.

du Bos, Charles. 1948. *Le Journal de Charles du Bos*. Paris: Corréa.

Echols, Alice. 1989. *Daring To Be Bad: Radical Feminism in America 1967–1975*. Minneapolis: University of Minnesota Press.

Edwards, James. [1980]. On Saint Genet. Paper presented at the Sartre Retrospective program of the Radical Caucus and the Society for Women in Philosophy at the December meeting of the American Philosophical Association.

Edwards, Paul, ed. 1967. *The Encyclopedia of Philosophy*. 8 vols. New York: Macmillan.

Ehrenreich, Barbara, and Deirdre English. 1978. *For Her Own Good: 150 Years of the Expert's Advice to Women*. Garden City, N.Y.: Anchor/Doubleday.

Ellison, Ralph. 1966. Richard Wright's Blues. In *Shadow and Act*. New York: New American Library.

Everley, Christine. 1996. War and Alterity in *L'Invitée*. Paper presented at Beauvoir conference, Trinity College, Dublin, September.

Fabre, Michel. 1985. Interview with Simone de Beauvoir [June 24, 1970]. In *The World of Richard Wright*. Jackson: University Press of Mississippi.

———. 1990. *Richard Wright: Books & Writers*. Jackson: University Press of Mississippi.

———. 1993. *The Unfinished Quest of Richard Wright*. 2nd ed. Trans. Isabel Barzun. Urbana: University of Illinois.

Fallaize, Elizabeth. 1997. A Saraband of Imagery: The Uses of Biological Science in *The Second Sex*. Paper presented at FAU/CARP Research Symposium on Beauvoir, Delray Beach, Florida, May.

Fanon, Frantz. 1967. *Black Skin, White Masks*. Trans. Charles Lam Markmann, New York: Grove.

Firestone, Shulamith. 1970. *The Dialectic of Sex*. New York: William Morrow.

———, ed. 1970. *Notes from the Second Year*. New York: Radical Feminists.

Fisher, Beverly. 1977. Race and Class: Beyond Personal Politics. *Quest* 3, no. 4 (Spring): 2–15.

Fitch, Noel Riley. 1983. *Sylvia Beach and the Lost Generation: A History of Literary Paris in the Twenties and Thirties*. New York: Norton.

Forster, Penny and Imogen Sutton, eds. 1989. Kate Millett. In *Daughters of de Beauvoir*. London: The Women's Press.

Francis, Claude, and Fernande Gontier. 1987. *Simone de Beauvoir: A Life, a Love Story*. Trans. Lisa Nesselson. New York: St. Martin's.

Friedan, Betty. 1981. *The Second Stage*. New York: Summit.

Fullbrook, Kate, and Edward Fullbrook. 1994. *Simone de Beauvoir: The Remaking of a Twentieth-Century Legend*. New York: Basic Books.

———. 1998. *Simone de Beauvoir: A Critical Introduction*. Malden, Mass.: Blackwell.

Gerassi, John. 1976. Simone de Beauvoir: *The Second Sex* 25 Years Later. *Society* 13, no. 2 (January/February): 79–85.

Gilligan, Carol. 1982. *In a Different Voice: Psychological Theory and Women's Development*. Cambridge, Mass.: Harvard University Press.

———. 1987. Moral Orientation and Moral Development. In *Women and Moral Theory*, ed. Eva Feder Kittay and Diana T. Meyers. Totowa, N.J.: Rowman & Littlefield.

Gilman, Charlotte Perkins. 1973. *The Yellow Wallpaper*. Old Westbury, N.Y.: Feminist Press.

Gilroy, Paul. 1993. *The Black Atlantic: Modernity and Double Consciousness*. Cambridge, Mass.: Harvard University Press.

Gornick, Vivian, and Barbara K. Moran, eds. 1971. *Woman in Sexist Society: Studies in Power and Powerlessness*. New York: Basic Books.

Grene, Marjorie. 1973. *Sartre.* New York: Franklin Watts.

Hammond, Judith, and J. Rex Enoch. 1976. Conjugal Power Relations among Black Working Class Families. *Journal of Black Studies* 7, no. 1 (September): 107–27.

Heineman, F. H. 1958. *Existentialism and the Modern Predicament.* Harper Torchbook. New York: Harper & Row.

Hole, Judith, and Ellen Levine. 1971. *Rebirth of Feminism.* New York: Quadrangle.

Holveck, Eleanore. 1995. Can a Woman Be a Philosopher? Reflections of a Beauvoirian Housemaid. In Simons (1995).

Jacobs, Sue-Ellen, and Karen T. Hansen. 1977. *Anthropological Studies of Women: A Course for Independent Study.* Seattle: University of Washington.

Jaggar, Alison M. 1983. *Feminist Politics and Human Nature.* Totowa, N.J.: Rowman & Allanheld.

Jaggar, Alison M., and Paula Rothenberg Struhl, eds. 1978. *Feminist Frameworks.* New York: McGraw-Hill.

James, C. L. R. 1962. *The Black Jacobins; Toussaint L'Ouverture and the San Domingo Revolution.* 2nd ed. New York: Vintage.

Johnson, Barbara. 1993. The Re(a)d and the Black. In *Richard Wright: Critical Perspectives Past and Present,* ed. Henry Louis Gates, Jr. and K. A. Appiah. New York: Amistad.

Jordan, June. 1974. On Richard Wright and Zora Neale Hurston: Notes Toward a Balancing of Love and Hatred. *Black World* (August): 4–8.

Kaufmann, Walter, ed. 1956. *Existentialism from Dostoevsky to Sartre.* New York: World Publishing. Revised ed., New York: New American Library, 1975.

Keefe, Terry. 1983. *Simone de Beauvoir: A Study of Her Writings.* Totowa, N.J.: Barnes & Noble.

Keller, Catherine. 1985. Feminism and the Ethics of Inseparability. In *Women's Consciousness, Women's Conscience,* ed. Barbara Hilkert Andolsen, Christine E. Gudorf, and Mary D. Pellauer, 251–263, New York: Harper & Row.

King, Mae C. 1973. The Politics of Sexual Stereotypes. *The Black Scholar* 4, nos. 6–7 (March-April): 12–23.

Koedt, Anne, ed. 1971. *Notes from the Third Year.* New York: Notes from the Second Year, Inc.

Kolodny, Annette. 1985. A Map for Rereading: Gender and the Interpretation of Literary Texts. In *The New Feminist Criticism,* ed. Elaine Showalter. New York: Pantheon.

Kruks, Sonia. 1990. *Situation and Human Existence: Freedom, Subjectivity and Society.* New York: Routledge.

———. 1995. Simone de Beauvoir: Teaching Sartre About Freedom. In Simons (1995).

Lamphere, Louise. 1977. Anthropology. *Signs* 2, no. 3 (Spring): 612–27.

Le Doeuff, Michèle. 1984. Sartre; l'unique sujet parlant. *Esprit—changer la culture et la politique* 5:181–91.

———. [1989] 1991. *Hipparchia's Choice: An Essay Concerning Women, Philosophy, etc.* Trans. Trista Selous. Cambridge, Mass.: Basil Blackwell.

Les Chimères. 1975. *Maternité esclave* [Enslaved motherhood]. Paris: UGE 10/18.

Lewis, Diane K. 1977. A Response to Inequality: Black Women, Racism, and Sexism. *Signs* 3 (2):339–61.

Lundgren-Gothlin, Eva. 1996a. *Sex and Existence: Simone de Beauvoir's* The Second Sex. Trans. Linda Schenck. Hanover, N.H.: Wesleyan University Press.

———. 1996b. Simone de Beauvoir's Ethics and its Relation to Current Moral Philosophy. Paper presented at Beauvoir Conference, Trinity College, Dublin, Ireland, September.

———. 1997. Simone de Beauvoir's Existential Philosophy and Philosophy of History in *Le Deuxième Sexe*. Paper presented at FAU/CARP Research Symposium on Beauvoir, Delray Beach, Florida, May.

Marcel, Gabriel. 1927. *Journal métaphysique* [Metaphysical Journal]. Paris; Trans. Bernard Wall. Chicago: Regnery, 1952.

Marks, Elaine. 1986. Transgressing the (In)cont(in)ent Boundaries: The Body in Decline. In *Simone de Beauvoir: Witness to a Century*, ed. Helene Vivienne Wenzel, a special issue of *Yale French Studies* 72:181–200.

Martin, M. Kay, and Barbara Voorhies. 1975. *Female of the Species*. New York: Columbia University.

Martinez, Elizabeth Sutherland. 1970. An Introduction. In Morgan 1970.

McBride, William. 1981. "Sartre and Lived Experience." *Review in Phenomenology* X, n.p.

Merleau-Ponty, Maurice. [1945] 1964. Metaphysics and the Novel. In *Sense and Non-Sense*, trans. Hubert L. Dreyfus and Patricia Allen Dreyfus. Evanston, Ill.: Northwestern University Press.

Millett, Kate. 1971. *Sexual Politics*. New York: Doubleday.

Morgan, Robin, ed. 1970. *Sisterhood Is Powerful: An Anthology of Writings from the Women's Liberation Movement*. New York: Random House.

Murphy, Julien. 1995. Beauvoir and the Algerian War: Toward a Postcolonial Ethics. In Simons (1995).

Myrdal, Gunnar, Richard Sterner, and Arnold Rose. 1944. *An American Dilemma: The Negro Problem and Modern Democracy*. New York: Harper.

Norton, Eleanor Holmes. For Sadie and Maude. In Morgan (1970).

Olafson, Frederick A. 1967. Sartre, Jean-Paul. In *The Encyclopedia of Philosophy*. Vols. 7 & 8, ed. Paul Edwards. New York: Macmillan.

Portuges, Catherine. 1986. Attachment and Separation in *The Memoirs of a Duti-*

ful Daughter. In *Simone de Beauvoir: Witness to a Century*, ed. Helene Vivienne Wenzel, a special issue of *Yale French Studies* 72:107–18.

Rabil, Albert Jr. 1967. *Merleau-Ponty: Existentialist of the Social World.* New York: Columbia University.

Raymond, Diane Barsoum. 1991. *Existentialism and the Philosophical Tradition.* Englewood Cliffs, N.J.: Prentice Hall.

Redding, Saunders. [1963] 1970. The Alien Land of Richard Wright. In *Five Black Writers*, ed. Donald B. Gibson. New York: New York University.

Reiter, Rayna R., ed. 1975. *Toward an Anthropology of Women.* New York: Monthly Review.

Riccio, Mary-Therese. 1978. If I've Upset You, You've Got the Message. *Quest* 4, no. 5 (Fall): 37–41.

Rich, Adrienne. 1976. *Of Woman Born: Motherhood as Experience and Institution.* New York: Norton.

———. [1980] 1989. Compulsory Heterosexuality and Lesbian Existence. In *Feminist Frontiers II*, ed. Laurel Richardson and Verta Taylor. New York: Mc-Graw-Hill.

Rosaldo, Michelle Zimbalist, and Louise Lamphere, eds. 1974. *Woman, Culture, and Society.* Stanford, Calif.: Stanford University.

Ruddick, Sara. 1982. Maternal Thinking. In *Rethinking the Family: Some Feminist Questions,* ed. Barrie Thorne and Marilyn Yalon. New York: Longman.

Sartre, Jean-Paul. [1943] 1966. *Being and Nothingness.* Trans. Hazel Barnes. New York: Washington Square Press.

———. 1945. Le problème noir aux États-Unis. *Le Figaro*, 16 juin, 30 juillet, n.p.

———. [1945] 1947. *No Exit.* Trans. Stuart Gilbert. New York: Vintage.

———. [1946] 1950. *Baudelaire.* Trans. Martin Turnell. New York: New Directions.

———. [1946] 1954. *Réflections sur la question juive* [Anti-Semite and Jew]. Paris: Gallimard. Trans. George J. Besker, New York: Schocken, 1948.

———. [1946] 1955. Materialism and Revolution. In *Literary and Philosophical Essays*, trans. Annette Michelson. New York: Collier.

———. 1948. Orphée Noir. Preface to *Anthologie de la nouvelle poésie nègre et malgache.* Paris: Presses Universitaires de France.

———. [1952] 1963. *Saint Genet.* Trans. Bernard Frechtman. New York: George Braziller.

———. 1983. *Lettres au Castor et à quelques autres.* 2 vols. Ed. Simone de Beauvoir. Paris: Gallimard.

———. 1984. *The War Diaries of Jean-Paul Sartre.* Trans. Quintin Hoare. New York: Pantheon.

Schlegal, Alice, ed. 1977. *Sexual Stratification: A Cross-Cultural View.* New York: Columbia University.

Schwarzer, Alice. 1984. *After* The Second Sex: *Conversations with Simone de Beauvoir.* Trans. Marianne Howarth. New York: Pantheon.

Schweickart, Patrocinio. 1986. Reading Ourselves: Toward a Feminist Theory of Reading. In *Gender and Reading: Essays on Readers, Texts, and Contexts,* ed. Elizabeth A. Flynn and Patrocinio P. Schweickart. Baltimore, Md.: Johns Hopkins University Press.

Simons, Margaret A. 1977. *A Phenomenology of Oppression: A Critical Introduction to* Le Deuxième Sexe *by Simone de Beauvoir.* Ph.D. diss., Purdue University.

———, ed. 1995. *Feminist Interpretations of Simone de Beauvoir.* University Park: Pennsylvania State University Press.

Simons, Margaret, and Azizah Y. al-Hibri, eds. 1990. *Hypatia Reborn: Essays in Feminist Philosophy.* Bloomington: Indiana University.

Singer, Linda. 1985. Interpretation and Retrieval: Rereading Beauvoir. *Hypatia* 3, a special issue of *Women's Studies International Forum* 8; reprinted in Simons and Al-Hibri (1990).

Smith-Rosenberg, Carroll. 1975. The Female World of Love and Ritual: Relations between Women in Nineteenth-Century America. *Signs: Journal of Women in Culture and Society* 1(1): 1–29.

Solomon, Robert. 1972. *From Rationalism to Existentialism: The Existentialists and Their Nineteenth-Century Backgrounds.* New York: Humanities.

Southern, David W. 1987. *Gunnar Myrdal and Black-White Relations: The Use and Abuse of* An American Dilemma, *1944–1969.* Baton Rouge: Louisiana State University Press.

Spelman, Elizabeth V. 1988. *Inessential Woman: Problems of Exclusion in Feminist Thought.* Boston: Beacon Press.

Spiegelberg, Herbert. 1982. *The Phenomenological Movement: A Historical Introduction.* 3rd ed. The Hague: Martinus Nijhoff.

Stack, Carol B. 1974. Sex Roles and Survival Strategies in an Urban Black Community. In Rosaldo and Lamphere (1974), 113–28.

Stimpson, Catherine. 1971. "Thy Neighbor's Wife, Thy Neighbor's Servants": Women's Liberation and Black Civil Rights. In Gornick and Moran (1971).

Stone, Pauline Terrelonge. 1979. Feminist Consciousness and Black Women. In *Women: A Feminist Perspective.* 2d ed., ed. Jo Freeman. Palo Alto, Calif.: Mayfield.

Tanner, Leslie, ed. 1970. *Voices from Women's Liberation.* New York: New American Library.

Vasquez, Enriqueta Longauex y. 1970. The Mexican-American Woman. In Morgan (1970).

Vieillard-Baron, Jean-Louis. 1985. Présentation. In Baruzi 1985.

Vintges, Karen. 1996. *Philosophy as Passion: The Thinking of Simone de Beauvoir.* Tr. Anne Lavelle. Bloomington: Indiana University Press.

Wahl, Jean. 1949. *A Short History of Existentialism*. Tr. Forrest Williams and Stanley Maron. New York: Philosophical Library.

Walker, Alice. 1977. Foreword: Zora Neale Hurston—A Cautionary Tale and a Partisan View. In *Zora Neale Hurston: A Literary Biography,* by Robert E. Hemenway. Urbana: University of Illinois Press.

———. 1983. *In Search of Our Mothers' Gardens: Womanist Prose*. New York: Harcourt Brace Jovanovich.

Walker, Margaret. 1988. *Richard Wright: Daemonic Genius: A Portrait of the Man and Critical Look at His Work*. New York: Amistad.

Wallace, Michele. 1979. Black Macho and the Myth of the Super Woman. *Ms* 7, no. 7 (January): 46.

Ware, Cellestine. 1970. *Woman Power: The Movement for Women's Liberation*. New York: Tower.

Webb, Constance. 1968. *Richard Wright: A Biography*. New York: G. P. Putnam's Sons.

Werner, Craig. 1990. Bigger's Blues: *Native Son* and the Articulation of African American Modernism. In *New Essays on Native Son*, ed. Keneth Kinnamon. Cambridge, Eng.: Cambridge University Press.

Wright, Richard. Papers. Beinecke Rare Book and Manuscript Library. Yale University.

———. [1937]. 1945. Le feu dans la nuée [Fire and cloud]. *Les Temps Modernes* 1(1)–1(2).

———. [1938] 1978. *Richard Wright Reader*. Ed. Ellen Wright and Michel Fabre. New York: Harper & Row.

———. [1940] 1993. *Native Son and How Bigger Was Born*. Introduction by Arnold Rampersad. New York: HarperCollins.

———. 1945. Introduction. In *Black Metropolis*, by St. Clair Drake and Horace R. Cayton. New York: Harper & Row.

———. [1946] 1969. The Man Who Went to Chicago. In *Eight Men*, by Richard Wright. New York: Pyramid Books.

———. 1947. Black Boy I-VI. *Les Temps Modernes* 2(16)-2(21).

———. 1948. Littéraire Noire Américaine. *Les Temps Modernes* 3:35.

Young, Iris. 1990. Humanism, Gynocentrism and Feminist Politics. In Simons and Al-Hibri (1990).

INDEX

abortion, 58–59
absolutes, 206, 224
African American women, 169–72
agrégation, 95, 126–27, 190, 219
Alain, 190
Alain-Fourier, 191
Algren, Nelson, 115, 119, 170
alienation, 157
All Said and Done, 136
alterity, 169, 173
ambiguity, 48
America Day by Day, 176–83
American Dilemma, 150, 171, 172, 175
anguish, 209, 213, 216, 220
Anti-Semite and Jew, 46, 51–53, 102, 172
Apuzzo, Ginny, 37
Aragon, Louis, 190
Aristotle, 130
Arland, Marcel, 191
Aron, Raymond, 200
Ascher, Carol, 113, 124
Atkinson, Ti-Grace, 145
Auclert, Hubertine, 64
Audry, Colette, 131
authenticity, 45, 130, 156, 160

bad faith, 172, 209–12, 221, 232. *See also* self-deception

Bair, Deirdre, xx, 71, 115–20, 130–31
Balzac, Honoré de, 163
Barbier, 225
Barnes, Hazel, 108
Barrès, Maurice, 191
Barrett, William, 106–8
Baruzi, Jean, 187, 188, 198–200, 225
Baudelaire, 49
Beach, Sylvia, 174–75
Beauvoir, Hélène (Poupette), 121–22, 134, 221, 222, 224
Beauvoir, Simone de: ambiguous gender identity of, 116–43; asceticism of, 192, 213; authors cited by, 171–72, 192–205; autonomy of, 13, 41–42; critique of reason by, 201, 204; diary, as philosophical tool of, 213; diary from 1927 of, 185–233; early Catholicism of, 191, 203–4, 211; education of, 55–56, 95, 188; egoism of, 209, 221, 228–30; ethics, of, 102, 179, 231–33, 224; existential phenomenology of, 69–71, 140; female friendships of, 14, 59, 115–43; in the feminist movement, 3–6, 114; on God, 193; and Husserlean phenomenology, 200–202; individualism of, 228–30; influences on the philosophy of, 170,

255

ABOUT THE AUTHOR

MARGARET A. SIMONS, professor of philosophy and coordinator of the women's studies program at Southern Illinois University at Edwardsville, was the editor of *Hypatia: A Journal of Feminist Philosophy* from 1985 to 1990. She is co-editor (with Azizah al-Hibri) of *Hypatia Reborn: Essays in Feminist Philosophy* (Indiana University Press, 1990), and editor of *Feminist Interpretations of Simone de Beauvoir* (Pennsylvania State University Press, 1995). She is currently co-editing (with Sylvie Le Bon de Beauvoir) a six-volume series of Beauvoir's philosophical texts in English translation (Indiana University Press, forthcoming).